FROM TERRORISM TO TELEVISION

This book unpacks the media dynamics within the socio-cultural, political, and economic context of Pakistan. It provides an in-depth, critical, and scholarly discussion of contemporary issues such as media, state, and democracy in Pakistan; freedom of expression in Pakistani journalism; Balochistan as a blind spot in mainstream newspapers; media control by state institutions; women and media discourses; TV talk shows and coverage of Kashmir; feminist narrative and media images of Malala Yousufzai and Mukhtaran Mai; jihad on screen; and Osama bin Laden's death on screen, to understand the relation between media and terrorism. The book covers diverse media types including TV, radio, newspapers, print media, films, documentary, stage performance, and social media.

Detailed, interdisciplinary, analytical, and with original perspectives from journalists as well as academics, this volume will be useful to scholars and researchers of media studies, Pakistan studies, politics and international affairs, military and terrorism studies, journalism and communication studies, and South Asian studies. It will also interest general readers, policy makers, and those interested in global journalism, mass media, and freedom of expression.

Qaisar Abbas is Advisor, SMU Human Rights Program at Southern Methodist University, Dallas, USA.

Farooq Sulehria is Assistant Professor at the Department of Liberal Arts, Beaconhouse National University, Lahore, Pakistan.

FROM TERRORISM TO TELEVISION

Dynamics of Media, State, and Society in Pakistan

Edited by Qaisar Abbas and Farooq Sulehria

Routledge
Taylor & Francis Group

LONDON AND NEW YORK

First published 2021
by Routledge
2 Park Square, Milton Park, Abingdon, Oxon OX14 4RN

and by Routledge
52 Vanderbilt Avenue, New York, NY 10017

Routledge is an imprint of the Taylor & Francis Group, an informa business

© 2021 selection and editorial matter, Qaisar Abbas and Farooq Sulehria; individual chapters, the contributors

The right of Qaisar Abbas and Farooq Sulehria to be identified as the authors of the editorial material, and of the authors for their individual chapters, has been asserted in accordance with sections 77 and 78 of the Copyright, Designs and Patents Act 1988.

All rights reserved. No part of this book may be reprinted or reproduced or utilised in any form or by any electronic, mechanical, or other means, now known or hereafter invented, including photocopying and recording, or in any information storage or retrieval system, without permission in writing from the publishers.

Trademark notice: Product or corporate names may be trademarks or registered trademarks, and are used only for identification and explanation without intent to infringe.

Disclaimer: The views and opinions expressed in this book are solely those of the authors and do not necessarily reflect those of the publisher. The text representations and analyses based on research material are intended here to serve general educational and informational purposes and not obligatory upon any party. The authors and publisher have made every effort to ensure that the information presented in the book was correct at the time of press, but do not assume and hereby disclaim any liability with respect to the accuracy, completeness, reliability, suitability, selection and inclusion of the contents of this book and any implied warranties or guarantees. The authors and publisher make no representations or warranties of any kind to any person or entity for any loss, including, but not limited to special, incidental or consequential damage, or disruption—physical, psychological, emotional, or otherwise—alleged to have been caused, directly or indirectly, by omissions or any other related cause.

British Library Cataloguing-in-Publication Data
A catalogue record for this book is available from the British Library

Library of Congress Cataloging-in-Publication Data
A catalog record has been requested for this book

ISBN: 978-0-367-42195-3 (hbk)
ISBN: 978-0-367-42582-1 (pbk)
ISBN: 978-0-367-82446-4 (ebk)

Typeset in Bembo
by Taylor & Francis Books

To Masoodullah Khan, Nasir Zaidi, Khawar Naeem Hashmi, and Iqbal Jafferi!

(Four brave journalists who were sentenced to flogging by the Zia dictatorship in 1978 for protesting restrictions on freedom of the press).

CONTENTS

List of illustrations   ix
List of contributors   x
Preface   xiii

1 Walking in circles: Democracy, state, and freedom of expression in Pakistan   1
  Qaisar Abbas and Farooq Sulehria

2 Journalism in the service of Jihad   26
  Faizullah Jan

3 Jihad on screen: The role of jihadi drama and film and their press coverage, 1979–89, in Islamising Pakistan   39
  Farooq Sulehria

4 The politics of pity and the individual heroine syndrome: Mukhtaran Mai and Malala Yousafzai of Pakistan   61
  Fawzia Afzal-Khan

5 TV news as merchant of war hysteria: Framing the Kashmir conflict in India and Pakistan   83
  Qaisar Abbas

6 Performing piety and sexuality in Pakistan   99
  Afiya Shehrbano Zia

7 The cost of doing their job online: Harassment of women
   journalists 117
   Ayesha Khan

8 Counter-terrorism perspective and the Pakistani TV channels: A
   case study of Osama bin Laden's assassination 135
   Amir Hamza Marwan

9 The journey of Pakistan's Oscar success: *A Girl in the River*: An
   insider's account 148
   Haya Fatima Iqbal

10 What freedom?: Reflections of a working journalist 163
   Farah Zia

11 Covering the periphery: Balochistan as a blind spot in the
   mainstream newspapers of Pakistan 177
   Adnan Aamir

12 Interviews with I. A. Rehman, Mehdi Hasan, and Eric Rahim:
   Freedom of expression and sham democracy 190
   Qaisar Abbas and Farooq Sulehria

Index *200*

ILLUSTRATIONS

Figure

5.1	Proposed model of news frames	86

Tables

1.1	Private and state media in 2018	15
1.2	Number of TV channels by theme and language	16
1.3	Timeline of political process and freedom of expression in Pakistan	18
1.4	Pakistan's ranking in the World Press Freedom Index	20
5.1	News frames and themes	95
7.1	Nature and frequency of threats and abuse received by women journalists in the Pakistani media, May–October 2016	124
7.2	Prevalence, reporting, and action taken	129
8.1	Decline in the strength of news coverage	139
8.2	Themes discussed in the introduction of the news item	141
8.3	First three additional themes discussed in the body of the story	143
11.1	Number of stories published about Balochistan before and after Hazaras bomb explosion	185
11.2	Press coverage of Balochistan before and after the financial scandal	186

CONTRIBUTORS

Adnan Aamir is a journalist, researcher, and analyst based in Quetta, Pakistan. He covers politics, economy, development, conflict, and security, with a special interest in the conflict in Balochistan and the Chinese projects in Pakistan. He has written for the *Financial Times, South China Morning Post, Asia Times, China-US Focus*, and *Business Standard*, among others. He is also founder and editor of *Balochistan Voices*, a community-based online newspaper covering the issues of Balochistan that are ignored by mainstream media.

Qaisar Abbas is Advisor, SMU Human Rights Program at Southern Methodist University, Dallas, USA. He received his doctoral degree from the University of Wisconsin-Madison, and Master's from Iowa State University, in Mass Communication. He has worked at several universities in the USA as professor and director, and was formerly Assistant Dean at the University of North Texas. He has contributed articles to major journals and newspapers. His research interests are political and international communication, development broadcasting, poetic discourse as resistance, postcolonial South Asia, and peace journalism. He has also worked in Pakistan as News Producer for Pakistan Television (PTV) and Information Officer to the Minister of Education in the province of Punjab.

Fawzia Afzal-Khan is Professor of English and Director of Women and Gender Studies at Montclair State University, USA. With a PhD in English Literature from Tufts University, her research interests include third-world postcolonial literature and theory, feminist theory, and cultural and performance studies. She is recognised as a University Distinguished Scholar, received a National Endowment for the Humanities grant for *The Nightingales of Pakistan* (2011), and was awarded a Fulbright fellowship to Pakistan in 2015–16.

List of contributors xi

Haya Fatima Iqbal is an Academy Award winner and Emmy Award-winning documentary filmmaker. Her work has been featured by HBO Documentary, CNN, BBC, Vice, Channel 4 UK, the Thomson Reuters Foundation, and Deutsche Welle (DW). Haya is the co-founder of the Documentary Association of Pakistan (DAP). She also teaches communication and journalism at Habib University, Karachi. She is an Acumen Fellow and a Fulbright alumna. She has a Master's degree in News and Documentary from New York University.

Faizullah Jan is Associate Professor in the Department of Journalism and Mass Communication at the University of Peshawar, Pakistan. He earned a PhD in Communication from American University's School of Communication, Washington, DC. His book, *The Muslim Extremist Discourse: Constructing Us vs. Them*, was published in 2016. He served *The Frontier Post*, an English national daily, as the Editor-in-Charge and Sub-Editor before he started teaching. He has also worked as Public Relations Officer (PRO) at the University of Peshawar.

Ayesha Khan is a journalist-turned-academic and holds a PhD in peace and war journalism from the University of Wollongong, Australia. Her first-hand exposure to conflict developed her research interest in war, conflict and peace, genocide, refugees, religious and sectarian violence, and feminism. In Australia she teaches at the University of Wollongong, the University of Sydney, and the University of New South Wales. She also contributes to SBS News in Urdu, English, and Pashto languages.

Amir Hamza Marwan is Lecturer in the Department of Journalism and Mass Communication at the University of Peshawar, Pakistan. He did his doctoral studies in Journalism Studies at the University of Sheffield, UK. His doctoral thesis was on the coverage of bin Laden's killing across the Pakistani, British, and American media. His academic interests revolve around the coverage of terrorism, issues concerning regional conflicts, and their impact on media freedom and journalists' safety.

Farooq Sulehria is Assistant Professor in the School of Liberal Arts and Social Science, Beaconhouse National University, Lahore, Pakistan. He has a doctoral degree in Development Study from SOAS University of London. In addition to his recent book, *Media Imperialism in India and Pakistan* (2018), he has authored almost a dozen book chapters and journal articles. He regularly contributes to national and international publications, including *Jacobin Magazine*. In the past, he has worked with mainstream Pakistani dailies such as *The News, The Frontier Post,* and *The Nation*.

Afiya Shehrbano Zia is a feminist scholar, activist, and author of *Faith and Feminism in Pakistan* (2018). She has authored over a dozen peer-reviewed essays for international journals. She has taught at the University of Toronto.

Farah Zia has been a print journalist for 27 years. She was editor of *The News on Sunday* for more than 12 years. She has a Master's degree in International Relations from SOAS, London. She has another Master's degree in English Literature from Government College Lahore, Pakistan, where she was editor of the college magazine the *Ravi*. She frequently writes on politics, literature, and culture, and appears as an analyst on the BBC Urdu's radio service.

PREFACE

Since the 1990s, embedded structures of information culture, particularly in South Asia, have been uprooted and transformed beyond recognition. Pakistan is no exception. However, scholarly literature exploring Pakistani media—an intellectual deficit—and their transformations since the late 1990s, remains embarrassingly scarce.

Therefore, the primary aim of this book is to document and analyse the changes in information culture often attributed, in an uncritical manner, to revolutionising information and communication technologies (ICTs). Consequently, our book embraces and explains the phenomenal expansion of the television spectrum after the liberalisation of the airwaves, which effectively ended from 2001–2002 onwards a long-established monopoly enjoyed by the state-run Pakistan Television (PTV).

Meanwhile, the internet's stupefying expansion has contributed yet another decisive factor in the form of social media. But in the midst of all-embracing digitisation, radio and the newspaper industry have registered a sad decline. While contemporary scholarship on Pakistan media continues centre-staging the boom, the bust is ignored.

In this context, our book is a timely intervention because it approaches the media transformations, mentioned above, critically. By criticality, we imply an attempt at establishing a difference between the form and essence.

This volume, the first anthology on media dynamics within the socio-cultural, political, and economic contexts of Pakistan, offers multiple perspectives with micro and macro analyses of media contents and their societal undercurrents. It provides an in-depth examination of media issues for a variety of audiences, including policymakers, communication scholars, and institutions of higher education. As a collection of research studies, it has been conceptualised keeping in mind students and scholars of South Asian studies, Pakistan studies, international communication, media and society, global journalism, freedom of expression, and political science.

Notably, three aspects manifest themselves beyond the text itself. They deserve a special mention, in particular, for the readership not intimately acquainted with Pakistan's socio-political and historical settings. First, our contributors represent all four of the country's federating units. Media discourses emerging in metropolitan Pakistan more often than not marginalise periphery voices. This book makes a conscious effort to include Balochistan and Khyber Pakhtunkhwa (KP) provinces, otherwise treated as an academic and intellectual periphery. Second, and importantly, the gender balance was paid special attention when designing this project. In fact, women contributors outnumber (and let us dare say, outshine) their male counterparts. Lastly, chapters have been contributed by media scholars as well as media practitioners. Likewise, there are members of the Pakistani diaspora as well as Pakistan-based contributors.

Hence, this book is not merely a scholarly effort. It is also an attempt to go beyond routine patterns. Traditionally, mass media research in Pakistan focuses mostly on the historical analysis of communication issues and surveys of the field related to print journalism. This volume, however, tries to look beyond traditional approaches and offers an in-depth, critical, and scholarly discussion of contemporary media issues in diverse media formats. This plurality and diversity, needless to say, would not have been possible without our contributors who accepted our invitations to contribute despite their exhaustingly tight schedules. A big thanks to them all.

We also owe special thanks to our Routledge colleagues, in particular, Shoma Choudhury and Rimina Mohapatra. Anonymous reviewers who made invaluable suggestions and the editors also deserve our thanks for diligently working with us to improve the manuscripts we submitted to Routledge.

We would like to thank prominent Pakistani journalists, scholars, and intellectuals who not only encouraged us to work on this project but also responded to our interview questions on the media issues and freedom of expression in Pakistan. These include Dr Mehdi Hasan, I. A. Rehman, Dr Eric Rahim, and Dr Pervez Hoodbhoy.

Finally, our families also deserve our gratitude; they fully supported our work on this four-year-long project, which took quality family time away from them. Nevertheless, they were so patient and supportive.

We sincerely hope this book proves a stimulus for further research on Pakistani media operating in an atmosphere of terror(ism), gags, and cultural constraints. Like media systems in neighbouring countries, the Pakistani media also constitute an interesting, challenging, and instructive case study.

1

WALKING IN CIRCLES

Democracy, state, and freedom of expression in Pakistan

Qaisar Abbas and Farooq Sulehria

The tagline that appears on the title page of the *Washington Post*, "democracy dies in darkness", perfectly signifies the existing symbiosis between the media and democratic norms. Although the claim that mass media act as a catalyst to modernity and progress for societies might be an exaggeration, most flourishing democracies in the twenty-first century also demonstrate a high level of freedom of expression. As media are no longer limited to a privileged group of people in this age, a free and thriving media system in any society signifies the level of its political openness, intellectual diversity, and cultural maturity. How true is it about Pakistan, a country shuttling between democratic transition and creeping authoritarianism?

Most international media thinktanks and human rights organisations have been labelling Pakistan as a nation where the mass media are moderately free. On the other hand, until the change of government in 2018, the mass media in Pakistan also offered "a robust media landscape; among the most dynamic and outspoken in South Asia" (Jan 2015). Since 2018, there has been a creeping censorship and attacks on media freedoms in Pakistan, yet the media in Pakistan courageously assert their independence in many ways. This dynamism and media freedom, however, have been achieved after a long history of struggle for free expression by journalists, media workers, and intellectuals during the last 70 years of the nation's existence.

This introduction explores the complexities of the political process as it hinders or fosters freedom of expression in Pakistan. It synthesises media dynamics against the backdrop of a schizophrenic political process within the context of historically determined milestones. First, it offers a theoretical framework, followed by a historical review of media censorship as a sign of state hegemony. After a detailed discussion on the growth of media structures and the transforming nature of freedom of expression, the final section offers an overall analysis of media polemics and implications. The aim is to provide a context to the debates in the chapters that follow.

Theoretical framework

We claim that a media system in a given country is grounded, as a rule of thumb, in its polity. It is, therefore, imperative that any theoretical perspective to analyse a media system[1] considers the character of the coterminous polity. Hence, we begin by characterising the Pakistani state. Pakistan as a nation-state offers some peculiar characteristics that differentiate it from other nations in South Asia, the region it shares cultural and historical legacies with. The very fact that the Pakistani state was created based on culture and religion different from the rest of the Indian territories makes it an ideological state. Hamza Alavi, in proposing a theory of the Pakistani state (Alavi 1972), argued that both primary and secondary versions of Marx's theory of state offer a reasonable conceptual framework to comprehend the nature of the Pakistani state as such. The primary version of this theory defines the modern state as "the organized power of one class for oppressing the other". Here, the state becomes an instrument in the hand of one class, which is dominant politically and economically. In another explanation, the state becomes a protector of economically and socially determined classes, not an instrument to suppress classes.

To Eric Rahim (2014), this Marxist definition of state can be applied to post-colonial states, also referred to as the "Bonapartist" state historically, referring to Napoleon Bonaparte who became patron of the dominant class in France. Also, for Alavi, the post-colonial state is relatively autonomous, mediating between the competing interests of foreign capital, the internal bourgeoisie, and the landed class. By doing this, the state works to preserve the social order on behalf of these three interests, safeguarding their stakes in private property and the capitalistic mode of production.

As a significant aspect of the theory, the internal system in Pakistan has become subordinate to a powerful military-bureaucratic institution. This is primarily due to, among other factors, the legacy of the former colonial system. Thus, this developed and relatively autonomous nature of the powerful military-bureaucratic institution tends to mediate the interests of these classes. Since other institutions are so weak, they allow this domination. In short, Alavi conceptualises the "overdeveloped state" as a top-down, centralised structure apexed by a triumvirate of feudal lords, the local bourgeoisie, and metropolitan capital. Furthermore, the military exploits the system of parliamentary democracy to dominate the state, and, consequently, the current dominance of the military-bureaucratic oligarchy benefits neo-colonialism in post-colonial Pakistan (Alavi 1972).[2]

Rahim (2014) also observes three factors that help comprehend the nature of the Pakistani state. First, the predominant socioeconomic structures in Pakistan were mostly tribal or feudal. While two provinces, Khyber Pakhtunkhwah and Balochistan, were predominantly tribal societies, the other two, the Punjab and Sindh, were primarily agrarian and feudal. Subsequently, the feudal aristocracy and *Sardars* (tribal chieftains) have become the dominant classes to rule the country in post-colonial Pakistan. Second, these areas historically did not experience the democratic process as compared to the other Indian regions. In the absence of this political and administrative experience, individual leaders became more central to the political process than the political parties that should have been at the centre of the democratic system. The political games after independence in 1947 were primarily played by this feudal aristocracy that promoted kinship, *baradries* (caste-based brotherhood), cronyism, and various kinds of socioeconomic fraternities.

However, criticising Alavi's (1972) notion of the "overdeveloped state", Zaidi (2014), while arguing that there is no feudalism in Pakistan, assigns the media a centrality in the transformed political economy of the Pakistani state.

No doubt, Alavi's thesis of overdeveloped state was the predominant model in the 1970s. However, some scholars believe feudalism has not been a critical force lately as its influence has been curtailed drastically due to the fast-changing socioeconomic conditions. Although still a vital force, feudalism has been weakening since the 1990s.

Sulehria (2019: 241–255), proposing an alternative explanation, argues that although the media have become an important institution, they hardly occupy a central place in the state structure now. Sulehria contends that the current Pakistani state can be best described as a praetorian state, while the media are dominated and managed by three institutions: the military, commercial interests, and the Urdu-Punjabi middle class.

Within the above theoretical context of the nature of the state, it should be easier to grasp the dynamics of media and society in Pakistan. Here, the predominant military-bureaucratic oligarchy, with the full support of the feudalistic structure and commercial interests, controls political, economic, and cultural institutions, including the mass media and education. Its primary function is to protect the interests of the dominant classes. As this alliance rules the country using democracy as a political umbrella, the mass media primarily serve the military-bureaucratic establishment, not the masses. There are several models of media systems that can be reviewed and analysed within the context of the contemporary nation-state of Pakistan.

For instance, Bilge Yesil (2014) refers to Hallin and Mancini's "polarised pluralistic" model of the freedom of the press, which proposes three significant strategies to manage and control media, including clientelism, political parallelism, and state intervention. First, by promoting clientelism, the state becomes a patron of controlling cultural resources of a society including the mass media. State clientelism protects the dominant institutions and classes to promote their viewpoints, predominantly through the mainstream media, effectively rejecting the counter-narrative of the marginalised sectors.

The process of political parallelism allows media outlets to work in collaboration with their favourite political parties, support them, and serve their purpose. This alliance serves media organisations and political parties at the same time. Political leaders and parties within the alliance get space in the media, and media organisations get economic and political perks.

The third strategy of state intervention becomes a practical approach where the government uses different tactics to mould media messages, including direct instructions, legal justifications, and threats to restrict media content (Hallin and Mancini 2012). In several cases, this also leads to self-censorship by media editors and reporters to avoid economic and legal repercussions. This pattern of direct intervention, however, is fast changing because of advancing media technologies and the increasing awareness of civil rights, as we will see in the following section.

In contrast to the traditional model of censorship, Yesil also notes the new model of "dispersion and displacement", where soft or hard censorship is imposed through a wide range of state apparatuses, rather than by a single government agency, which has been the traditional method. Formal, informal, direct, and indirect methods are used to employ internal self-censorship and impose state laws to mould media content.

Contrary to the above postulations of censorship and freedom of expression, several theoretical propositions also focus on how the media are becoming powerful, especially where democratic systems are in the process of maturation. Freedman (2015), for instance, talks about four paradigms of media power within the context of how media systems function: consensus, chaos, control, and contradiction. While the consensus paradigm explains mechanisms of western democracies where media become part of creating consensus, the chaos paradigm also notices the emergence of social media which have challenged the traditional control paradigm by shifting power from media owners and the state to the ordinary citizens who can communicate in their own time and space as they wish. It has altered the communication process from top-down to bottom-top, where citizens take the central place.

The control and contradiction paradigms, combined, better explain the dynamics of media in Pakistan which are controlled by the state and non-state institutions. However, within the same system, the media also tend to contradict the traditional patterns of control and power by providing space to the marginalised segments of society. Although most of the time the media outlets serve the dominant establishment, they occasionally give voice to the poor, minorities, and exploited groups of the society. When issues such as honour killings, missing individuals, and child labour make their way into the media, they are part of this contradiction within the media system. Additionally, this arrangement also works because media outlets need to maintain a façade of credibility, and there are media workers who, despite the political economy of a given media system, bring in dissenting voices.

Based on the above discussion, we can offer the following propositions as a theoretical framework for this volume:

1. As Pakistan has become a praetorian state, the military-bureaucratic oligarchy has become the sole protector of dominant interests in society in alliance with the feudal aristocracy and commercial interests.
2. The mass media, in these circumstances, have become an effective tool in the hands of this ruling oligarchy, mainly to serve the powerful military, commercial interests, and the Urdu, Punjabi middle class that manages the media systems.
3. The "dispersal" and "replacement" model can also explain the process of media censorship, where, in addition to the establishment, multiple state and non-state agencies use numerous strategies to mute the media voice to promote their narrative. In addition to the traditional and modern approaches of

censorship employed by the civil and military establishment, there are several non-state institutions and vested interests that pose severe threats to free expression and media autonomy in Pakistan.
4. Media censorship utilises the strategies of clientelism, political parallelism, as well as direct government intervention. Media outlets are only partly independent as they are aligned with political parties and the powerful establishment which is so apparent from their contents.
5. The control and contradiction paradigm seems to work simultaneously by supporting the dominant narrative and counter-narrative at the same time. Cyberspace, with its social media, has pushed the media outlets to include alternative narratives where the mainstream media, in addition to promoting the dominant discourse, also include the marginalised communities and their issues on a limited basis.

These theoretical propositions can be further elaborated within the dynamics of media growth and freedom of expression throughout the history of Pakistan.

Theoretical implications

First, the military-bureaucratic oligarchy appears to be the sole protector of dominant interests in society in alliance with the feudal aristocracy. The security establishment never allowed the political process to take root, making sure its control and power over the process never diminish.

The mass media, as a result, became a powerful tool in the hands of the military junta, mainly to serve the dominant interest of foreign capital, the internal bourgeoisie, and the landed aristocracy. And it worked both ways. The international capitalistic centre gained its military and geopolitical goals, and the military establishment further strengthened its internal control and power with the timely funding and weaponry of the capitalist system.

Also, as we have seen in the preceding sections, media censorship can be explained within the "dispersal" and "replacement" model, where, in addition to the establishment, multiple state and non-state agencies use numerous strategies to mute the media voices to promote their narrative. In addition to the traditional and modern approaches of censorship employed mostly by the military establishment, there are several non-state groups that pose severe threats to freedom of expression and media in Pakistan. More recently, we have seen different censorship patterns that work perfectly for the junta, including clientelism, political parallelism, and direct governmental intervention.

Interestingly, a recent report by the Committee to Protect Journalists (CPJ) notes that although constitutional guarantees for freedom of the press are provided in Pakistan, "true press freedom is elusive. While the military is not solely responsible for the pressures facing the media, its hands can be found almost everywhere" (CPJ 2018).

Finally, the control and contradiction paradigm seems to work as the coercive military tactics allow the media to include the mainstream discourse while including marginalised communities and their issues as part of the media discourse. Censorship only comes into action if the media try to change or criticise the dominant military discourse.

Coercive tactics have led to a permanent state of mind among journalists and writers to protect their livelihood and life. A 2018 survey of working journalists found that 88% of respondents had censored what they had written, while 72% said this trend of self-censorship had increased over time. Also, 7 in 10 journalists said the strategy makes them feel safe, and 6 in 10 journalists said they would tend to use censorship while writing on the security establishment and religion, and 83% said they would likely censor information about the militancy and terrorism (Media Matters for Democracy 2018a).

Having proposed a theoretical framework for this volume and its implications, in the next section a historical survey of media dynamics along with related issues will help grasp the proposed theoretical postulations.

State hegemony and censorship

At the time of independence, Pakistani society was pre-industrial and pre-literate (Kurian 1982) and the mass media were in a developing stage. Newspapers and radio were a significant source for disseminating news and views to a substantial number of audiences. For the educated middle and upper classes, readership was not just limited to Urdu-language newspapers; it also included some special-interest magazines devoted to children, women, and literature. Ever since, the print media have gradually grown to a large industry where national, regional, and local newspapers provide information, analyses, and news to readers who can read and write (literacy in Pakistan remains far from universal).

With this humble beginning in 1947, 103 dailies were added during the first decade of independence. In 1970, the number rose to 117 and 121 by 1986. With the opening of new universities and improvements in literacy, the growth of Urdu-language dailies was three times that of the English press. Although the English-language readership was limited to urbanised and well-educated professionals, the quality of English-language journalism was far better than the Urdu press.

As the print media were privately owned in the beginning, they enjoyed relative freedom in the reporting and analysis of social, political, and economic issues. But they increasingly came under state pressure or direct control. Not even books, let alone the press, were free from restrictions throughout the national history. From the outset, civil as well as military governments used legal mechanisms and extreme administrative measures to curb any broadsheet that refused to toe their line, while rewarding those who supported them (Gunaratne 1970).

Although English-language publications offered more mature and professional journalism than the Urdu press, historically these remained highly monopolised by a limited number of strong media organisations including the three well-established—Jang, Nawa-i-Waqt, and Dawn—media houses.

Developments in technology tremendously improved the appearance of newspapers, which in turn attracted more readers. Emphasis was given to pictorial journalism, large headlines, short editorials, and simplicity of language. Technological advancements, including computers and the internet, not only enhanced the physical appearance of Urdu-language newspapers, but they also contributed to a faster pace of printing and reporting.

The post-independence period also marked the beginning of a prolonged period of media control and censorship. The Muslim League, the political party which led the liberation movement for Muslims in colonial India, tried to mute political voices in post-colonial Pakistan. Instead of repealing colonial laws widely used by the British authorities, the new rulers of Pakistan imposed additional legal frameworks to control the press. The Pakistan Public Safety Act and the West Punjab Safety Act were introduced within two years of independence. The Security of Pakistan Act was imposed in 1952 to control journalism in the name of national security, which became an intimidating weapon to curb the free press. Using these laws, numerous newspapers were banned during the first seven years of independence (Abbas 1990). Zamir Niazi, in his seminal work on censorship in Pakistan, documents numerous instances of arresting journalists, imposing fines on newspapers, and banning publications temporarily or permanently that deviated from the official standpoint of the ruling Muslim League. According to him, 50 publications were given warnings, and 32 were asked for security deposits in only one year, 1952–53 (Niazi 2010).

With the imposition of the first martial law in 1958, the first military ruler General Ayub Khan used multiple methods to suppress media outlets by introducing the West Pakistan Maintenance of Public Order Ordinance in 1960, the Press and Publication Ordinance (PPO) in 1963 and the formation of the National Press Trust (NPT)[3] in 1964.

In addition to using legal provisions, censorship was being imposed through a widely used practice of press advice where just a phone call from the Press Information Department (PID) would have been enough for editors to kill or modify any news story. All these methods led to self-censorship among the editors and journalists, not only in the state-owned media but also in the privately owned press.

With the low literacy rate, however, readership was not as high in rural areas where opinion leaders read newspapers to a group of farmers. While interpersonal communication was the primary mode of communication instead of written words, the lack of good infrastructure and transportation facilities also became physical hurdles to communicate with the rural masses in interior areas. For these reasons, radio filled the gap of communicating to the rural masses.

Once upon a time, radio reigned supreme

With the invention of radio transistors in 1960, which made reception of radio programmes cost-effective and user-friendly, the radio became a popular medium not only in the rural but also in urban centres by 1970. "It was technological advancements which, to a great extent, enlarged the radio spectrum. Radio, satellite communication, FM radio, and the inexpensive transmitting equipment, made radio accessible to small communities and organizations" (Abbas 1990: 36).

The apparent objectives of radio broadcasting in Pakistan were to promote "democratic, religious, moral, and social values and projecting the state policies on national issues both in its home and external broadcasts" (Said 1996). Radio broadcasting was thus developed as a state-controlled medium with a centralised administration. A network of radio stations throughout the country was established, and by 1974, 70% of the population and 33% of the area were covered by the medium-wave broadcasting system. Pakistan Broadcasting Corporation (PBC) established a network of 16 radio stations which transmitted about 53,000 hours annually. With this rapid growth of broadcasting, radio covered 95% of the population and 75% of the area by the 1980s. PBC presently covers 98% of the population and 80% of the area (PBC 2018) with its 42 stations across the country which broadcast 322 hours daily on medium wave, short wave, and FM in 20 languages and dialects. Its external service broadcasts 30 hours daily in 17 languages for 70 countries in Asia, Africa, and Europe.

While radio content largely targeted urban centres, the PBC also introduced rural programs in the sixties "as an instrument of social change, education, and information" (Said 1996). Farm forum programmes became part of the rural transmissions with the objectives of providing technical information on farming, motivating farmers to adopt modern farming techniques and livestock and dairy farming, to keep farmers informed on the activities of the Department of Agriculture, and finally to motivate them to adopt cooperative farming.

Aligned with the first military regime's rural development initiatives, specific programmes were offered for rural areas, mostly as part of an open listenership strategy for at least 12 languages for such lingual groups as Punjabi, Pashto, Barahavi, Balochi, Pothohari, Saraiki, Sindhi, Balochi, Brashistki, Balti, Hindko, and Chitrali. These programmes are generally in the format of talk shows with two or three characters speaking in the local languages. Topics range from health to weather, farming, scientific information, market reports, religion, national issues, and folk and cultural activities. Radio Pakistan also conducted several surveys to assess listening patterns of its rural programmes. One of the surveys for its rural programmes produced by the Rawalpindi station in the 1990s revealed that the programme was liked by over 60% of listeners, who were over 35% male and 46% female, and 60.64% of these listeners were illiterate (Said 1996).

Being a state medium, radio widely supported the regime of the day, and because of this linkage it became a tool of government propaganda. During national crises or war, the official viewpoint was widely supported by radio, without including alternative perspectives. During the 1965 war with India, for instance, "Pakistan's state-controlled media generated a frenzy of jihad, extolling the virtues of 'Pakistan's soldiers of Islam' who were said to have received divine help" (Ispahani 2015). This unusual but one-sided worldview became the hallmark of state-controlled electronic media in Pakistan, even in the case of Pakistan Television (PTV), launched in 1964 as a state-run channel.

The idiot box arrives in Pakistan

For developing nations, TV has proved to be a modern medium which can be used to promote national unity as noted by Hedebro: "Many developing nations invest much in building television systems. The motives for this may differ, but whatever the reason, television has been given high priority. One objective seems to be present in most countries: that of promoting indigenous national culture and strengthening feeling of one people, one nation" (Hedebro 1982).

Compared to radio, TV became an overnight obsession for viewers and rulers, as a magic box that combined sound, light, and colourful visuals mesmerising its captive audiences. Realising the immense power of this new medium, both military and civilian governments exploited it to the utmost. Although national integration was the primary reason behind establishing television, it became an astonishing instrument not only as a propaganda tool through news and current affairs, but also as a medium for disseminating state ideologies through entertainment and educational programmes.

The introduction of TV in Pakistan primarily contributed to undermining radio broadcasting, especially in urban areas. The Pakistan Television Corporation, commonly known as PTV, became a commercialised state organisation. Although a corporation, the government controls most of its shares, while it works under the Ministry of Information, Broadcasting, National History, and Literary Heritage.

Six PTV production centres in the country, including two in Islamabad and one each in Lahore, Karachi, Quetta, Peshawar, and Quetta, were connected through a vast network of boosters and microwave, satellite, and cable systems. This network is also connected to the outside world through its earth satellite station in Karachi. PTV has contributed quality entertainment programmes rooted in technologically skilled professionals and well-trained producers.

Starting from limited facilities and staff, PTV covered 34.6% of the area and reached 82% of the population by 1986 and "compared to 60 hours and 49 minutes of telecast per week in 1985–86, the TV programmes in 1986–87 amounted to 66 hours and 40 minutes" (Government of Pakistan 1987). PTV broadcasts entertainment, drama, news, current affairs, sports, and religious and educational programmes.

Unlike the current TV viewership patterns in Pakistan with the popularity of news and current affairs programmes, it was PTV's entertainment programmes that became popular among the masses, not only in Pakistan but other countries, including India, in the 1970s and 1980s. As news and current affairs segments lost credibility, being the government's mouthpiece, plays, sports, and music, became very popular based on their quality and portrayal of social issues of society at large. A doctoral dissertation reported in 1990 that PTV's "Drama series have become a regular and popular genre in Pakistan Television (PTV) productions since 1975" (Suleman 1990).

Unfortunately, the mass media were not only becoming an easy target of military dictators, they were also widely and comfortably suppressed by political leaders. Zulfikar Ali Bhutto (ruled 1972–77), the first democratically elected leader who championed democratic values, human rights, and freedom of expression, not only continued the existing legal framework but also introduced new measures. Two martial law orders were issued to bring the NPT publications under his direct control when he assumed responsibility as Martial Law Administrator in 1972. Allocation of government advertisements and newsprint quotas were fully utilised to pressurise the press economically. Several publications were banned, permanently or for a short period, and editors were barred from writing or owning print media between 1971 and 1977.

Another military dictator, General Zia-ul-Haq, imposed martial law in 1977, which took the nation to an unprecedented level of coercion and censorship. Apart from the usual tactics of jailing journalists and banning publications, the regime introduced some innovative methods. Under the new pre-censorship strategy, newspapers, magazines, and even literary periodicals were scrutinised before publication. Resistance and disagreement with the government were liable to severe punishment which also came in the form of flogging, jailing, and torturing journalists. Four journalists, Nasir Zaidi, Masoodullah Khan, Iqbal Jafferi, and Khwar Naeem Hashmi, were sentenced to lashes by a military court in 1979.

The autocratic regimes of Ayub Khan and Ziaul Haq tightened the grip on news and current affairs programmes, with stringent policies to control the state media, especially television. The Islamised ideological thrust of Zia's regime severely decreased the popularity of television, which was effectively filling the gap of limited entertainment opportunities in the social life of the middle and poor classes (Shaikh 2007).

News and current affairs, as a result, became untrustworthy sources of information, mostly seen as an instrument of official propaganda. That's why, during national crises or war, people always switched to international news media, including the BBC Urdu radio service.

The next, civilian, government of Benazir Bhutto (1988–90) allowed freedom of the press to some extent. Despite this openness, however, state-controlled radio and TV started excluding major news stories from their news shows, while the press was reporting them. This contradiction exposed the democratically elected government's claims of freeing the media but not allowing free flow of news through the state media. The later civilian governments of Nawaz Sharif (or his party the Pakistan Muslim League-N)[4] and Benazir Bhutto again (1993–97) were not less inclined to use their power for muting media voices, although they allowed comparative freedom to media outlets, especially the print media during the democratic interregnum (1988–99).

PTV monopoly ends

As the nation approached the twenty-first century, two significant trends, one national and one global, were taking place. Internally, the country failed to develop an appropriate political system based on universal democratic norms. The security establishment, as it grew in leaps and bounds to become a well-organised political party and a gigantic economic conglomerate, never allowed political and cultural institutions to grow as it fully controlled the media in order to strengthen its power and control. On the other hand, global technological and media dynamics were changing fast. Because of the emerging communication technologies of the internet, satellite communication, cell phone, and social media, the traditional media, especially television, became part of a global system technologically and programmatically.

The cyber age brought new challenges and opportunities in Pakistan as the emergence of social media has widened the communication space not only to a national but a global audience at an unprecedented speed. As internet technology and social media were transforming the traditional media of communication, the government came under tremendous pressure to liberate the conventional media.

These emerging media also posed a significant challenge for military and civil governments. For them, the main question was how to control the flow of information when social media provide an alternative discourse while the state media tend to provide a one-sided official worldview. Realising this, it was the military establishment which decided to privatise electronic media and bring the internet into its grip to serve its purpose. Also, to counter the ever-increasing influence of global and regional media outlets, the military had realised that during the limited war with India in Kargil the privately owned and commercially driven Indian channels were more successful in telling the world their story than the Pakistani state-controlled media (Sulehria 2018: 93–95).

Ironically, it was a dictator, Pervez Musharraf, who privatised the electronic media in 2002, realising that the security establishment was not being served well by the state media in comparison to the privately owned TV channels in India. He realised too late that the privatised TV channels were becoming a monster, challenging his power and control.

In the later part of his rule, Musharraf started showing his true colours by declaring an emergency on 3 November 2007 and imposing draconian laws to curb media messages. His administration suspended TV shows, blocked websites, raided media offices, including newspapers, radio, and TV stations, and censored newspapers. During the Musharraf regime, the Pakistan Electronic Media Regulatory Authority (PEMRA) was formed to regulate electronic media and issuing licenses through auctions to electronic media, cable operators, cyber media providers, and non-commercial radio services for educational purposes. Subsequent governments in Pakistan have exploited PEMRA to gag TV channels.

Finally, it was the civilian government of Nawaz Sharif that devised a legal framework in 2016 to put the privatisation jinee back in the bottle, in the name of curbing terrorism, national security, and law and order. The Cyber Crime Act, introduced to tame the unleashed tiger, thus provided broad authority to the government to cancel media licenses, ban content, and punish media workers at will. The Act, however, came under severe criticism from activists and scholars (Khan 2016).

Meanwhile, we have witnessed a surge in electronic media, including FM radio and TV channels of all kinds all over the country. Between 2002 and 2018 electronic media became a booming business for both the government and media owners. The government earned millions through auctioning radio and TV licenses and distributing rights, while media owners pocketed profits through the ever-growing consumerism and commercialisation in society. While the stated purpose of privatising the mass media was to allow easy media access to all strata of society, including low-income populations in urban and rural areas, media ownership is highly concentrated in urban areas, mostly in Punjab and Sindh provinces. The presence of commercial media in Baluchistan and Khyber Pakhtunkhwah is highly limited.

This privatisation has also helped media organisations to gain some freedom from government sponsorship as they started depending on private commercials. Currently, TV channels have 47% of commercial revenue, print media 33%, outdoor advertising 11%, and radio 2% (Khan 2009). In the cutthroat media competition, however, media managers are increasingly adopting cheap tactics to gain audiences. Producing talk shows with shouting contests, provoking participants to insult opponents, and avoiding in-depth discussions on issues have become common tricks of gaining popularity these days.

Civilian martial law

The security establishment was well equipped to practice new strategies of controlling the media after experiencing four military dictatorships over the last 70 years. Motivated by the establishment's intentions to control the outcome of the 2018 general election, its agencies started using extreme measures. Media organisations faced threats and direct attacks, while abduction of bloggers and journalists rose to an unprecedented level.

As the security establishment came in direct conflict with the third Nawaz Sharif-led government (2013–18) and his party, media were caught between the two conflicting institutions in the 2018 general election. The security establishment used unimaginable tactics to control information which did not favour its institutions or policies. According to a primary survey of overt or covert brutalities, 28 incidents of various types, from direct violent attacks to hidden threats, were reported. Of these, 11 physical attacks on writers and reporters, one arrest, two abductions, three blockades, five censorships, five intimidations, and one legal action against media personnel were reported (Media Matters in Democracy 2018b).

In the case of Pakistan, the security establishment increasingly implicates the country's military. A trend that deserves a special mention in the context of this book's theme is the growing control and influence of the Pakistan military over Pakistani media, including TV, film, and social networks. The next section explores precisely this theme.

Military as the media manager

Ayesha Siddiqa's seminal work on the Pakistan military's business ventures, *Military Inc.*, hit the stalls in 2007. The book was immediately banned by the Musharraf dictatorship, triggering global curiosity and censure. The tome is well researched and well argued, and it is a foundational work because it broached a topic hitherto taboo, uncharted terrain in Pakistan. In 2017, the second edition of *Military Inc.* rolled out. In the latest edition, the author has appended two chapters. While the penultimate chapter documents the military's control of governance, the last chapter is suggestively titled "From Military Inc. to Media Inc.".

The expansion in media, she claims, has allowed the military to systematically encourage a narrative that is not merely friendly in relation to the security establishment but has also allowed the military to develop "a new nationalist discourse to keep its institution relevant not only for the state but for society as well" (Siddiqa 2017: 328). She agrees that the media are not as strictly controlled as was the norm in previous decades when airwaves were a jealously guarded state monopoly. However, she adds a caveat: "Yet, such openness is riddled with a bias for the military. While there are endless talk shows discussing the corruption of politicians, there is very little about similar acts by military men" (Siddiqa 2017: 325).

The military's corruption is not merely edited out, the media either never broach topics the military would find unpalatable or do not deviate from the military-dictated narrative on such strategic questions as Balochistan, Kashmir, Afghanistan, and the Taliban. Of late (since 2019), the Pashtun Defence Movement (PTM), a rights-based social movement that emerged in the region bordering Afghanistan, has become the latest taboo. In an op-ed for the *Washington Post*, suggestively titled, "Why Pakistan's crackdown on the press is getting worse by the day", Steven Butler at the Committee to Protect Journalists (CPJ) claims: "The government and military now share the view that the media should support the Pakistani state, not criticize it. As a result, no one's left to put the brakes on measures, legal or extra legal, taken against journalists who report news authorities don't like. The military's in charge, without a coup" (Butler 2019).

The fact of the matter is, the expansion in the television spectrum, after the liberalisation of the airwaves from 2001 onwards, has allowed a systematic militarisation of the media. Arguably, there are four good reasons to explain the militarisation of the Pakistani media in the last decade.

First, the military, as the architect of the media market's liberalisation, was able to shape and guide policies for electronic media. The PEMRA was brought into being by the Inter Services Public Relations (ISPR), which serves as the public relations arm of the armed forces in Pakistan. Likewise, the Frequency Allocation Board (FAB), allocating frequencies to television channels, is overrepresented by the government, and channels require clearance from the security agencies to get their licenses. Most importantly, the military has a history of shaping, disciplining, and manipulating the media owing to its political role.

Second, the military commands a substantial infrastructure to influence, infiltrate, and manipulate the media. The ISPR serves as a legitimate platform to interact and penetrate media houses. Owing to a particular political situation whereby spasmodically the military is directly ruling the country, the ISPR has grown in size, scope, and capacity. There is also a shift in the ISPR's operational routines. "Many journalists bitterly remember how they were mistreated, sometimes even badly manhandled, by intelligence officials in the 1990s only for reporting on high-level staff shuffles in the army. Reports about such shuffles now reach newsrooms as an official press release, mostly delivered as an email or a tweet," reports Umer Farooq, a seasoned journalist (Farooq 2016).

Most importantly, the ISPR has learnt to maintain a functioning distance and deploy an operational ambiguity to retain an element of credibility. For instance, when the ISPR wants favourable coverage for the military, it engages "private consultants—some of them journalists-turned-analysts—to coordinate with reporters and desk editors". Likewise, ambiguity is maintained in a crafty manner. A certain "Pak Army Channel", for instance, propagates pro-army content. However, the ISPR disowns such obscure accounts and sites (Farooq 2016).

As if the military does not trust its ISPR-Goebbels, there is also a "Media Cell" at the Inter-Services Intelligence (ISI) headquarters. While accessible to friendly journalists and researchers, the "media cell" operates in a phoney manner. Hence, it is indeed challenging to document infiltration of Pakistani media by the ISI's media cell. Anecdotal evidence slips through cracks that appear in the rock-solid multi-storey concrete and steel structures housing the ISI establishment at Islamabad's Zero Point. For instance, Zaid Hamid—a pro-military hawk dominating the TV screens as a "defence analyst"—is a spurious character in many ways. In 2013, Imad Khalid, Hamid's secretary, in a sensational press conference, accused his boss of receiving from the ISI over half a million rupees monthly for propagating his views on mainstream and social media.

Third, the element of ideological affinity between the military and on-screen celebrities has further facilitated the hegemonic khaki hold over television screens. This ideological affinity is further enabled by a generalised rightwards ideological shift in the country since the late 1980s. In an ideological milieu charged with religiously motivated anti-Americanism, veritable conspiracy theories are crudely deployed to diffuse any crisis tainting the military image.

Finally, when carrots do not serve the purpose, the stick is deployed to discipline an anchor person/channel gone berserk[5]. In 2011, Salim Shahzad was murdered. His tortured body was recovered from a canal. Before his death, he had informed various human rights and journalist bodies that the ISI had warned him. A year earlier, Umer Cheema, another reporter working for *The News*, was kidnapped, tortured, and sexually assaulted. Again, the finger was pointed at the ISI. In 2014, noted anchor person with a considerable fan following, Hamid Mir, was shot at and critically injured. His family blamed the ISI chief, which led to a bitter row between GEO network, Mir's employer and the country's leading network, and the military establishment. Najam Sethi, a noted anchor person and owner of an influential weekly, *The Friday Times*, also points out a "wonderful mechanism" to silence the news channels: "the military intelligence agency just calls up the cable operators in every part of the country and tells them to take such-and-such channels off the air" (Butler 2019). In this manner, nobody can either prove the military's involvement or name them.

A combination of all the factors described above has transformed the privately owned commercial channels into mouthpieces of the military establishment.

Growth of mass media and freedom of expression

Two paradoxical trends were emerging in Pakistan's scenario of media and politics. While the forces of power and control were busy controlling the means of communication, the media were also experiencing a consistent pattern of growth. This was possible for two reasons. First, censorship was not a blanket phenomenon as it was only meant to boost the governmental view and mute voices of resistance. For this reason, criticism was allowed on socio-cultural, administrative, and political issues.

Second, media workers, journalists, and writers never lost hope of attaining freedom of expression, and they continued protesting and raising their voices against the government control of the media. Consequently, from a strictly controlled press to independent media outlets, Pakistan has also been witnessing a consistent growth of mass media during the last 70 years.

The All Pakistan Newspapers Society (APNS) reported 466 total publications in 2018, based on its membership, comprising 384 dailies, 60 monthlies, 18 weeklies, and 4 fortnightly magazines. Although there might be additional publications which are not APNS members across the country, this indicates a growing interest of readers in daily newspapers as compared to magazines (see Table 1.1). Of the total number of dailies (384), the overwhelming majority of newspapers (252) are published in the national language Urdu. Next come the English dailies at 84, followed by Sindhi 43, Pushto 3, Seraiki 1, and Balochi 1 (APNS 2018).

The following top 15 Urdu dailies had substantial advertisement revenue in August 2017: *Jang, Express, Nawa-i-Waqt, Dunya, Khabrain, NaiBaat, Ausaf, Aaj, Mashriq, Kawish, Pakistan, Ummat, Jehan-E Pakistan, Din,* and *Jasarat.* The top nine English dailies in the same period were *Dawn, The News, Business Recorder, Express Tribune, The Nation, Pakistan Today, Pakistan Observer,* and *The Frontier Post* (PAS 2017). Publication of political, social, and specialised magazines in Urdu also increased based on their popularity in the specific audience.

TABLE 1.1 Private and state media in 2018

	State TV (PTV)	State radio (PBC)	Private satellite TV	Private cable TV license	Private FM radio	University FM radio	Internet TV (IPTV) license
Number and type of media outlets	6 TV stations	42 Radio stations	90 Channels	22 Licenses	143 Radio stations	45 Education radio	3 Licenses
Reach and main features	Covered 89% population	Covered 98% population	Thematic TV channels	Mostly in urban areas	In urban and rural areas	Radio for education and training	To distribute internet-based TV

Source: PEMRA, PBC, and PTV

The privatisation spree in 2002 changed the media dynamics so fast that by 2018 the Pakistani media industry became a mix of state-controlled radio and TV and privatised electronic media, which included a variety of TV outlets and FM radio stations, in addition to internet-based social media outlets.

Table 1.1 indicates an interesting scenario where 6 state-controlled TV stations and 42 radio stations were losing their audience by 2018, while a diverse group of 90-odd private TV channels and 143 FM radio stations, supported by cable and satellite technologies, were ready to challenge the political system, if not the establishment. The content of these media outlets is currently distributed by 22 licensed cable operators, mostly in urban centres of the country.

But what about the reach of these media outlets in society at large? A 2018 Gallup Pakistan survey reveals some interesting trends in the penetration of media and communication technologies in society. The survey results indicate that 65% of Pakistanis use mobile phones, 11% report having access to the internet, and 15% have access to a computer. Almost two-thirds of Pakistanis claim to watch television, which is a 24% increase since 1987 (43% in 1987 and 67% in 2018).

As TV viewership increased, newspaper readership declined from 39% in 1987 to only 18% in 2018. A similar trend has been noticed in radio listening as its listenership was 48% in 1987, declining to 9% in 2018 (Gallup Pakistan 2018). Clearly, television has captured a large share of the audience, becoming the most popular medium in Pakistan, and offering a variety of themes in local languages. Table 1.2 indicates the number of TV channels in the country by theme and language. Of the total TV outlets being offered currently, 39 are devoted to local news followed by 10 channels for religion, indicating that the audience has a

TABLE 1.2 Number of TV channels by theme and language

TV channels by theme		*TV channels by language*	
Local News	39	Urdu	17
International News	7	Punjabi	2
Religion	10	Sindhi	4
Sports	3	Pashto	2
Children	2	Hindko	1
Urdu Movies	1	Balochi	1
English Movies	3	Kashmir/Gilgit/Baltistan	1
Music	4	English	1
Health	1		
Food	2		
Education	2		
Business	1		
Fashion	1		

Source: Gallup Pakistan (2015)

predominant interest in domestic news and religion. Additionally, there are seven international news channels, three sports, two children's, one Urdu movies, three English movies, four music, one health, two food, two education, one business, and one fashion.

Although state radio and TV offered programmes in native languages on a limited basis, privatisation has offered new opportunities for TV channels devoted to local languages. A total of 29 TV channels now offer entertainment programmes in 8 languages including 17 in Urdu, the national language. Additionally, there are two Punjabi channels, four Sindhi, one Pashto, one Hindko, one Balochi, one English, and one for local languages in Kashmir, Gilgit, and Baltistan.

The evolution of media organisations and Pakistan's political process can be better explained within the context of the changing scenario of freedom of expression, which kept transforming along with the tumultuous political process. As freedom of expression represents a wide variety of perceptions, it needs a robust definition. Dr Mehdi Hasan, former dean of communication and media expert in Pakistan, subscribes to a cultural and historical view of the concept in an interview conducted for this study:

> Every nation defines freedom of expression within the context of its history and cultural traditions. In Pakistan, unfortunately, freedom of expression is defined by the establishment that elaborates this constitutional right to protect its interest. All administrations in Pakistan, military or civilian, have justified censorship on the pretext of national security, religious sanctity, and good relations with other countries. In fact, they were only interested in strengthening their power and control.
>
> *(Hasan 2016)*

Freedom of expression also includes national and international perspectives. Universally accepted as a basic human right, freedom of expression also comes with moral and ethical responsibilities. Whatever the approach, the concept includes culturally defined and legally implemented rights and limits of public discourse in each society. The social responsibilities of communicators and journalists become a widely accepted "code of ethics" in most societies.

Table 1.3 offers a historical view of the political process, tools of media control employed by civilian and military regimes, and the corresponding level of freedom of expression. We can see two distinctive patterns of freedom of expression in Pakistan during the two historical periods: the first 53 years, 1947–2000, and from 2000 onwards. Although there were four military dictatorships and six democratically elected regimes in the first period, the military establishment became the strongest political and economic institution, undermining the growth of political institutions and weakening the political process. Increasingly, the concept that dissent is a healthy ingredient of democratic societies did not gain support from the rulers. Consequently, all the regimes used an overall policy of curbing opposing viewpoints and suppressing media outlets, mostly using legal provisions, press advice, censorship, and pre-censorship, as well as using government advertisements and newsprint quotas as exploitative tools.

TABLE 1.3 Timeline of political process and freedom of expression in Pakistan

Year	Regime type and leader	Freedom of expression level and tools of censorship
1947–1958	**Civilian Rule** Various leaders of Muslim League ruled.	**Moderately Controlled:** 1923 Safety Act continued. Pakistan Public Safety Act, West Punjab Safety Act, and Security of Pakistan Act introduced.
1958–1969	**Military Dictatorship** Gen. Ayub Khan.	**Strictly Controlled:** APP, newspapers, and publications nationalised. NPT formed, PPO and new laws imposed. Self-censorship and press advice began.
1969–1971	**Military Dictatorship** Gen. Yahya Khan.	**Partly Free:** Free media in the first year. Media restrictions during the 1971 war. Most media outlets toed the government line.
1971–1977	**Civilian Rule** Prime Minister Zulfiqar Ali Bhutto.	**Moderately Controlled:** West Pakistan Maintenance of Public Order Ordinance and press laws introduced. NPT came under Bhutto.
1977–1988	**Military Dictatorship** Gen. Ziaul Haq.	**Strictly Controlled:** Press advice. Martial law regulations and laws used. Intimidation, arrests, public flogging, and pre-censorship for public and private media introduced.
1988–1990	**Civilian Rule** Prime Minister Benazir Bhutto.	**Moderately Free:** State radio and TV excluded opposition parties.
1991–1993	**Civilian Rule** Prime Minister Nawaz Sharif.	**Moderately Free:** State radio/TV. Comparatively free press.
1993–1996	**Civilian Rule** Prime Minister Benazir Bhutto.	**Moderately Free:** State-owned electronic media. Press moderately free.
1997–1999	**Civilian Rule** Prime Minister Nawaz Sharif.	**Moderately Free:** Some restrictions on print media. EMRA formed.
1999–2008	**Military Dictatorship** Gen. Pervez Musharraf.	**Moderately Controlled:** PEMRA formed to regularise electronic and cyber media. PTA formed to regularise telecommunications. Emergency imposed. Non-state groups built up pressures.
2008–2013	**Civilian Rule** Prime Ministers Yusuf Gilani and Pervez Ashraf.	**Moderately Free:** Free media with strong non-state coercion by terrorists and political activists.
2013–2018	**Civilian Rule** Prime Ministers Nawaz Sharif and Khaqan Abbasi.	**Covertly Coerced:** Cyber Crime Act introduced. Overt freedom with covert military coercion. Attacks by non-state organisations. Self-censorship increased.
2018–Present	**Civilian Rule** Prime Minister Imran Khan.	**Covertly Coerced:** Covert military control on media. Self-censorship increased.

Source: Author

Note: Partly Free=Mostly free media with some restrictions; **Moderately Controlled**=Mostly controlled with some freedom; **Moderately Free**=Free and controlled media at the same time; **Strictly Controlled**=No tolerance for any dissent; **Covertly Coerced**=No apparent censorship but strong covert actions/violence leading to self-censorship. **NPT**=National Press Trust; **EMRA**=Electronic Media Authority; **PEMRA**=Pakistan Electronic Media Authority; **PTA**=Pakistan Telecommunication Authority; **PPO**=Press and Publication Ordinance; **APP**=Associated Press of Pakistan news agency.

The political scenario, however, drastically changed in the aftermath of 9/11. As all the previous military regimes were fully supported by the West, specifically the United States, they also strengthened the Musharraf regime with funding and armaments. The country, because of these geopolitical conditions, became the target of a prolonged reign of terrorism and violence by non-state groups.

By this time, telecommunications and global media technologies were already experiencing the new cyber age. Amid these internal and international dynamics, the military became extremely protective of its institutions from 2000 onwards, more than the previous dictatorial regimes. The security establishment thus developed direct but undeclared devices which became more dreadful and dangerous for intellectuals, social media activists, and journalists.

The two civilian governments post-Musharraf were forced to operate under extremely oppressive conditions as their elected prime ministers were sent home frequently, ostensibly by the judiciary but covertly by the military and its agencies. The mass media were thus extremely pressured and coerced by the establishment and non-state forces of militants and political activists. The use of the legal and administrative approach in muting the media, a hallmark of the first period, were conveniently replaced with direct and fatal attacks, financial blackmailing, abductions, intimidation, and torture.

The media came under renewed attack ahead of the general elections in 2018. However, the gagging of the media reached an acute crisis a year after the election and the formation of a government headed by Prime Minister Imran Khan.

Consider the following incidents in July 2019. On 8 July three news channels, Capital TV, 24 News, and Abbtak, were simultaneously blocked for almost one day. GEO News was pulled off the air just ahead of Prime Minister Imran Khan's US visit on 22 July. GEO is viewed as a belligerent voice both by Mr Khan and his party, Pakistan Justice Movement (PTI). GEO also has a history of a run-in with the Pakistan military. Meanwhile, on 1 July, GEO stopped broadcasting an interview with the former president, Asif Zardari, after a few minutes of airing the interview. Likewise, on 11 July, Hum channel stopped mid-way an interview with Maryam Nawaz Sharif, daughter of former prime minister Nawaz Sharif. Also, in July 2019, an online campaign was orchestrated to harass journalists deemed critical of the PTI and the Pakistan military. In response to the call of media workers' unions, demonstrations were staged across Pakistan by journalists to protest the attempts to stifle the media (Butler 2019; Jabeen 2019).

Table 1.4 represents Pakistan's overall press freedom ranking among 180 countries on the World Press Freedom Index, calculated annually by Reporters Without Borders. As a smaller number indicates a better ranking, Pakistan stands almost in the middle of the world index above Bangladesh, Thailand, Iran, and some Arab countries. With Norway at the top, most of the Western countries, including the United States, are in the top half of the grid. Although its ranking has improved from 159 in 2013 to 142 in 2019, the overall ranking still shows Pakistan in a "difficult situation" category when it comes to freedom of the press.

TABLE 1.4 Pakistan's ranking in the World Press Freedom Index

Year	Ranking
2019	142/180
2018	139/180
2017	139/180
2016	147/180
2015	159/180
2014	158/180
2013	159/180

Source: Reporters Without Borders, RSF 2019

Media workers, however, were not merely agitating against the gagging of the media. Massive redundancies at media houses across Pakistan have further aggravated the precarious situation for media workers. These layoffs, however, also mirror the fact that the media system in Pakistan is economically in crisis too.

At the turn of the century, there were 20,000 media workers, 3,000 of them journalists. Presently, the media industry employs 250,000 workers, 20,000 of them journalists. During 2018–19, roughly 10,000 media workers, including 3,000 journalists, lost their jobs. In some instances, the media workers accepted 40–60% cuts in their wages to avoid layoffs. In 2019, workers at such major media houses as Jang and Nawa-i-Waqt were not paid their salaries regularly. In some cases, payments were delayed for three to four months.

The media bosses have blamed an overall economic crunch as well as the PTI government for the job losses. On the one hand, advertising spend has shrunk. The advertising spend in 2016 was Rs 87 billion (US$500 million). It shrunk by 7% in 2017–18. It was expected to shrink by 30% (Jabeen 2019). On the other hand, the PTI government has slashed the rates for media advertisements. The government ads constitute a significant source of income for the Pakistani media. For instance, during 2013–18, the federal government spent Rs 15 billion on media advertisements (Jabeen 2019). However, blaming the economic downturn is an inadequate explanation for workers' redundancies. A key reason behind workers' redundancies is the crisis of trade unionism in the media sector (Sulehria 2017: 354–356).

Conclusion

Privatisation is sometimes confused with media independence. On the contrary, private media organisations appear to be highly vulnerable to coercive state manoeuvring and non-state elements. Thus, in the case of Pakistan, the state is not the sole institution today, as multiple forces have emerged to manipulate media outlets.

Media professionalism also seems to be declining as media owners, as well as organisations of editors and reporters, are responsible for the lack of professional maturity and absence of a robust code of ethics. As it is, the whole media industry is suffering from on-the-job-training syndrome, without providing training opportunities for journalists. It is like sending a soldier to the battlefield without weapons training. It is the responsibility of news managers to offer proper training to young journalists in media ethics, professional skills, and social responsibilities.

Despite these limitations, there have been some positive advancements in the field. The provincial governments of Sindh, Punjab, and Khyber Pakhtunkhwa have enacted right-to-information laws which allow journalists and citizens to have access to government information. Likewise, the Sindh government has appointed a focal person to monitor crimes against journalists and provide arbitration between security agencies and reporters (PPF 2017). In the wake of increasing atrocities against media workers, some crucial steps have been taken to create a safe working environment. Safety Hubs have been introduced in several cities, including Lahore, Islamabad, Karachi, and Quetta to assist journalists who are under pressure from state and non-state institutions by providing information, mediation, and training.

The Nawaz Sharif government removed the ban on YouTube in 2016 after five years and introduced a safety bill for journalists in parliament in 2017 which proposed payments to affected journalists, appointing a special prosecutor for media, and widening the definition of a journalist. A WhatsApp group of 30 editors, "Editors for Safety", was founded in 2015 to assist media personnel who are under pressure from state institutions and non-state groups.

In addition to these efforts, there exist many advocacy, training, and research organisations to support and inform media personnel. Media Matters for Democracy, the Pakistan Press Foundation, and the Freedom Network are three such organisations which help raise awareness for freedom of expression with different approaches.

As strengthening democracy promotes the free flow of ideas and tolerance, freedom of expression flourishes with the growth of the democratic process in any society. Unfortunately, periodic military interventions, terrorism, and the strong will of rulers to control the media have contributed to weakening the fourth estate of democracy since independence.

Overall, the news about the status of the media in Pakistan is good and bad. Despite the unprecedented growth of the media and achieving a level of freedom, the media still face state and non-state coercion, while a substantial number of journalists and reporters lack professional maturity and finesse.

Pathetically, little has changed so far when it comes to freedom of expression and professionalism. It explains why BBC Urdu, along with global TV channels, is still the most trustworthy news medium, while the Pakistani media lack credibility among the masses at large. What has changed is the variety and number of media outlets that have emerged in the aftermath of the privatising spree.

Organisation of the book

This book is organised around the following five themes: Terrorism and television content; freedom of expression and media-state relations; women journalists and gender bias; media coverage of peripheral areas; and finally, coverage of interstate crises.

The editors of this book, Qaisar Abbas and Farooq Sulehria, set the tone of the current volume in Chapter 1 by defining its theoretical framework, drawing upon the historical contexts of how media evolved in the country. Exploring the complexities of the political structure and how it hinders freedom of expression in Pakistan, it offers a thorough survey of the growth of media industries in Pakistan and the transforming nature of censorship.

In Chapter 2, Faizullah Jan examines newspapers and magazines of extremist/militant organisations with the aim of understanding how they define Pakistan and its society; how they construct the socio-political reality of the world; what discourse(s) they draw on to represent the world; and what discourse(s) they create.

Chapter 3 looks at Pakistan Television (PTV) drama and Lollywood films that promote a jihadi discourse. Farooq Sulehria, in this chapter, establishes reciprocity between jihadification of television drama/Lollywood productions and a deepening Islamisation of the country which in turn strengthened the Pakistan military's hegemony. Additionally, a juxtaposition of jihadi plays and Islamisation foregrounds the importance of culture in the spread of Islamic fundamentalism in Pakistan.

In Chapter 4, Fawzia Afzal Khan, comparing two different media types, Malala Yousufzai's book and a stage performance on the life of Mukhtaran Mai, explores these and other relevant questions: Does it reproduce the image of the "third world woman as monolith"—or did it allow for the figure of Mukhtaran to speak to the audience assembled at Baruch Performing Arts Center in ways that brought forth the historical context of Pakistani and US politics? Does Malala's self-representation in her memoir, her staging of herself as the "voice" of a young Pakistani woman, similarly exemplify the competing motives animating the spectacle of being placed in the centre of a supposedly "universalist" human rights discursive framework?

Chapter 5 looks at the TV news coverage of an interstate crisis within the theoretical framework of frames. Qaisar Abbas, in this chapter, textually analyses how GEO TV of Pakistan and NDTV of India covered the 2016 Kashmir crisis supporting their state narrative. It concludes that talk shows of both channels covered the Indian "strategic strike" inside the Pakistani-administered Kashmir in terms of coloniality, warmongering, construction of reality, and a patriotic thrust.

Afiya Shehrbano Zia, in Chapter 6, offers a condensed summary on some diverse trends related to the performativity of women's piety as observed in various media forms after 2001. In order to highlight how contested this terrain is, it contrasts the political discourses that are transcoded in other trends, such as the rising expressions of sexuality and sexual autonomies by and within Pakistan's feminist movements and which are received as anti-piety and anti-Islam, or counter-cultural. A variety of media sources are referenced to demonstrate the range of cultural spaces that are influential on these themes in Pakistan today.

In Chapter 7, Ayesha Khan investigates the types and levels of online threats, harassment, and abuse faced by women journalists in Pakistan. It is based on the hypothesis that women journalists, particularly those demonstrating a higher level of press freedom through their choice of beat and other journalistic work, are exposed to online misogyny. This study uses the objectivist and epistemological framework to investigate the nature of abuse, threats, and harassment targeted at women journalists publishing their work online in Pakistan.

Chapter 8 evaluates the American attack inside Pakistan in 2011, killing Osama bin Laden, as seen by three Pakistani TV channels. Amir Hamza Marwan examines the hypothesis that TV news did not cover the Abbottabad Operation from a counter-terrorism perspective (Marwan 2015). On the other hand, they tried to rescue the Pakistan military from public criticism of its inability to defend against border violation by the USA.

Chapter 9 provides an insider's view on the motivation behind Pakistan's Oscar-winning documentary *A Girl in the River: The Price of Forgiveness* by exploring the interactions between the film crew and the documentary subjects, and the production process of the documentary itself. Haya Fatima Iqbal, in this chapter, also narrates the shifting focus of media after receiving the award from the efforts to improve legislation to a smear campaign by public opinion leaders.

In Chapter 10 Farah Zia traces the trajectory of the media within the context of personal reflections of the author's professional work in the print media. The author looks at the mechanisms of press censorship and the hardships women journalists go through working in a male-dominated field. It also discusses the transformations the media went through after privatisation in 2002, the post-9/11 dynamics, and the relationship between media and political institutions in the country.

Chapter 11 explores the nature and issues related to the media outlets in Balochistan and analyses the coverage the province gets in the national press. Analysing two newsworthy events in the province, Adnan Aamir argues that the national media, most of the time, look for economic benefits rather than valuing the historical and geopolitical heritage of the area. As a result, the overall coverage of the province in the national press is marginalised or overlooked.

Chapter 12 offers views of three known Pakistani communication experts and journalists on journalists' working conditions, code of ethics, and the nature of freedom of expression in the country. The editors of this volume Qaisar Abbas and Farooq Sulehria interviewed I. A. Rehman, a senior journalist; Dr Mehdi Hasan, a former dean of communication; and Eric Rahim, a former journalist who became an academic scholar in England. In a unique format, responding to the same questions, these scholars offer their individual perspectives on the dynamics of media, state, and society at large.

Notes

1 By media system, in line with Sulehria (2018: 5), we imply not merely its political economy, but also audience practices as well as "content production, technological dependence/independence, media policy, media training and education, and entrenchment in the global media system". Media workers provide backbone to the entire system.
2 Alavi's thesis has been hotly debated in a recently published title: McCartney, M. and Zaidi, S.A (2019) *New Perspectives on Pakistan's Political Economy*. New Delhi: Cambridge University Press.

3 The NPT was handed over to two media houses, left-wing Progressive Papers Limited (PPL) and the Mashriq group of publications, "nationalised" by the Ayub regime on assuming power. The staunchly anti-communist Ayub regime otherwise followed economic policies preached by the Chicago Boys. However, in the case of the press, he went for partial "nationalising".
4 Nawaz Sharif served as the prime minister twice in the 1990s: first 1990–93, then 1997–99. He was deposed on October 12, 1999 in a military coup led by General Musharraf (ruled 1999–2007).
5 That many media moguls have corruption cases pending in the National Accountability Bureau (NAB), an institution established during the Musharraf era to investigate corruption cases, makes the task of the "media cell" easy. Any media house not toeing the line can be summoned through the NAB.

References

Abbas, Qaisar. 1990. *Radio Broadcasting and Development: A Strategy for Pakistan*. Unpublished Doctoral Dissertation. The University of Wisconsin-Madison.
Alavi, H. 1972. "The state in post-colonial societies: Pakistan and Bangladesh". *New Left Review*, 1(74) July–August.
APNS. 2018. List of members. All Pakistan Newspapers Society (accessed 8 October 2018), http://apns.com.pk/member_publication/index.php.
Butler, Steven. 2019. "Why Pakistan's crackdown on the press is getting worse by the day". *Washington Post*, 22 July 2019 (accessed 21 September 2019), www.washingtonpost.com/opinions/2019/07/22/why-pakistans-crackdown-press-is-getting-worse-by-day/?fbclid=IwAR1Invi88fmPTP4CgCaYN4Za6Gr9Tyab3-MkdE1k4uVZ2g5Rdwu19V5_GNw&utm_term=.9d52ca53ea65.
CPJ. 2018. "Acts of intimidation: In Pakistan, journalists' fear and censorship grows even as fatal violence declines". *Committee to Protect Journalists*, 12 September 2018 (accessed 2019), https://cpj.org/x/73ff.
Farooq, U. 2016. "Enter the General". *Herald* (accessed 30 May 2017), http://herald.dawn.com/news/1153264.
Freedman, Des. 2015."Paradigms of media power". *Media, Culture and Critique*, 2(8): 273–289.
Gallup Pakistan. 2018. *Gallup Pakistan Short Report on Media Landscape in Pakistan*, 19 September (accessed 13 March 2020), https://mail.google.com/mail/u/0/#search/sulehria+gallup/FMfcgxvzKtcHfSPTFXfLzzKfhzPZTtTp?projector=1&messagePartId=0.1.
Gallup Pakistan. 2015. "Television, primary sources of information, March 4" (accessed 9 October 2018) http://gallup.com.pk/primary-source-of-information-2/.
Government of Pakistan. 1987. *Economic Survey, 1986-87*. Islamabad: Economic Advisor's Wing, Ministry of Finance.
Gunaratne, S. 1970. "Press in Pakistan under Ayub Khan". *Gazette*, 16(1).
Hallin, C. Daniel and Mancini, Paolo. 2012. *Comparing Media Systems Beyond the Western World*. New York: Cambridge University Press.
Hasan, Mehdi. 2016. "Email interview with Dr. Mehdi Hasan", 1 November 2016.
Hedebro, G. 1982. *Communication and Social Change in Developing Nations*. Ames: Iowa State University.
Ispahani, Farah Naz. 2015. *Purifying the Land of the Pure: Pakistan's Religious Minorities*. Noida, India: HarperCollins, 80.
Jabeen, Ismat. 2019. "Pakistani media ka bohran, Shafi 'bhokay mar rahay' hain". *DW* (accessed 30 July 2019), https://p.dw.com/p/3MAPY.

Jan, Faizullah. 2015. *The Muslim Extremist Discourse: Constructing us Versus Them*. Lanham, MD: Lexington Books.
Khan, Atif Muhammed. 2009. "The mediatization of politics in Pakistan: A structural analysis". *Pakistaniaat: A Journal of Pakistan Studies*, 1(1): 30–47.
Khan, Raza. 2016. "Cyber Crime Bill passed by NA: 13 reasons Pakistanis should be worried". *Dawn*, 11 August 2016 (accessed 24 October 2018), www.dawn.com/news/1276662.
Kurian, G. 1982. *World Press Encyclopaedia, Volume 2*. New York: Facts on File.
Marwan, A.H. 2015. *One Death, Three Regions and Two Stories. A Study of the Media Coverage of the Killing of Osama bin Laden in Pakistani, British and American Media*. PhD thesis, University of Sheffield.
Media Matters for Democracy. 2018a. "Surrendering to silence: An account to self-censorship among Pakistani journalists" (accessed 5 October 2018), http://digitalrightsmonitor.pk/wp-content/uploads/2018/05/report-1.pdf.
Media Matters for Democracy. 2018b. "Violence, journalism and elections. An overview of threats against media in run up to elections 2018" (accessed 5 October 2018), https://drive.google.com/file/d/15PE9pTaQ64rwxnQN05OJEIPmwfDmLtaL/view.
Niazi, Z. 2010. *The Press in Chains*. Karachi: Oxford University Press.
PAS (Pakistan Advertising Society). 2017 (accessed 4 October 2018), http://pas.org.pk/print-media-analysis-august-2017/.
PBC. 2018. "Radio Pakistan" (accessed 16 October 2018), www.radio.gov.pk/pbc-family.
PPF. 2017. *Pakistan Press Freedom Report, January 1, 2016–April 30, 2017*. Pakistan Press Foundation, 3 May.
Rahim, Eric. 2014. Characterizing the Pakistani state. Was Marx 100% materialist and other essays from a Marxist perspective (accessed 9 November 2018), http://ericrahim.co.uk.
Reporters Without Borders (RSF). 2019. "World press index" (accessed 13 March 2020) https://rsf.org/en/pakistan.
Siddiqa, A. 2017. *Military Inc: Inside Pakistan's Military Economy*. London: Pluto.
Said, Mansur. 1996. "Letter from Pakistan Broadcasting Corporation Islamabad, on radio programs to Qaisar Abbas, dated October 10, 1996".
Shaikh, Mohammad Ali. 2007. *Satellite Television and Social Change in Pakistan: A Case Study of Rural Sindh*. Karachi: Orient Book Publishing House.
Sulehria, Farooq. 2019. "Overdeveloped state to praetorian Pakistan: Tracing the media ", in M. McCartney and S.A. Zaidi (eds) *New Perspectives on Pakistan's Political Economy*. New Delhi: Cambridge University Press.
Sulehria, Farooq. 2018. *Media Imperialism in India and Pakistan*. New York: Routledge.
Sulehria, Farooq. 2017. "Globalisation of media marginalising workers: The case of India and Pakistan". *Marxism 21*, 14(1): 335–365.
Suleman, Saleha. 1990. *Representation of Gender in Prime-Time Television: A Textual Analysis of Drama Series of Pakistan Television*. Unpublished Doctoral Dissertation, University of Wisconsin-Madison.
Yesil, Bilge. 2014. "Press censorship in Turkey: Networks of state power, commercial pressures, and self-censorship". *Communication, Culture and Critique*, 7(2) June.
Zaidi, S.A. 2014. "Rethinking Pakistan's political economy: Class, state, power and transition". *Political Weekly*, 49(5).

2

JOURNALISM IN THE SERVICE OF JIHAD

Faizullah Jan

This chapter examines the role of four key jihadi publications in boosting extremism by way of constructing jihadi identities through a jihadi discourse. Deploying a post-structuralist tradition of discourse analysis, I argue that the jihadi publications explored for the purpose of this study address their audience in a "ritualistic" manner of communication, by employing the following multi-fold discursive repertoire: (a) rooting for a subjective reality; (b) an analogical reading of history; (c) self and the other and the great divide; (d) a mirroring of the self; (e) monolithic Other; and (f) enemies near and far.

Geographically, the study is limited to the Khyber Pakhtunkhwa province and the erstwhile Federally Administered Tribal Areas (FATA) region bordering Afghanistan.[1] Ethnically dominated by Pashtuns, this region has been in the throes of militarised violence ever since 9/11. In the absence of independent life choices, the youths have been left vulnerable to a reactionary culture of war and violence. Using James Carey's (1989) concept of the ritual view of communication, this chapter examines how the jihadi publications[2] construct a discourse as a ritual form of communication in which the otherwise progressive spirit of journalism is represented to suit the retrogressive ideological needs of Pashtuns, especially jobless youth.

How a ritual form of extremist discourse is constructed can be understood from an anecdotal example of a young man like Abdullah, whose life could have taken any number of trajectories; however, the hierarchy of tradition came into his way to push him on the way to jihad. At 23, like most youth in Pakistan to whom little career counselling, guidance, and opportunity are available, Abdullah's outlook and vocation were chosen and shaped by the aspirations of parents—in most cases, the father, who as family-head and breadwinner has a greater say in what a son or a daughter should make of their lives. This traditional form of social upbringing itself contributes to extremism, inviting attention towards the role of jihadi publications and organised militant and religious forces out to prey on young impressionable minds by offering "guidance and counselling" in every nook and corner of the country.

It all started with *Al Qalam* and *Zarb-i-Momin*, weekly newspapers published by apparently proscribed militant organisations in the country—Jaish-e-Muhammad and Al-Rashid Trust, respectively (details below). Abdullah's father chose his career for him. It may not have been driven by a desire for material riches but, then, in the vocation of jihad, worldly possessions are rarely a consideration. "I have been an avid reader of *Al Qalam* and *Zarb-i-Momin* for the last 12 years", says Mohammad Ilyas, Abdullah's father. "After reading these [weekly] newspapers, I made up my mind to send my son for jihad". In 2014, Abdullah went to Indian-administered Kashmir for jihad, where he was killed by the Indian troops.

Al Qalam and *Zarb-i-Momin* are two of the scores of newspapers published by militant organisations in Pakistan. These publications, the majority of which are openly distributed, often free, are distinct from the mainstream press in outlook, content, and rhetoric. Published in the country's metropolitan cities such as Karachi and Lahore, these are readily available at news stalls and bookshops all over the country. Theirs is a focus defined by pernicious indoctrination increasingly influential in the radicalisation of Pakistani society. They find a predisposed audience and willing converts in a milieu that puts much stock in religiosity, its symbols, and rituals, but more importantly, large sections of which are already susceptible to the radical worldview these publications and their publishers and patrons propagate. Compared to mainstream media that dabble in all manner of information, their communication and information agenda can be easily pigeonholed—one dedicated to, and characterised by, misinformation that undermines tolerance and democracy by demonising non-Muslims and the West. Like repressive radical media (Downing et al. 2001), these newspapers maim the public's ability to understand the world and their place in it. "Neither critical reflection nor any genuine increase in personal or collective freedom are on the radar screen of such media" (Downing et al. 2001: 89).

Like Abdullah, scores of youth, all over the country and the border region, read and follow the ideology these publications promote, a ritual form of communication in which life after death is celebrated and associated with a jihadi cause that has been actively pursued and supported by the state's foreign policy interests in neighbouring Afghanistan and India since the early 1980s.

Echoing a Manichean mass

While inculcating a jihadi outlook has always been part of the training of security forces in Pakistan to lend fighting and war a religious zeal and cause, it is the systematic transfer and consequent adoption of that cause by larger Pakistani society, including youth like Abdullah, through the creation and patronage of a jihadi media by the state that is the issue that concerns this chapter.

In the wake of the Afghan jihad through the 1980s, the state, flushed with success over the vanquished Soviet Russia (USSR) in Afghanistan, sought to bring strategic lessons from that war—recruiting, training, and arming the Mujahideen in camps for proxy wars, using jihadi media and literature for religious indoctrination to find favour, support, and willing recruits among the citizenry for unconventional wars of attrition it waged against "the enemy" in Afghanistan and India. This chapter takes into account the role of the jihadi media in radicalising larger society as they were pressed into the active service of the state to pursue the strategic lessons of the Afghan War as an integral part of its foreign policy. This chapter is an attempt to understand the worldview that these newspapers attempt to construct in their discourse. To this end, I analyse four newspapers that are published by militant organisations in Pakistan. They are *Daily Islam*, *Zarb-e-Momin*, *Al-Qalam*, and *Jarrar*. For examining the content and objectives of these newspapers, this chapter draws on American communication theorist and media critic James W. Carey (1934–2006).

In *Communication as Culture*, Carey explains that in a ritual view of communication, reading a newspaper is "less sending or gaining information and more like attending a mass: a situation in which nothing new is learned but in which a particular view of the world is portrayed and confirmed" (Carey 1989: 20). The militant newspapers carry less news and more views. Their target audience is not the casual, unrelated reader, but an ideologically committed supporter; news reading and writing, in this case, is a ritual act and a dramatic one. "What is arrayed before the reader is not pure information but portrayal of the contending forces in the world" (Carey 1989: 20). And the contending forces are offered as "good versus bad".

The newspapers under study create an echo chamber in which arguments appealing to a "victimhood mentality" emanating from the oppression of the Muslims in Palestine and Kashmir create a social reality that articulates Muslims and non-Muslims in an equation of "us versus them". Their message is simplistic and Manichean, defining the world in terms of black and white. To understand the worldview of the militants and extremists, it is imperative to deconstruct and understand the discourse of their publications because mass media do not produce only news and information; they produce "particular forms of consciousness by making available a range of positions to understand the world" (Williams 2003: 149). Every position offered by way of information or communication creates a different and distinct understanding of the world and a different set of actions. This means that any social reality that is constructed by the mass media has real-life consequences.

Over the years, Pakistan has been ranked as the most dangerous place for journalists. According to UNESCO, no fewer than 73 journalists have been killed in different parts of the country between 2001—when the United States and its allies launched a global "War on Terror"—and 2018. The majority of the journalists killed were reporters belonging to FATA and Balochistan, the restive south-eastern province of Pakistan that also lies on the border with Afghanistan.

This elusive "War on Terror", launched in neighbouring Afghanistan, spilled over into parts of Pakistan, especially the former FATA. These tribal districts, administered until 2019 under parallel laws, became a safe haven and a hotbed for militants. It was from here that they sought to establish a Taliban Emirate across the rest of Pakistan. However, long before 9/11 and the associated "War on Terror", the former FATA region had become a base camp for Afghan jihad. The genesis of jihadi media, in fact, can be traced to Afghan jihad.

Little is known about the news/media publications and religious teachings of thousands of orthodox Arab militants who contributed immensely to instilling and propagating the jihadi worldview among the Afghan mujahideen. To keep these jihadists motivated, charity organisations from different Arab countries set up printing presses in the Nasir Bagh area of Peshawar, also home to sprawling Afghan refugee settlements. Initially, these printing presses propagated the doctrine of Dr Abdullah Azzam, one of al Qaeda's founding fathers.

The mushrooming of militant media did not stop with the end of the Afghan war in 1989. To bleed India after the Red Army rolled out of Afghanistan, the focus shifted to "jihad" in Indian-administered Kashmir. In the post-9/11 context, as the battleground expanded from Afghanistan and India to the US and NATO allies, so did the focus of the militant media: the US was the new nemesis, and publications promoting this mindset proliferated even when Pakistan was the frontline ally of America.

While the objective of mobilising jihadi elements to fight the Western armies in Afghanistan was motivation enough for militant publications, another factor that led to their strengthening was the emergence of private media in 2002 and its expansion from there onwards. The private media brought to the fore a diversity of opinions and perspectives that often challenged the state's policies on its eastern and western borders, and inside Pakistan, as jihadi groups turned on the state itself.

Diverse narratives defied the homogeneous discourse that the state had single-mindedly constructed over the decades, and such views needed to be tamed, confronted, and silenced. Hence, post-9/11, a discursive change is evident in the narratives peddled by the jihadi media. But with improved ICTs, one also witnesses a technological shift registered by the militant media where social media and multimedia formats are employed freely to reach out to a broader audience beyond the restrictions of literacy as imposed by print.

The militant media now include more sophisticated forms of expression such as DVDs, CDs, and websites—in Urdu, Pushto, English, Arabic, and Persian—which are, at times, aimed at global audiences. As one commentator states, "The radical media is no longer part of a specific cause, restricted by time and space, but espouses the unending cause of global jihad" (Ashraf 2012.

The struggle between conflicting narratives emerging from the decades-long militarisation of the country has increasingly polarised Pakistani audiences along liberal and conservative lines. The publications run by militant organisations, who have their stakes in silencing voices that do not fit into their scheme of things, often criticise the mainstream media for being "hostage to secular-minded writers/reporters and dub them as advocates of obscenity" (Khan 2004: 450).

Conditions in the country seem favourable for the further growth of jihadi media. With a new regime of restrictions on the mainstream media from 2018 onwards, the space and audience for the Manichean outlook that the jihadi media push has considerably increased. Pressure tactics or applicable laws can tame or regulate the mass media, but the jihadi media can say what they want with little fear of retribution. There was an apparent crackdown on jihadi publications in 2001 and then again in 2006. Since then, however, it has been more or less business as usual because the crackdown on jihadi media is as duplicitous as the ban on various jihadi outfits.

Despite their broad influence within the local population (Khan and Jan 2007), only a few attempts have been made to examine these publications in a systematic manner to know what they contain and determine precisely to what purposes these newspapers are being put. As a consequence, we have a less empirical understanding of the issues, stories, and narratives that predominate texts, and thus less understanding of what writers see as key to encouraging terrorism.

Methodology

This chapter analyses the system of representation offered in publications such as *Al-Qalam, Zarb-i-Momin, Daily Islam,* and the now-defunct weekly *Jarrar*. The broadsheets were selected for two reasons. First, they all had a large circulation and second, these were mouthpieces of influential jihadi organisations.

Al-Qalam, an eight-page weekly, is published by Jaish-e-Muhammad (Army of the Prophet) from Peshawar and is available on news stalls. *Zarb-i-Momin,* also an eight-page weekly, is published by proscribed Al-Rashid Trust from Karachi. Al-Rashid Trust also publishes the *Daily Islam* from six different cities. *Jarrar* was published as a weekly by banned Jamaat-u-Da'awa from Lahore. Except for *Jarrar*, they are available on news stalls and have e-editions as well (for more details see Jan 2015).

Methodologically, this study deploys tools of post-structuralist traditions attributed to Michel Foucault, as well as Ernesto Laclau and Chantel Mouffe, to analyse data gathered for this study. The analysis through these tools is in turn informed by James Carey's theoretical perspective, especially his concept of communication as ritual, discussed above.

The purpose of the above method is to analyse the above-mentioned four newspapers to understand how the militant organisations construct the social-political reality of the post-9/11 world, especially in the context of Us versus Them. Arguably, one way of constructing social reality is constructing the Self and the Other through discourse. In this case, it is the text of the above four broadsheets.

How identities of the Self and the Other are constructed as the effect of discourse are discussed below through offering an examination of meta-narratives such as *umma*—a word that also has a pan-Islamic connotation in that it creates a sense of belonging to a brotherhood beyond borders. These meta-narratives serve the ritual form of communication, guiding people to act in specific ways and not others.

It will be interesting, at the outset, to notice that a distinctive feature of these publications is their rhetorical and highly symbolic titles anchored in Quranic/Arabic symbolism. For example, *Zarb-i-Momin* derives from an Arabic compound word that means "the blow/strike of the Muslim", which couches both its image and message in martial—in this case, jihadi—context and terms. The provocative title is poised to strike a blow to the infidel, who is no other than the West and non-Muslims, but could be anyone supporting the West in the Muslim world, or anyone not subscribing to the jihadi worldview.

It is also notable that these publications avoid human pictures, considered un-Islamic. However, images of inanimate things such as destroyed buildings, roads, and tanks, etc. find enough space in their pages. Weaponry and Islamic holy sites occupy pride of place. Most importantly, the editorial content, in general, is either religious in nature or concerns Muslim hotspots such as Palestine, Iraq, Afghanistan, Kashmir, Myanmar, and Chechnya, etc.

In the following section, I deploy the post-structuralist tradition of discourse analysis to develop a multi-fold empirical understanding of identity construction in the jihadi publications under investigation, which in turn helped galvanise religious extremism.

Rooting for a subjective reality

In the post-structuralist tradition, reality can never be reached outside of discourses; therefore, discourse itself has become the object of analysis. If one were to follow Laclau and Mouffe (1985), this conceptualisation has severe implications for Pakistan and the larger world where the militant discourse demonises the Other and legitimises violence in the name of jihad. This is also important because human behaviour depends on the subjective interpretation of reality, and not on the objective reality of a situation. People produce their understanding of the world and their place in it before they choose to act in a certain way. As Dunn (2008: 82) observes, "People are guided to act in certain ways, and not others, by their discursively produced understanding of the world and their place in it".

Militant newspapers use Islam as a nodal point. Islam, being a totalised system or "pure signifier" (Zizek 2008), encompasses culture, civilisation, dignity, etc. These elements, which are floating signifiers, refer to Islam to recognise themselves in their unity. That is, they acquire their meaning from their relationship with Islam. Thus, an "attack on [the] culture and sovereignty" of Pakistan becomes an attack on Islam, and threatening Pakistan or Muslims is equated with threatening Islam.

Within the universe that the militant newspapers construct, Muslims are in a "state of siege", and the only solution is to choose between total submission, which is equated with "humiliation", or fighting back, which is jihad. Mbembe (2009), in his classic article on necropolitics, explains that escape from "the state of siege and occupation" is through "the logic of martyrdom". Embracing death becomes the only option open to the one under siege, who in the process takes away other people's lives too. This philosophy drives the suicide bomber, who goes in a blaze of glory, taking with him or her the infidels or their supporters, who do not deserve to live because they contribute to the oppression of the faithful.

In this context, the militant discourse makes a hegemonic intervention in favour of a "legitimised violence" in the name of jihad by excluding alternative equivalences. By this construction of socio-political reality, the militant discourse takes one step towards confrontation with the Other. Chief of the Afghan Taliban Mullah Muhammad Omar, in one of his rare interviews soon after 9/11, sketches a similar scenario when he says, "Americans will not be able to prevent such acts [9/11 attacks] … because America has taken Islam hostage" (The Guardian 2001).

Thus, representations of reality have real implications: certain paths of action become possible within distinct discourses, while others become unthinkable. As Omar continues in the same interview: "In their pain and frustration, some [Muslims] commit suicide acts. They feel they have nothing to lose" (*The Guardian* 2001).

An analogical reading of history

The militant discourse is legitimised by invoking the Qur'an, *Hadith*, contemporary scholarship, and history of early Islam. History is used as a tool of validation to emphasise the fatality and perpetuity of the attack by the Other. Salwa Ismail (1994), in her analysis of the militant discourse in Egypt, has noted that jihadi discourse erases the boundaries marking the "here and now" from the "there and then" by way of analogical reasoning.

This logic is at work when the militant newspapers' discourse equates the assassination of bin Laden with the Battle of Badr and the anti-Islam YouTube video, *Innocence of Muslims*, with the *Crusades* (an existential threat), while child activist and Nobel laureate Malala Yousafzai's shooting is articulated as a "declaration of war" against Islam. For instance, *Daily Islam* argues in an editorial about the film *Innocence of Muslims*: "This [film] is not an isolated mischievous act of a single individual; such blasphemous acts are continuations of the Crusades. The Christian world has always shown its resolves to destroy the Muslims, their power and their religion" (18 September 2012). By articulating the anti-Islam film with the Crusades, *Daily Islam* attempts to establish that this is not an individual or isolated act that happened in the present. It is portrayed as the continuation of a series of different acts and events, committed by the infidel West, or Christians and Jews, who have been at war with Islam for centuries. Seen from this angle, any such act is not random or isolated but carries the weight of history.

Likewise, when Malala was embraced as an icon by the West, the militant discourse created another system of equivalences. Her shooting by the Taliban was articulated in association with the US drone war, portrayed as an extension of the "War on Terror" in FATA. So instead of condemning the act of shooting a child, *Daily Islam* argues, "Media has made a spectacle out of the Malala event. It seems as if a war has been formally announced against the religious section" (*Daily Islam,* 26 October 2012). This argument is further extended in *Jarrar*: "Everybody has their ax to grind in the name of Malala" (*Jarrar,* 26 October 2012). According to *Zarb-i-Momin*, "Pakistani victims of the US drone wars find no space in the media, while Malala is being projected because she has been allegedly shot by the Taliban" (*Zarb-i-Momin,* 19 October 2012).

By implication, Malala as a symbol of resistance against extremists was equated with drone attacks in these publications. In the process, the following system of equivalences is constructed: the drone attacks violate the "sovereignty" of Pakistan, their constant presence in Pakistani air space is "encircling" Pakistan and Muslims, which would finally lead to the "annihilation" of Muslims/Islam. Thus, the shooting of Malala and her turning into a universal symbol of resistance became a "drone" that violates Pakistan sovereignty and kills "innocent Muslims".

Self and the Other: The great divide

To construct identities of the Self and the Other, the militant discourse constitutes two socio-political spaces which exist in an antagonistic relation. The world is divided into "the land of Islam" and "the land of the infidel". The land of Islam is rooted in a moral value system based on divine revelation, while the land of the infidel is anti-divine, with moral values drawn from a human-constructed knowledge system. A case in point: *Al Qalam* makes a moral value judgement to emphasise the difference between the Muslims and infidel West in the following excerpt: "Society in America and other Western European countries is lacking those moral values which are derived from Godly revelation—the true source of knowledge. … Therefore, they don't care about the glory of God and dignity of the Prophet" (*Al-Qalam*, 14 September 2012).

Here the newspaper claims that only Muslims, being custodians of Godly revelation, i.e., the Qur'an, have moral values. At the same time, it passes judgement against modern scientific knowledge created in the West by juxtaposing it to the knowledge that is contained in the divine book, i.e., the Qur'an and the traditions of the Prophet Muhammad. Thus, one represents the Kingdom of God and the other the kingdom of Evil (Ismail 1994). These two poles are constituted in a relationship of contradiction whereby the Other is not merely an adversary, with whom one can coexist, but an Other whose presence prevents the Self from being totally itself (Laclau and Mouffe 1985). As Laclau (1977) elaborates: "Discursive antagonisms are constructed when differential positive characteristics which, in a genetic discourse, are represented as a system of differences, come to be constituted as a system of equivalence and signify negativity. In other words, discursive antagonism is a relation of contradiction between a pole of positivity 'A' and a pole of negativity 'non-A'" (89–91).

Thus, the two entities are not just different from each other in a relationship of contrariety; one negates the existence of the other. In other words, the Self cannot be totalised as long as the Other is present. Similarly, in the extremist discourse, the YouTube film is not an individual act; the producer is articulated into the realm of the Other, which is constituted as his abettor in "agonizing Muslims by hurting their religious sentiments" (*Jarrar*, 14 September 2012).

Mirroring the Self

The militant discourse creates equivalent identities that express a pure negation of the discursive system and the Other. The construction of a particular identity involves a process of its affirmation in opposition to other identities. Therefore, in the constitution of *umma* as the Self, the overriding concern of the militant discourse is to exclude other identities such as sectarian, ethnic, and racial, etc. In other words, the Self is created as a monolithic entity by collapsing internal differences around a pole of positivity. As Bucholtz and Hall (2005: 383) explain, to form a united front, "potentially salient differences are set aside in favor of perceived or asserted similarities". For example, *Daily Islam* argues, "Muslims across the world—Palestine, Chechnya, Lebanon, Kashmir and Afghanistan—face extermination at the hands of Christian and Jewish forces who have made a common front to eliminate the *umma*" (*Daily Islam*, 15 September 2012). Jarrar makes a similar argument that "the infidels are out to wipe out Muslims of *every shade* from the face of the earth" [emphasis mine] (*Jarrar*, 14 September 2012).

The militant discourse aims to establish a collection of common entities unified by their common reference to the nodal point of Islam. "Umma everywhere is being persecuted" (*Al-Qalam*, 25 September 2012); "Umma is being deprived of its freedom, be it in Kashmir, Afghanistan, Palestine and Chechnya" (*Zarb-i-Momin*, 15 September 2012). If Laclau and Mouffe's term for "society" is replaced with *umma, umma* is always partially structured. When Muslims of different denominations identify themselves with *umma,* it is not because *umma* is objectively constituted, but because there has been a temporary closure whereby other possibilities for identification are marginalised or excluded. *Umma* as a totality is a floating signifier which is invested with different contents through different articulations. It is an imagined totality that provides a common platform to the various discourses within Islam and at the same time delimits what is meaningful to be discussed and in which manner.

Umma, as a subject of discourse, is produced in different chains of equivalences in the discourse of these publications. *Umma* is defined only in religious terms (non-Muslims excluded invariably) and in identity with the "victim", the "oppressed", the "subjugated", and finally the "mujahid" or fighter. Thus, *umma* is a victimised Self. This construction of the Self as a victim that faces a threat to its existence has serious implications. It represents the Other as an enemy and justifies violence as a tool of survival. This construction of reality imagines no scope for coexistence with the Other and conceptualises its existence in the elimination of the Other.

The construction of *umma* is also a result of the discursive construction of a common enemy. The discursive operation, according to Al-Azmeh (1993), that sanctions construction of the enemy involves a double displacement, according to which the Crusades are conceived as the early manifestation of colonialism, and imperialism is conceived in terms of a cultural invasion. Therefore, when the militant discourse constructs the "War on Terror" as the "Crusades", it produces the West in identity with colonialism. Similarly, when it defines the West as imperialist, it signifies as a cultural attack. This construction takes the present to the past and brings the past to the present to make the confrontation with the Other historical and perpetual, as in the following excerpts: "Christians and Jews have been inveterate enemies of the *umma* since the times of our Prophet" (*Jarrar*, 5

September 2012); "Jews and Christians can never be friends of Muslims, it is a historical fact" (*Islam*, 25 September 2012); "From the day one, Christians and Jews have been plotting against Muslims" (*Jarrar*, 12 September 2012); "Christians and Jews will never stop damaging the *umma;* it is in their genes" (*Al-Qalam*, 30 September 2012).

The monolithic Other

The Other is constructed in multiple identities: the "Christian", the "Jew", and the "Hindu". These multiple identities ultimately coalesce into a singular entity, that is, "the West" by collapsing all other identities of the constituent signifiers. After creating this monolithic "West", militant discourse—in another chain of equivalence—creates a pole of negativity. Now the "West" is produced in identity with the "imperialist", the "colonialist", the "arrogant", the "disrespectful", and the "unjust". While the West was always viewed through that lens in the pre-9/11 world by organisations and media of religious or militant persuasion, it is now solely defined by the "War on Terror," drone attacks, and cultural attacks signalled by the anti-Islam book, Rushdie's *The Satanic Verses*, and Danish cartoons of the Prophet Muhammad (pbuh).

In the articulation of a negative pole, the extremist discourse represents modern education as well as the mainstream Pakistani media as tools of Western cultural imperialism. This articulation constructs the West as an enemy that has infiltrated Muslim institutions in disguise. It also emphasises the "fact" that the enemy is lurking within the ranks of the Muslims and "slips poison in the honey". This construction of reality announces that the enemy has already encircled *umma*. As Burke (2003) argues, "the main objective of Muslim extremists is not conquest, but to beat back what they perceive as an aggressive West that is supposedly trying to complete the project begun during the Crusades and colonial periods of denigrating, dividing, and humiliating Islam" (18).

The militant discourse also articulates secular education and the mainstream media of Pakistan in identity with the Other. Therefore, in the construction of the West, financial aid, training, and exchange programs, etc. become illegitimate activities. By withdrawing this legitimacy, the militant discourse creates another socio-political pole of negativity. Intellectuals, journalists, writer guilds, and cultural organisations, being recipients of training and funding, are identified with the Other.

Enemies near and far

Militant newspapers identify the West as the "far enemy." Muslim rulers/governments that ally with the West are constructed in their identity with the West. This makes them the "near enemy" to be targeted first in their struggle against the Other. These newspapers construct the identity of rulers in Muslim countries as "corrupt", which has made them spineless in the face of foreign threats, and hence they are unrepresentative of the people. For example, *Daily Islam* notes: "It is bad luck that political rulers care more about their power and [personal] interests … while the nation is caught between a rock and a hard place". Corruption of the rulers, "who have sold out their conscience to get dollars" (*Al-Qalam*, 20 May 2011), has created a gulf between the government and the public. As a result, "the rulers have lost the confidence of the people" (*Islam*, 20 May 2011). "Apathy, delinquency, and greed of the rulers" (*Al-Qalam*, 13 May 2011) have made them susceptible to compromises with Western countries and international financial institutions like the World Bank and the International Monetary Fund (IMF). Thus, "Pakistan is no more an independent and sovereign country" (*Al-Qalam*, 20 May 2011) because it is an ally of the United States in the "War on Terror" and a regular recipient of the World Bank and IMF's loans. Here too, the militant discourse, through chains of equivalences, constructs two poles of antagonism. The "people" are constructed as a positive pole which is in contradiction with the negative pole. The positive pole represents *umma*, while the negative pole is comprised of Muslim rulers/governments and their functionaries. Thus, again, two socio-political identities are constructed which exist in a relation of contradiction.

The identity of the Muslim rulers/governments is constructed by their association with the West, especially the United States. Muslim rulers are disarticulated from the body of *umma* and, by their association with the West, are rearticulated in the body of the Other. Muslim rulers/governments are constructed as corrupt, who seek support from the West to stay in power. Their dependence on the West leaves them spineless to challenge Western aggression against Muslims. Unlike the rulers, *umma* is brave enough to stand up to the West and safeguard its sovereignty. This disconnect between *umma* and Muslim governments renders the rulers and state institutions like the parliament—unrepresentative.

It would be erroneous to assume that the militant discourse exists on the fringes in total isolation from the mainstream media discourse. This discourse is, in fact, nested in the discourse of the mainstream Pakistani media (Hassan 2014). These publications also reproduce content from the mainstream Urdu media, which indicates that the two discourses conflate considerably, at least in their sentiments against American policies towards the Muslim world. It poses a severe challenge to the Pakistani state's efforts to win the hearts and minds of mainstream society by weaning people off extremism. The mainstream Pakistani media is not immune to the effects of the militant discourse. The militant discourse represents modern institutions, including news and entertainment media, in association with the West, which undermines their credibility. When this discourse hegemonises the discursive field of democracy, human rights (especially women rights) and the development, plurality of opinion, and diversity in media content gives way to Manichaeism. Thus, the mainstream media have to fight for their credibility and relevancy to the everyday life of Pakistani people and for ensuring that different opinions get their due share in public debate on different issues of public interest.

In the socio-political reality that the militant discourse constructs, the West in general and the United States in particular, are defined in terms of the "War on Terror," drone attacks, and Guantanamo military prison. Thus, the terms in which the West is defined are devoid of social, political, and cultural content, which are the source of its "soft power" (Nye 2004). The rising sentiments against American policies in Pakistan show that the socio-political reality that the militant discourse creates is not an oddity. It is generally spread across the different segments of Pakistani society (see Afzal 2013a,b). Assuming that this construction of reality resonates with the more significant moderate segments of the Pakistani population, the United States has to create a fair balance between what is says and what it does. In other words, understanding this reality can prove helpful for the US government and its different institutions in reaching out to mainstream Muslims and in countering the extremist discourse more effectively.

Conclusion

The chapter shows how the jihadi press constructs a ritual form of discourse to build a history of the present, reproducing the state-sponsored jihad of the past through jihadi publications. Using meta-narratives, the ritual form of discourse does not liberate individuals; it only reinforces history, a status quo, the purpose of which is to maintain hatred and not to transcend it. This retrogressive discourse might be based on hatred against the West, but its immediate target is all democratic and liberating values in the country. Mixing traditions with religion and then celebrating this cocktail by calling it Islamic values, i.e., *umma*, these publications construct a discourse which contributes to a hierarchical form of society, a community of faithful in which relationships do not go beyond other than what we have seen in the chapter's introduction between Abdullah and his father, Mohammad Ilyas.

Notes

1 In 2019, the state of Pakistan—through constitutional amendment—merged FATA with Khyber Pakhtunkhwa (formerly North Western Frontier Province or NWFP), thus effectively ending the British colonial legacy under which the region was ruled through a parallel law that did not allow fundamental rights as enjoyed by the citizens of mainland Pakistan.
2 Publications run by militant organisations are referred to by different nomenclatures: some commentators call these jihadi newspapers, while others "militant". In this chapter, I use the two nomenclatures interchangeably.

References

Afzal, M. 2013a. "Drone strikes and anti-Americanism in Pakistan". 7 February (accessed 2 August 2019), www.brookings.edu/research/opinions/2013/02/07-drones-anti-americanism-pakistan-afzal.
Afzal, M. 2013b. "On the Pakistani anti-Americanism" (accessed 2 August 2019), www.brookings.edu/research/opinions/2013/11/14-pakistani-anti-americanism-afzal.
Al-Azmeh, A. 1993. *Islams and Modernities*. London: Verso.
Ashraf, I. 2012. "We all share responsibility". *British Journalism Review*, 23(4): 5–7. www.bjr.org.uk/archive+we_all_share_responsibility.

Bucholtz, M. and Hall, K. 2005. "Identity and interaction: A sociocultural linguistic approach". *Discourse Studies*, 7(4–5): 585–614.
Burke, J. 2003. *Al-Qaeda: Casting a Shadow of Terror*. New York: I. B. Taurus.
Carey, J.W. 1989. *Communication as Culture*. New York: Routledge.
Downing, J.D.H. et al. 2001. "Religion, ethnicity, and the international dimension", in *Radical Media: Rebellious Communication and Social Movements*. London: Sage Publications: 75–87.
Dunn, K.C. 2008. "Historical representations", in A. Klotz and D. Prakash (eds) *Qualitative Methods in International Relations*. New York: Palgrave Macmillan, 78–92.
Guardian, The. 2001. "Mullah Omar—in his own words". 12 September (accessed 23 September 2019), www.theguardian.com/world/2001/sep/26/afghanistan.features11.
Hassan, K. 2014. "The role of private electronic media in radicalizing Pakistan". *The Round Table: The Commonwealth Journal of International Affairs*, 27 January: 65–81.
Ismail, S. 1994. "Confronting the other: Identity, culture, politics, and conservative Islamism in Egypt". *International Journal of Middle East Studies*, 30(2): 199–225.
Jan, F. 2015. *The Muslim Extremist Discourse: Constructing Us versus Them*. Maryland: Lexington Books.
Khan, A.U. 2011. *News Media and Journalism in Pakistan*. Saarbrucken, Germany: LAP LAMBERT Academic Publishing.
Khan, A. and Jan, F. 2007. "Alternative print media in Pakistan: Reacting to the mainstream". *The Journal of Humanities and Social Sciences* (Faculty of Arts and Humanities, University of Peshawar), xv(2): 55–68.
Khan, Z. 2004. "Cyber jihad: Fighting the infidels from Pakistan", in S. Gan, J. Gomez and U. Johannen (eds) *Asian Cyber Terrorism*. Bangkok: Friedrich Naumann Foundation, 442–470.
Laclau, E. 1977. *Politics and Ideology in Marxist Theory*. London: New Left Books.
Laclau, E. and Mouffe, C. 1985. *Hegemony and Socialist Strategy*. London: Verso.
Mbembe, A. 2009. "Necropolitics". *Public Culture*, 15(1): 11–40.
Nye, Josef. 2004. *Soft Power: The Means of Success in World Politics*. New York: PublicAffairs.
Williams, K. 2003. *Understanding Media Theory*. New York: Oxford University Press.
Zizek, S. 2008. *The Sublime Object of Ideology*. London: Verso.

3

JIHAD ON SCREEN

The role of jihadi drama and film and their press coverage, 1979–89, in Islamising Pakistan

Farooq Sulehria

An endless debate goes on in Pakistan to ascertain if Pakistan was created in the name of Islam, as a "Muslim Zion", or as a land for Muslims. However, the country did not embrace Islamisation until 1977. It was under the military rule of General Zia-ul-Haq (ruled 1977–88), largely to legitimise martial law, that a process of Islamising the state and society was unleashed. While various factors in the rise of Islamisation in Pakistan have been explored, no study has been conducted to examine the role of state-sponsored television and film production in relation to Islamisation.

Notably, in the 1980s, jihadi themes became a drama genre on mini-screen as well as silver screen in Pakistan. Was it an incidental paradigm shift or reflective of a wider systematic process of Islamisation of society? How, if at all, did the military benefit from jihadification of drama and film? To examine these questions I present a case study of Pakistan Television (PTV) drama, and films produced by the Pakistani film industry (called Lollywood) from 1977 to 1999. Further, I look at their presentation in two Urdu-language newspapers, *Jang* and *Nawa-i-Waqt*, by examining coverage in these papers of jihadi plays and films.

It is the contention of this chapter that the Islamisation of Pakistani society was manufactured by the Pakistani military through its control and dominance of the cultural apparatus, among other factors. For instance, while Pakistani and Saudi funding of madrassas (seminaries) and militant groups was significant, it cannot account for the hegemonic nature of Islamisation in Pakistan.

I argue that while the Pakistani state before 1977 had used television and film production for its ideological purposes, this practice became the norm rather than the exception once General Zia came to power in 1977 (Hussain 2007: 7).

Before Zia, I note, PTV and, in particular, Lollywood were cosmopolitan and pluralistic. While Islamic themes and characters are present, they do not hold hegemony. However, from Gen. Zia's time onwards Islamisation became the official policy. It had two important functions for Zia and the military. First, it supported Pakistan's use of non-state actors in Kashmir and Afghanistan (what are often termed "jihadis"). Second, it functioned to provide ideological legitimacy to the Zia regime (Toor 2011; Siddiqa 2007).

Since there does not exist any research focusing on jihadification of cultural apparatus in Pakistan under the guidance of the Pakistan military, I will start by sketching out a model. This model makes an attempt to conceptualise jihadi drama and film. This concept in turn provides a framework for research as will be shown below.

Conceptualising jihadification of cultural apparatus

The concept of jihad cannot be understood in isolation from the notion of Islamisation. While Islamisation is a difficult phenomenon to define, I use the term here to refer to the process by which the Wahabi textual interpretive tradition comes to take supremacy over the political, cultural, and social horizons of a population.

Wahabism is a revivalist cult attributed to eighteenth-century preacher Muhammad ibn Abdul Wahab. A revivalist zealot from the Saudi town of Uyayna, ibn Wahab was appalled to see Arabia "sunk into corruption". The solution, he concluded, would be a return to, by force if necessary, puritan Islam (Lacy 1984: 59).

The Wahabi interpretation of the Qur'an, then, supersedes all local forms of knowledge, the constitution, and the legal apparatus. It becomes, de facto, the final authority on all matters. In turn, clerics of the Wahabi tradition become the interpreters of right and wrong, legal and illegal, moral and immoral. While jihad is a central theme of Islamisation—as defined above—jihad itself is a contested discourse in Islam, yet it is implied here as a political and social philosophy, advocated by jihadi outfits, urging armed mobilisation against "unbelievers" to undo an imagined "injustice" (Rashid 2002: 2). This philosophy justifies the use of violence against "infidels", while there is a conception of paradise as reward for such work. In other words, while jihadification issues from Islamisation and they are concomitant, I have not employed these terms as synonyms.

I define jihadi drama and film as drama serials and films that promote a Wahabi discourse while focusing on the glorification of violent jihad and presenting "us" Muslims/Pakistanis engaging in holy war with the non-Muslim "others". In other words, jihadification and otherfying of non-Muslims are the two defining characteristics of jihadi drama and films. This characterisation of these plays and films has been based on the analysis of the discourses promoted in them. The twin characteristics, jihadification and otherfication (of non-Muslims), also provided the parameters for the design of the first part of the research. In the subsequent part, a combination of methods has been employed to examine and analyse the logic behind jihadification of cultural apparatus from 1977 onwards. The next section lays out this two-step methodology.

Research methodology and literature review

This chapter is based on extensive fieldwork conducted during 2011–12 in Pakistan. I have depended upon primary as well as secondary sources. The data was collected at PTV archival centres in Lahore, Islamabad, and Karachi. I also consulted the libraries at Mass Communication departments of the University of Punjab, Lahore, and Allama Iqbal Open University, Islamabad. Mass Communication students have written dissertations on PTV in the past that proved helpful in gathering the necessary data otherwise not available at the PTV archives. I also accessed newspaper archives of the daily *Jang* and the daily *Nawa-i-Waqt* in my bid to locate the coverage of jihadi plays in these two broadsheets.

To date, no research has been conducted to examine the role of jihadi film and drama in the Islamisation of Pakistani society. While a few books exist on the Pakistani TV and film industry, they have limitations. Mushtaq Gazdar's *Pakistan Cinema:1947–1997* is the only full-length study of Pakistani cinema ever written. This book looks closely at the changing trends of cinema 1947–97. Besides chronicling the history of cinema on the Indian subcontinent, it features a review of cinema classics, trivia, and cinema lore. The book juxtaposes the artistic development of the cinematic world with the overall social development in the country. It shows how the narrow self-interest of the various military regimes clashed with the creative potential of the artistic world, stifling originality and all but destroying the film industry. An index of films made during the period 1947–1997 is also included. However, the work is aimed at a general audience and is full of generalisations that are not backed up by evidence.

Two books exist on PTV: Nasreen Pervez's *Pakistan Television Drama and Social Change* (1998) and Agha Nasir's *This is PTV: Another Day, Another World* (2009). Nasir only partially covers PTV drama, while Pervez's research, conducted during 1987–92 in Karachi, looks at the popularity of different genres of PTV drama among different communities and income and age groups. While both these tomes provide data for my present study, they are limited in many ways. Nasir offers a personal account of his time with PTV and the work lacks a scholarly approach. It is anecdotal rather than academic or systematic, thus making it impossible to verify his data. Pervez provides a systematic approach but limits herself to Karachi. The present study, therefore, is the first of its kind in its ambition.

Owing to the paucity of literature and research, I conducted interviews with four former PTV officials as well as a spokesperson at the ISPR, or Inter Services Public Relations, the military's department for public relations. The ISPR was pivotal in orientating PTV towards jihad in the 1980s onwards. From the ISPR, I interviewed Colonel Mansoor Rashid, now retired. He was involved in some of the projects described as jihadi plays in this paper. From PTV, I interviewed former Managing Directors in the 1980s, Aslam Azhar and Agha Nasir. Two PTV directors, Salim Tahir and Muhammad Azim, who directed jihadi plays, were also interviewed.

To provide interpretive context, interviews were conducted with two leading cultural critics and writers on military affairs, Ayesha Siddiqa and Masood Raja. Siddiqa is an independent social scientist with expertise in civil–military relations. She has a doctorate from King's College, London, and has authored two books on the military and Pakistani politics. Raja is an Assistant Professor of Postcolonial Literature and Theory at the University of North Texas.

Similarly, five former members of jihadi groups who participated in "Afghan jihad" or "Kashmir jihad", were also interviewed to establish if jihadi film and drama played any role either in motivating them to join jihad or if such plays were shown at jihadi training camps. Two of them were interviewed via e-mail and I met the other three at their places of work. However, in view of possible consequences that their public identification might entail, ethical commitment requires that I conceal their real names and identities.

The data gathered is analysed in two ways. First, the plays described as jihadi drama or films in this essay were watched (most of them available on YouTube or in the PTV archives) or their manuscripts were read from the viewpoint of discourse analysis. Hence, this essay will offer case studies based on discourse analysis, whereby the twin characterisations of jihadi genre, jihadification and otherfication, were examined. Second, on the basis of secondary sources and interviews conducted for this research, the evidence is analysed to establish that jihadi genre played a role in recruiting mujahideen, on the one hand, and perpetuating discourses which in turn helped solidify the military's hegemony, on the other.

The essay covers the period 1979–99. I begin with 1979 for two reasons. First, 1977 marks the beginning of a state-sponsored Islamisation programme. Second, in 1979 the USA began covert intervention in Afghanistan against the Soviets, by sponsoring jihad. Thus, 1979 can be considered the year in which local and international support for Islamisation converged (Mir 2004: 19–20).

The case study ends in 1999, also for two reasons. In 1999, General Musharraf staged another military coup and this was welcomed in Pakistan according to Ali (2002). I interpret this "welcoming" as a reflection of the military's hegemony. The military, at this stage, had gained near total hegemony and thus was revealing its dimensions with greater clarity. This hegemony would not have been possible without harnessing the cultural apparatus.

Second, though heavily regulated, a private channel was allowed to air in competition with PTV in 1990 (Frontier Post 1990). Private channels were further encouraged by the Musharraf dictatorship from 2003 onwards, effectively ending the monopoly PTV had enjoyed since its founding in 1964. Therefore, to continue the case study beyond 1999 would not isolate PTV and thus any correlation between cause and effect would be impossible to establish.

However, before we examine PTV and Lollywood productions from 1977 to 1999, it would be useful to lay down some political background to the period under investigation. Therefore, I will begin by contextualising the debate by delineating PTV's trajectory and how it was determined by Pakistan's chequered political history. In this section, I also explore jihadi plays and their role. I then present coverage of jihadi plays in *Jang* and *Nawa-i-Waqt*. Finally, I raise various paradigms and engage with various theoretical questions before concluding the study.

Taking jihad to screen

PTV was launched in 1964 under the first military regime in a bid to meet the growing propaganda needs just ahead of controlled presidential elections (Nasir 2013: v–vii) being held first the time since the birth of Pakistan.

Born in 1947 as a homeland for Indian Muslims, Pakistan appeared on the world map as a "parenthesis state" consisting of East Pakistan (now Bangladesh, which constituted 56% of the population) and West Pakistan. Official Pakistani nationalism ascribes the country's creation to the "two-nation theory" according to which Indian Muslims were always a distinct community from Hindus (Munawwar 1993). The anxiety between the claims of Muslim nationalism and the achievement of a territorial state was never resolved, confounding Pakistan's struggle to define an identity that is both Islamic and national (Jalal 2011: 11). The first expression of contested identity was language riots in East Pakistan. Muhammad Ali Jinnah, Pakistan's apocryphal founding father, wanted Urdu as the state language. East Pakistan wanted both Urdu and Bengali as state languages. From February 1948 onwards, the language issue began dominating politics in East Pakistan. The federal government finally capitulated to East Pakistan's demand in 1952, but several language activists were killed during the movement (Toor 2011: 18). In 1958, civil unrest over living standards fuelled the demands for general elections. The government announced it would hold the first general elections in March 1959. In October 1958, General Ayub imposed the first military rule to thwart a possible electoral victory by the left-wing National Awami Party (NAP) in the projected elections (Paracha 2011).

Even before the military began interpellation of the country's politics, an acrimonious debate over national identity had erupted in West Pakistan between members of the left-leaning Progressive Writers Association (PWA) and the liberal but staunchly anti-communist "patriots" (Toor 2011: 69). The PWA declared: "We announce that we will teach people to hate the capitalist system. We will make our literature the translator and herald of the democratic struggle" (Toor 2011: 222). The state set out to marginalise PWA's socialist vision for nation-building through repression. Key PWA members, including Pakistan's poet laureate Faiz Ahmed Faiz, were incarcerated on charges of conspiring to overthrow the government in 1951.

The story of the cultural war further unfolded under the Ayub regime. He had sought legitimacy by casting himself in the role of a great moderniser. The project of cultural and social modernisation involved a successful bid to control the cultural sphere through a combination of the takeover of the existing institutions and formation of new ones. While the left-leaning chain of newspapers, Progressive Papers Limited, was nationalised (Niazi 2010: 127), a National Press Trust, financed by 24 industrialists, was established to "monitor and smother any traces of independent thought" (Noman 1988: 29). The regime also initiated the Writers Guild, a "trade union for writers" to address their financial problems. The Guild was a thinly disguised attempt by the regime to co-opt writers (Toor 2011: 88). On the other hand, all the leading progressives—Faiz Ahmed Faiz, Ustad Daman, Habib Jalib, Sibt-e-Hassan, Sajjad Zaheer—were harassed and interned under the regime (Ali 1983).

Ayub even attempted to modernise Islam in his bid to manage Islamists. The idea was for the state itself to formulate a particular take on Islam. The lure to use Islam proved too seductive to ignore, however, when confrontation with the left heated up (Toor 2011: 94–95). However, a massive democracy movement humbled Ayub in March 1969. He resigned and General Yahya replaced him as the new military ruler.

In 1970, the first-ever general elections gave a single majority to the Awami League, a party from East Pakistan. Fearing a government in control of East Pakistan, the military annulled the results and a military operation was launched in East Pakistan. A civil war led to the creation of Bangladesh. In West Pakistan, the military handed over power to the Pakistan Peoples' Party (PPP), headed by Zulfiqar Ali Bhutto. Bhutto's most progressive contribution was in the cultural and ideological realm. Never before had socialist ideas and symbols enjoyed official support. Socialist iconography was ubiquitous in public places (Ahmed 1983: 105). However, the culturally liberal propertied classes were isolated by Bhutto's adoption of socialist accoutrements (Toor 2011: 123). In 1977, the military staged yet another coup. In 1979, Bhutto was hanged. In a bid to seek legitimacy, the third military regime, headed by General Zia, vowed to Islamise Pakistan (Toor 2011: 6).

In the case of PTV, "policy directions were issued about themes, dress code and even camera treatment of female actors". Zia's interest in PTV was so intense that the PTV staff began to call him "super programme manager" (Nasir 2013: 81–95). In November 1977, he ordered:

> I would like radio and TV to seriously consider broadcasting good religious programmes … I would like you to start … daily programmes at intervals to convey the basic Islamic teachings like offer prayers, give Zakat, speak the truth, love the poor, adopt simplicity and abstain from ills like theft, hoarding, black marketing and profiteering … Introduce Azan [call for prayers] on radio and television.
>
> *(Nasir 2013: 79–80).*

Ulema (theologians) were appointed as members of the National Film Censorship Board and they begin to sit on all five PTV stations to vet the PTV programmes (Toor 2011: 133–153). Except "male folk dances", any kind of dance was forbidden. Music entertainment was reduced to a minimum. Male-female duets were proscribed. The singers were told not to move their bodies while singing (Nasir 2013: 80).

In line with foreign policy adjusted to accommodate US engagement in Afghanistan, Pakistan began to encourage Pakistani youth to join jihad (Hussain 2007; Mir 2004). To mobilise youth for Afghan jihad, PTV drama became a tool in this struggle. PTV drama enjoyed mass popularity (Pervez 1998), unlike PTV news which was always seen as the incumbent regime's propaganda (Sohail 1989).

With Gen. Zia's mysterious crash in 1988, democracy was restored. But the democratic process remained fragile and the Pakistan Army kept calling the shots from behind the scene. From 1988 to October 1999, Benazir Bhutto, daughter of Ali Bhutto, and Nawaz Sharif, a protégé of Gen. Zia and head of the conservative Muslim League, alternatively won and formed the governments after general elections in 1988, 1990, 1993, and 1997. Every time, their governments were removed on various disagreements with the military. For instance, in 1999, to sabotage Sharif's move to normalise relations with India, the military started a war with India in the Kargil region of Kashmir. Kashmir is an occupied territory, almost evenly occupied by both India and Pakistan. The war not merely derailed the normalisation process, the civil-military dispute over the Kargil War paved the way for the fourth military coup led by General Musharraf on October 12, 1999. The coup did not meet any resistance. On the contrary, major political parties and sections of civil society greeted the Musharraf regime.

While the role PTV played in establishing the military hegemony from 1977 onwards will be explored below, I will begin by establishing that PTV was Islamified from the start.

Islamified from the start

The Islamification of PTV drama preceded its jihadification. Islamification of PTV here implies televangelist aggrandisement of Islam. Islamisation, as noted above, does not necessarily imply jihadification. However, one can argue that Islamisation helps cultivate jihadification. The very first programme aired from PTV, *Baseerat* (Pervez 1998: VII), was a religious talk show. Already in 1967, Gen. Ayub had directed PTV to lay "emphasis on Islamic ideology" (Nasir 2013: 75). PTV displayed, for the first time, its jihadist potential during the 1965 India-Pakistan War. According to Agha Nasir, during the 1965 War with India PTV daily aired a 15-minute play. These plays, however, were called motivational and not war plays. This practice was repeated during the 1971 war with India. PTV was advised to stir up anti-India feelings. Scripted by Munno Bhai, PTV started a serial titled *Platform*. Under this title, every week a story of a Muslim family that arrived in 1947 from India was narrated (Nasir 2011: Interview).

In the 1980s, every genre of PTV programme began to belligerently accommodate themes that were either televangelist or jihadist. For instance, *Al Huda* (1981) was a series of lectures by the late Dr Israr Ahmed, known for his jihadist views, while talk shows hosted politicians like Mian Tufail Muhammad, chief of Jamaat-e-Islami (Party of Islam), at a time when opposition politicians were banned on PTV. By the early 1980s, PTV drama also began to assume a jihadist and televangelist colour. The following 36 serials or special plays that were aired 1979–1999 can be classified as jihadist:

Akhari Chattan (*The Last Rock*)
Tareekh-o-Tamseel (*History and Fiction*)
Panah I (*Refuge*)
Panah II
Shaheen (*Eagle*)
Anokha Safar (*A Unique Journey*)
Apnay Hisay ka Bojh (*Sharing the Burden*)
Platform
Ghazi Ilam Din
Muhammad bin Qasim
Grift (*The Grip*)
Apnay Apnay Mahaz Per (*At One's Own Front*)
Wasal (*Meeting*)
Muqadama-e-Kashmir (*The Case of Kashmir*)
Mohasra (*The Siege*)
Wafa (*Fidelity*)
Manzil (*Destination*)
Laag (*Candid*)
Zameen Badar (*Exiled from Earth*)
Angar Wadi (*Valley of Amber*)
Taloh (*Dawn*)
Eindhan (*Fuel*)
Yatra (*Pilgrimage*)
Char Chinar (*Four Trees of Chinar*)
Laho Say Kar Kay Wazo (*Ablution with Blood*)
Sahar Honay Tak (*Till it Dawns*)
Aag (*Fire*)
Sonahary Din (*Golden Days*)
Alfa Bravo Charlie

Nishan-e-Haider series: Nishan-e-Haider is the highest military award granted posthumously to acknowledge the courage of a military soldier or officer. This series was initiated on the advice of Gen. Zia's information minister (Nasir 2011: Interview). The following five plays were broadcast as part of the Nishan-e-Haider series: *Captain Sarwar Shaheed, Rashid Minhas, Major Tufail Shaheed, Major Aziz Bhatti Shaheed, Lance Naik Muhammad Mehfooz Shaheed*. For details, see the Appendix.[1]

To offer a glimpse into the discourse employed by jihadi dramas, I will briefly narrate the case of *Mohasra*. This four-episode serial is apparently based on a true story. In 15 October 1993, the Indian forces laid the siege of Dargah Hazrat Ball, a shrine, in Srinagar. This revered shrine hosts a strand of the Prophet Muhammad's hair. Indian authorities believed that "terrorists" had taken refuge at the holy site. The siege came to an end a month later when 65 besieged "pilgrims" were arrested peacefully.

Among the besieged people shown in *Mohasra*, there is Zehra and her mother-in-law Baigan. Zehra is expecting a baby, hence, she, along with Baigan, has come to pray at Hazrat Ball when the army lays the siege. She is stranded there for days but is allowed to leave in view of her pregnancy. Meanwhile, various characters depicting Kashmir "resistance" visit or get engaged with the besieged shrine. Brief extracts from the text will show how India is delineated as brutal "other" while Islamist identity is stressed:

BAIGAN: It is vital to pay a visit to Dargah. After all Allah is blessing your prayers after 13 years. It is a must that we visit Dargah every Friday.
ZEHRA: But I will visit to pray for one more blessing [from Allah].
BAIGAN: And what is that?
ZEHRA: That my son is born in an independent and Islamic Kashmir. Zehra, when allowed to leave the shrine for being pregnant, comes out of the shrine and yells at the Indian troops: "Bloody beasts! I spit on your humanism".

ISPR arrives at PTV

Sonahary Din and *Alfa Bravo Charlie* were unlike other PTV plays since both were produced and financed by the Inter-Services Public Relations (ISPR), the military's public relations department.

Sonahary Din (1991) was "an instant hit. While this play was being broadcast, the army was getting great response" (Rashid 2011: Interview). This serial depicts the training of army officers at the Pakistan Military Academy (PMA), a site that later gained global notoriety when Osama bin Laden was hunted in its vicinity. The serial was filmed at original locations and some actors were real-life military men. The play was aimed at attracting talented young men to the army. In fact, by the end of the 1980s, many talented young men were making careers in other fields instead of the army. *Sonahary Din* changed it all. I interviewed Colonel Mansoor Rashid, a former ISPR official. He was in charge of the *Sonahary Din* and *Alfa Bravo Charlie* projects. He said that before *Sonahary Din* the number of aspiring officers filing job applications was roughly 2,000. It shot up to 30,000 after *Sonahary Din*. *Alfa Bravo Charlie* (1998) was a sequel to *Sonahary Din*. However, it may also be called a mini-screen precursor to the real-time Kargil War as it depicted war in that region. Like *Sonahary Din*, *Alfa Bravo Charlie*'s cast also included some army men and it was filmed at actual military installations and locations (Rashid 2011: Interview).

Paradoxically, the Islamification and jihadification of PTV went on even after the sudden end of the Zia dictatorship. In fact, the military's domination of society, as articulated in Gramsci's conceptualisation of hegemony (Gramsci 1988), did not end with the end of direct military rule. In Pakistan's case the military represents a key pole of power politics. Continued domination in power politics, in turn, is linked with control of society, which also depends on intellectual control. The jihadi plays were one of the Althusserian "ISAs" employed by the army to maintain its control over society.

Louis Althusser suggests that any state has two state apparatuses it could use: the Ideological State Apparatuses (ISAs) and the Repressive State Apparatuses (RSAs). According to Althusser, the ISAs consist of "the education system, the family, the legal system, the political system, the trade unions, the media, and the culture". The RSAs include "the government, the administration, the army, the police, the courts, the prisons, etc", which function "by violence at least ultimately (since repression, e.g. administrative repression, may take non-physical forms)" (Althusser 2001: 96). In Pakistan the army, which is supposed to work as an RSA, has successfully controlled the ISAs in its bid to jihadify what Benedict Anderson (2006) calls the "imagined community" that constitutes the Pakistani "nation".

Pakistan was founded as an ultimate delineation of an imagined community of faithful Muslims. Munawwar, a historian whose highly canonised book on Pakistan history issued to the officers of all three services of Pakistan military (Raja 2010: xii), explains:

> According to Western political theories it is generally a state which gives birth to a nation, i.e., a nation is known, normally, with reference to a state. But in Islam it is religion that creates and builds states. The Muslims of the sub-continent were a nation separate from Hindus on account of religion. They demanded a state to be their independent homeland. They fought for its achievement. And they got it.
>
> *(Munawwar 1993: 29–30)*

Given that it is an imagined community, it clearly has to be imagined by someone. In Pakistan's case, this work is done by the military. The control of the cultural apparatus by the Pakistani military allowed it to "imagine" and form a concept of nationhood and statehood for its own interests.

The Pakistani military, for instance, presents itself as a modernist force contributing to the country's economy through its commercial activities while presenting itself as a saviour, defending the country against an external threat, i.e. India (Siddiqa 2007). Hence, jihad on screen continued post-Zia as a hegemonic project driven by the Pakistan military (this aspect will be further explored below). However, the military regime did not harness only PTV in its hegemonic project; the film industry was also employed in the service of Khaki interests. The next section will explore the role the Pakistani film industry played in promoting jihad.

Lollywood calling

The state control of ISAs became even more structured when Gen. Ayub came to power (see Gazdar 1997: 73–74). The strategy of using documentary filmmaking for government propaganda was enforced. The first major project was *Nai Kiran* (*A New Ray of Light*), an hour-long feature-length film. *Nai Kiran* had the well-defined objective of dismissing politicians and politics as corrupt while projecting Gen. Ayub as a saviour. Through the martial law orders, it was made mandatory for every cinema house to run the film, free of cost, for a week. During the 1960s, over 50 films were produced defaming politics and politicians, creating antagonism towards democracy, and hailing the imposition of martial law (Gazdar 1997).

In 1973 Bhutto's government, realising the deteriorating condition of the film industry, established the National Film Development Corporation (NAFDEC). However, when the Bhutto government was overthrown, the Zia regime struck a crushing blow to the film industry. In 1979, all Pakistani films produced in the preceding three years were banned, causing a void. A new film policy was formulated and the Motion Pictures Ordinance 1979 was promulgated. The Ordinance was so restrictive that it became virtually impossible to express new ideas through form, content, or artistry in a film. While Bhutto's government had not allowed the demolition of cinema houses, Zia facilitated it by relaxing the rules; hence hundreds of cinema houses were converted into shopping malls.

Likewise, to set the ideological direction under the Zia regime, a film based on Nasim Hijazi's novel *Khak aur Khoon* (*Dust and Blood*) was produced by NAFDEC. *Khak Aur Khoon* presents Muslims as disproportionate victims of violence during Partition in 1947. The next venture was *Stand Up from The Dust*, a film on the life of Muhammad Ali Jinnah. The project began as a response to the success of Richard Attenborough's *Gandhi*. Though the project was shelved, the instructions passed to the director explicitly express Gen. Zia's cultural policy. The film opens with a shot of Arab warriors, riding on horses and led by a young man, all carrying swords in their hands, appearing from the Arabian Sea. The commentary informs the audience that it was young Arab General Muhammad bin Qasim who conquered Sindh and that was the genesis of Pakistan (Gazdar 1997: 184–192).

The following jihadi films were produced between 1979 and 1999 (see Filmography for details):

Khak aur Khoon (*Earth and Blood*)
International Gorillay (*International Guerrillas*)
Changa te Manga (*These are Two Names*)
Mujahid (*Holy Warrior*)
Aalmi Ghunday (*International Ruffians*)
Hum Panch (*We Five*)

An example of the genre is *International Gorillay*, which was released in the context of Salman Rushdie's novel *The Satanic Verses*. I am citing the case of *International Gorillay* here also because of the global significance it achieved. The film got international attention when it was denied a certificate by the British Board of Film Classification (BBFC). Citing the threat to Rushdie's life as an argument for refusing the certificate, the BBFC's refusal sparked a media controversy. However, Salman Rushdie himself opposed the BBFC ruling. The ban was overturned.

International Gorillay portrays Salman Rushdie as its main villain. The film was rated as a business success in Pakistan (Goreja 2003). The protagonists are three Pakistani brothers. In a dramatised version of the Islamabad police firing on a mob on 12 February 1990, when 5 demonstrators were killed and 83 injured, their younger sister is killed by the police while demonstrating against Rushdie. The three brothers decide to avenge her and Islam's honour by killing Rushdie, portrayed as a criminal mastermind, working for an international organisation devoted to destroying Islam. Hiding in the Philippines, guarded by a private army led by an Israeli general, he seeks pleasure in torturing Muslims by making them listen to readings of *The Satanic Verses*. The protagonists arrive in the Philippines and start their hunt for Rushdie, who escapes them repeatedly thanks to the use of multiple decoys. The Israeli general's sister is sent to seduce one of the Muslim guerrillas but ends up falling in love with him and ultimately converting to Islam. The film ends with a gunfight opposing the four Pakistani "guerrillas" and Rushdie's army. The heroes defeat the villains and, as Rushdie attempts to flee the scene, three giant copies of the Qur'an appear in the sky and fire energy beams at the blasphemous author of *The Satanic Verses*, incinerating him.

The message communicated by jihadi films and PTV productions was amplified by the vernacular press. In the next section, I will document the positive coverage jihadi plays received in the two largest vernacular dailies.

Press amplifies jihad

This section investigates how *Nawa-i-Waqt* and *Jang* negotiated with jihadist plays. Both these chain-papers have enjoyed their largest circulations since the 1980s.

Founded in 1940, *Nawa-i-Waqt* (*Voice of Time*) is published simultaneously from Lahore, Karachi, and Multan. It had a daily circulation of 400,000 during the time covered by this study. Its owner Majid Nizami claimed that his paper was committed "to ideology of Pakistan" (Akhtar 2000: xxvi–ii). *Jang* (*War*), founded in 1941, is published from Lahore, Karachi, Quetta, Rawalpindi, and London. It enjoys the highest circulation, i.e. 500,000, in Pakistan (Akhtar 2000: 89).

During the period under investigation, jihadi plays received rave reviews in both these dailies. Notably, when a review is critical, it is critical for not projecting an Islamic message. *Nawa-i-Waqt*, for instance, was critical of *Wasal* for giving Kashmir resistance a "patriotic colour" instead of confessional (see Yazdani 1994). Likewise *Alfa Bravo Charlie* was flayed by Saifullah Sipra (Sipra 1998) since "Alfa Bravo Charlie includes serving army officers in its cast. These officers have been shown engaging in romance. This is tarnishing army's image". The author of this review, however, received a "harsh" call from an army official. A day later, *Nawa-i-Waqt* published another review contradicting its previous position.

Besides these exceptions, *Nawa-i-Waqt* remained steadfast in its support for jihadi plays, even demanding the production of more films on Kashmir, more TV coverage of Kashmir, and more space in the media for the Kashmir cause (Cultural Reporter 1992). *Jang*, likewise, remained receptive to jihadi plays. In view of the space available, here I will restrict myself to the coverage of plays on Kashmir and the Nishan-e-Haider series.

Covering jihadi plays

Muqadama-e-Kashmir received admirable reviews in *Jang* and *Nawa-i-Waqt*. The latter declared it the "best post-mortem of history". However, *Nawa-i-Waqt* was slightly critical of the fact that Pandit Nehru, India's first prime minister, was presented as a great orator. "If real-life Nehru were to watch the way [PTV's] Nehru delivered the speech marked by fluency and anger, he would have gone mad with happiness" (Abbas 1991).

Both *Jang* (Qureshi 1990) and *Nawa-i-Waqt* (Behzad 1990a) were initially critical of *Wasal*. However, Nawa-i-Waqt (1990) began to approve of it after the third episode of the play was aired. For instance, *Nawa-i-Waqt* ran a statement by *Wasal*'s director, Shahid Nadeem, saying, "Meaningful plays like *Wasal* would highlight the Kashmir question" (Behzad 1990b). Even before *Wasal* was telecast, *Nawa-i-Waqt* was critical of PTV authorities for delaying its broadcast. "Azad Kashmir is nervous on *Wasal* not being telecast on April 30," claimed Nawa-i-Waqt (1990).

Mohasra was eulogised by *Jang* as a "praise-worthy play" (Awan 1994) while *Nawa-i-Waqt*, besides running a friendly review (see Riaz 1994), devoted a full page to a "forum" it organised in honour of the *Mohasra* team. The Kashmir Action Committee, a government body on Kashmir, was also invited on the occasion (Saghar 1994).

Wafa was also highlighted approvingly by *Nawa-i-Waqt* (see Shumar 1994), while *Jang*'s Sunday Magazine ran a full-page interview with actress Saba Pervez about her role in *Wafa* (Pervez 1994).

Angar Wadi was granted full-page coverage in *Nawa-i-Waqt*. The play was declared a "true picture of today's Kashmir" (Yazdani 1995). *Nawa-i-Waqt* ran another review when *Angar Wadi* concluded. "The play was successful" (Shumar 1995a), *Nawa-i-Waqt* declared. However, *Angar Wadi* was criticised by *Nawa-i-Waqt* columnist Nusrat Mirza (Mirza 1995). He thought an Indian general in *Angar Wadi* was cast in a positive manner. *Jang* ran actor Khawaja Salim's interview about his role in *Angar Wadi*. Salim declared that the play did not show "even ten percent of the atrocities actually being committed in Kashmir".

Aag was declared a "wonderful symbolic" play by *Jang* (see Qureshi 1995), while readers were informed that it would be telecast again on 29th June. *Eindhan*, while it was being aired, was declared a success (see Shumar 1995b) by *Nawa-i-Waqt*. *Aag* "is an attempt at highlighting the Kashmir cause", (Cultural Reporter 1998) declared *Jang*.

The *Nishan-e-Haider* episodes, likewise, received excellent reviews: *Rashid Minhas Shaheed*, "left tears in the eyes" (Hussain 1985), *Nawa-i-Waqt* declared. *Major Tufail Muhammad Shaheed* was reported about in *Jang* even before it was aired. The report was titled, "*Major Tufail Muhammed* will prove another milestone in PTV history". The report informs its readers that the play was filmed under the supervision of Raja Muhammad Ali, a retired army officer. Zil-e-Subhan, playing the lead role, told *Jang*: "I was meted out a VIP treatment by the army men to the extent that I have started behaving like one" (Jafri 1985). A day after *Major Aziz*

Bhatti Shaheed was aired, *Jang* carried an interview with Nasir Shirazi, the actor playing the lead role, while *Nawa-i-Waqt* praised the play as an "effective and meaningful" play (Shumar 1995c).

Discussion and analysis

Pakistan can be characterised as a praetorian state (Siddiqa 2007) defined by Perlmutter (1974: 93) as a state that "favors the development of military as the core group and encourages the growth of its expectations as a ruling class". Likewise, it is important to note that a social formation that does not reproduce the conditions of production at the same time as it produces, does not last. "The ultimate condition of production is therefore the reproduction of the condition of productions". The reproduction of conditions is granted through RSAs as well as ISAs (Althusser 2001: 86).

In praetorian Pakistan, the military as core group has not merely emerged as the dominant section of the RSAs, but has successfully established its hold over the ISAs. In the process, Pakistan not merely emerged as a praetorian state but also a state where society has been deeply jihadified (Hussain 2007). The military's hegemony would not have been smooth in the absence of the jihadist phenomenon. In the form of jihadis, the military has created a permanent ally. When the military is not directly conducting politics, it deploys jihadis to advance its agenda.

In fact, Khaled Ahmed (2009: 10) claims that unlike other states that have three mutually balancing centres of power, i.e. the legislature, the executive, and the judiciary, Pakistan has six "existential" pillars of the state: "Legislature, Executive, Judiciary, Army plus Establishment, Media, and Jihadi Organisations". Though his claim is not nuanced, it depicts a widespread impression among the liberal intellectual elite in the country.

Jihadification was assisted by controlling PTV, vigilantly monitoring Lollywood, and strictly censoring the press. Did the audience receive it all passively?

There are signs of resistance. For instance, *Khabarnama* [9 pm news] was a highly discredited programme. *Jang*, for instance, reports, "Whoever was in power, *Khabarnama* never became credible" (Sohail 1989). Similarly, the press was not readily believed in. PTV drama was, however, a subtle affair. Artistic expression may have propagandist intent. However, if artistically made, it outdoes the crude propaganda often conducted through documentaries, news, and talk shows. The case of *Platform*, for instance, shows that it was aimed at presenting India in a bad light. However, it was given the colour of human tragedy and it was a popular drama serial.

Din (2004: 59) provides proof of agenda-setting with regard to jihadi plays on Kashmir. He notes, "All the dramas on Kashmir, including *Angar Wadi*, have been highlighting the governmental viewpoint. Not merely permission was sought in advance from the ISPR, the ISPR was also encouraging and helping such plays". Similarly, the *Nishan-e-Haider* series was launched on the suggestion of Gen. Zia's Information Minister (Nasir 2011: Interview). Similarly, I have shown how *Sonahary Din* was conceived by the military apparatus to boost its image among prospective recruits.

That India and Pakistan fought a war over Kashmir three months after their birth established the primacy of a national security agenda. As the military began to take hold of the country's politics, stress on the imagined community's confessional basis assumed added importance. This project of Islamifying and jihadifying the state and society, however, became particularly imperative in view of foreign policy compulsions as well as the domestic politics of the Zia regime as was examined above.

Therefore, the process of jihadification was electrified under Gen. Zia's military rule. In the case of PTV, not only was drama jihadified, the entire TV milieu was Islamified. Islamisation of television preceded and accompanied the jihadification of PTV drama. For instance, *Mishal-e-Rah* in 1974 was the only Islamic programme. By 1984, there were eight such programmes. While televangelist programmes were granted 8.33% of the total transmission time in 1978–79, by September 1984, such programmes constituted 16.84% of the total transmission time (Imran 1984: 102–104). Even jihadist drama was telecast in unison with Islamified drama. For instance, *Akhari Chattan* was preceded by *Aur Dramay* (1980). *Akhari Chattan* preached jihad while *Aur Dramay*, scripted by Ashfaq Ahmed, was a serial "themed on pure Islamic values and true Pakistani ideology" (Murad 1990: 210).

However, PTV plays directly or indirectly subversive of the Islamisation project were reprimanded. Based on the English novel *The Fountain Head, Tesra Kinara*, for instance, was stringently criticised in *Nawa-i-Waqt*: "An extremely dangerous TV play *Tesra Kinara* is being telecast these days. Its basic theme is absolute freedom. Adopted from English, this Urdu play is an anathema to both Islam and Pakistan" (Murad 1990: 210–213). Similarly, *Show Time*, a popular comedy, was accused of "spreading class hatred" (Butt 1987). The jihadification of PTV transmission, in connivance with the press, marginalised every alternative discourse by, for instance, imposing an unwritten ban on undesirable writers, poets, and journalists (Nasir 2013: 81).

In the 1990s, when PTV was belligerently telecasting plays on Kashmir, the Indian film industry, or Bollywood, produced a number of films categorised as "hate-Pakistan" films. *Muqadama-e-Kashmir* (1991) was the first play that mentioned India by name. Similarly, in the 1990s, Bollywood gave up the past practice of mentioning Pakistan in the abstract. The "ISI", the Pakistani spy agency, became a catchphrase in Bollywood productions. A future study investigating a link between Bollywood's "hate-Pakistan" productions and PTV's jihadi plays would be useful both in understanding PTV/Lollywood as well as Bollywood, for the two sides reacted to each other.

Paradoxically, in the longer run, PTV and the film industry have become the victims of the jihadification they helped spread. Performing art, considered an obscenity by jihadists, is increasingly under attack. Militants had already in the 1990s begun to plant bombs at Lahore's cinema houses and theatres. Simultaneously, Lollywood, producing over 100 films a year in the 1980s, was able to release only 10 films in 2010. Likewise, the PTV rating has badly suffered since its monopoly on the airwaves foundered from 2003 onwards. Thus, the hegemony that exploited the cultural industry to strengthen its monopoly has, unintentionally, consigned the same cultural industry to ruin.

Conclusion

The aim of this study was to foreground the importance of the media and cultural apparatus in explaining military hegemony. This study showed that the Islamisation of PTV and Lollywood, alongside press censorship, not merely constrained the political imagination of ordinary Pakistanis but also helped change the country's political landscape per se.

However, it was Gen. Zia's military rule that carefully harmonised PTV transmission, Lollywood, and the press with the regime's political projects and foreign policy goals in mind. A strict censorship to silence the press and a new code of conduct for the film industry was introduced alongside the jihadification of TV drama. The Islamisation project won over the mosque as Gen. Zia's natural ally. Hence, all major ISA tools were harnessed in the service of the military regime which helped solidify military hegemony over Pakistan.

The entire process helped, on one hand, establish Islam's primacy in determining its national identity while, on the other hand, it shaped a new discourse of power whereby glorified jihadis—military men being the ultimate delineation of jihad—appeared as the natural claimant to power in an Islamic polity and state. This was manifested in practice when in October 1999 the fourth military coup did not meet any resistance. Besides isolated incidents of sweet distribution, all the major political parties welcomed the coup. The lack of resistance manifested the naturalisation of the military's hegemonic role.

Note

1 In a couple of cases, such as *Wasal* or *Aag*, one may consider these productions as borderline cases in the context of this study. However, I have included them here because the time period is important, as is the fact that PTV was promoting the jihadi genre.

Appendix

Akhari Chattan (1981) tells the story of a Central Asian king resisting Genghis Khan's invading armies. It is based on Nasim Hijazi's novel. Director: Qasim Jalali. Cast: Talat Iqbal, Shaista Qaiser, Salim Nasir, Subhani Bayunus, Rafiq Nawaz.

Tareekh-o-Tamseel (1981) depicted Muslim/Arab conquerors. Some of the plays, aired under the title *Tareekh-o-Tamseel*, included:

1. *Tariq bin Ziad*. Director: Qasim Jalali. Script: Talat Hussain. Date of telecast: 26 November 1981. Cast: Imtiaz Ahmed, Talat Hussain, Samina Peerzada, Wakil Farooq, Mohammad Yusuf, Zil-e-Subhan. Tariq bin Ziad was the Berber general who conquered the Iberian peninsula.
2. *Chand Bibi*. Director: Iqbal Ansari. Script: Shahid Kazmi. Date of telecast: Not Available. Cast: Tahira Wasti, Muhammad Yusuf, Aslam Lattar, Zil-e-Subhan. Chand Bibi was a 16th-century Muslim queen and warrior who ruled India.

3. *Al Tamash.* Director: Qasim Jalali. Script: Fatima Surriya Bajia. Date of telecast: Not Available. Cast: Mehmud Masood, Tahira Wasti, Javed Sheikh, Marriana Hassan, Kamal Irani, Ayesha Khan, Ishrat Hashmi. Altamash was a Muslim king who ruled India and founded a dynasty.
4. *Bakht Khan.* Director: Bukhtiar Ahmed. Script: Intizar Hussain. Date of telecast: Not Available. Cast: Mehmud Ali, Khalid Zafar, M. Warsi, Ishrat Hashmi, Taj Haider, Begum Khurshid Mirza, Shahzad Raza. Bakht Khan was a Muslim soldier who participated in the War of Independence 1857 against the East India Company.
5. *Suleman Alishan.* Director: Qaiser Farooq. Script: Shahid Kazmi. Cast: Salim Nasir, Anil Chudhry, Mushtaq Ahmed, Subhani Bayunus, Aslam Lattar, Mehmud Ali, Azra Sherwani, Sarwat Sultana. Suleman Alishan, known in the West as Suleman the Magnificent, was a 16th-century Ottoman caliph.

Panah I, *Panah* II (1983–84) depict the Afghan "resistance" against Soviet intervention in Afghanistan. Director: Shahzad Khalil. Script: Shahid Kazmi. Cast: Uzma Gilani, Talat Hussain, Khalida Riyasat, Zil-e-Subhan, A. R. Baloch, Noor Muhammad Lashari.

Shaheen (1984), a serial based on Nasim Hijazi's novel, depicts the situation of the Muslims at the time of the Inquisition in 1492. Producer: Mohsin Ali. Cast: Ismail Shah, Shakeel Ahmad, Mazhar Ali, Tahira Wasti, Subhani Ba Younis.

The *Nishan-e-Haider* series: The following four plays were broadcast in the name of Nishan-e-Haider (every play depicts the life of a Nishan-e-Haider recipient):

1. *Captain Sarwar Shaheed* (1984) was the first episode of the *Nishan-e-Haider* series. Director: Kanwar Aftab. Script: Colonel Ismail Siddiqi. It was aired on 7 September 1985. Cast: Salim Nasir, Sakina Sammo, Talat Husain, Usman Pirzada, Shakeel, Syed Imtiaz Husain, Imran Pirzada, Agha Wahid-ur-Rehman, Khalid Hafeez, Afzal Latifi.
2. *Rashid Minhas* (1985). Director/Script: Shehzad Khalil. Cast: Pilot Officer Farooq Iqbal, Nayyar Kamal, Pilot Officer Shahid Alvi, Marina Khan, Tasnim Ismail, Huma Akbar, Wing Commander Iqbal Haider, Squadron Leader Sohail Butt, Flight Lieutenant Adil Rashid, Squadron Leader Asif Jabbar.
3. *Major Tufail Shaheed* (1986). Director: Qasim Jalali. Script: Zaheer Bhatti. Aired on 17 August 1985. Cast: Munawwar Saeed, Zil-e-Subhan, Z. A. Zulfi, Sikander Shaheen, Mumtaz Ali, Tahira Wasti, Qasim Jalali, Asif raza Mir.
4. *Major Aziz Bhatti Shaheed* (1995). Director: Salim Tahir. Script: Asghar Nadim Syed. It was aired on 12 September 1995. Cast: Usman Peerzada, Nasir Shirazi.

Anokha Safar (1988–89) presents Muslim scientists and philosophers of the past. It is debatable whether this play can be classified as jihadist; however, there was a great stress on "us" and "them", hence this serial can qualify as a jihadi serial. *Anokha Safar* consisted of "Ibn-e-Batuta" (aired on 13 July 1988), "Ibn-e-Khaldoun" (20 July 1988), "Bo Ali Seena" (27 July 1988), "Ibn-e-Hesham" (3

August 1988), "Naseer-ud-Din Tosi" (10 August 1988), "Ahmed Jalil" (17 August 1988), "Yakub al-Kundi" (28 September 1988), "Abu Asarkat Baghdadi" (2 October 1988), "Hana ben Ishaq" (26 October 1988), "Ali ben Tibri" (2 November 1988), "Ahmed Taseer Faraghani" (30 November 1988), "Ibn-e-Rushd" (7 December 1988), "Abu Rehan Al-Bairouni" (14 December 1988), "Muhammad ben Jabir al-Astani" (21 December 1988), "Ali ben Eisa" (28 December 1988, 4 January 1989, 11 January 1989), "Yusuf ben Manzar" (18 January 1989), "Araib Qurtabi" (1 February 1989, 8 February 1989, 15 February 1989), "Jaish ben Hassan" (1 March 1989), "Abu al-Wafa Bozjani" (8 March 1989, 22 March 1989, 10 April 1989).

Apnay Hisay ka Bhhoj (1990) is a special play telecast on 6 September, 1990. It shows Pakistani forces attacking "enemy lines". *Nawa-i-Waqt* praised the play for an "original presentation of attack on enemy lines" (*Behzad* 6 September 1990). Director: Nusrat Thakur. Script: Amjad Islam Amjad. Cast: Not Available.

Wasal (1990). Directed and scripted by Shahid Mehmood Nadim, *Wasal* was aired on 28 May 1990, 4 June 1990, 11 June 1990, and 18 June 1990. Cast: Feryal Gouhar, Asim Bokhari, Jamil Fakhri, Abdul Hafiz, Sajjad Kishwer. The theme is Kashmir "resistance".

Muqadama-e-Kashmir (1991). Producer/director Bukhtiar Ahmed also scripted this play. It has also been published in book form under the same title. The three-episode series was broadcast on 6, 13, and 20 July 1991. For the first time, India was named in a PTV play. Abdul Ahad, the protagonist, represents the Kashmir case before the "court of international conscience". Not only is his entire family, including infants, killed by the Indian army, he himself is finally gunned down by the Indian troops. Major characters from the history of the Indian sub-continent like Lord Mountbatten, Pandit Nehru, Sheikh Abdullah, Hari Singh, Partab Singh, and Gulab Singh appear before the court. The Dogra dynasty is depicted as brutal and anti-Muslim, while Lord Mountbatten and Nehru are painted as biased towards Muslims. Nehru is prejudiced because he is a Hindu, while having an affair with Edwina Mountbatten. Sheikh Abdullah is accused of secularism, ladeeniat (heresy), and connivance with India.

Platform (1991), is a remake of *Platform* (1971) discussed in the text. Script: Munno Bhai.

Ghazi Ilam Din (1991) is the story of a Muslim youth who killed, in Lahore, back in the 1930s, a Hindu publisher on the charge of blasphemy. It was part of a series, *Wafa kay Paikar* (*Delineation of Fidelity*), that in every episode depicted a Muslim warrior. In 1978 and in 2003, Lollywood produced films on Ilam Din. The PTV play was given good coverage in *Jang* (15 January 1991). *Nawa-i-Waqt* (21 May 1991) praised *Wafa key Pekar* as "an excellent series".

Sonaharay Din (1991) Director/Script: Shoaib Mansoor. Cast: Salim Sheikh, Aliya Kazmi, Hameed Wayne, Mumtaz Ashraf, Azra Mansoor, Malik Faraz. It has been discussed in the text.

Muhammad bin Qasim (1992) narrates the story of an 8th-century Muslim/Arab general who conquered parts of India. He was the first Muslim general to set foot in India. It is based on a novel by Nasim Hijazi. Other details are not available.

Apnay Apnay Mahaz Par (1992). This play was telecast to mark 6 September, "Defence Day". Script: Dr Tariq Aziz. Other details are not available.

Wafa (1994) was an 11-episode drama serial. It shows the Kashmiris' struggle for independence from India. Director: Muhammad Azim. Script: Shehzad Ahmed. Cast: Mustafa Qureshi, Saba Pervez, Mehmud Aslam, Farooq Zamir, Khalid Osman, Lala Rukh, Jazba Sultana. It was aired on 17 July 1994, 24 July 1994, 7 August 1994, 21 August 1994, 28 August 1994, 11 September 1994, 18 September 1994, 25 September 1994, 2 October 1994, 9 October 1994, and 16 October 1994.

Mohasra (1994) Written and directed by Shahid Mehmood Nadeem, this four-episode play was telecast in April and May 1994. This play has been discussed earlier.

Angar Wadi (1995) Directed by Tariq Meraj, Angar Wadi's script was penned by Rauf Khalid. This 13-episode play was a joint production of Cosmos Television and PTV. The first episode was aired on 23 June 1995. *Angar Wadi* has also appeared as a book.

Char Chinar (1995) Director: Shahid Iqbal. Script: Hamid Kashmiri. Cast: Mazhar Ali, Shakil, Mehmud Akhtar. Date of telecast is not available.

Aag (1995) is a long play. Director/script: Muhammad Azim. It is a mystical play set in the background of a fire at a Kashmiri shrine.

Manzil (1995–96) depicts the struggle for independence in Kashmir. It was aired on 27 December 1995 and 5 February 1996. Director: Muhammad Azim. Script: Sajjad Tirmizi. Cast: Jazba Sultana, Samina Ahmed, Arshad Khan, Zubair Khan, Jamil Jaral, Nisar Qadri, Javed Baber, Rozeena Khalid.

Laag (1998) broke the previous rating records of any PTV drama. It was directed and produced by Rauf Khalid. It highlights the "Indian atrocities" in Kashmir and the freedom struggle of the Kashmiri Mujahideen. Cast: Rauf Khalid, Zeba Bukhtiar, Nadia Khan, Fareedullah, Azra Aftab, Sohail Asghar, Nayyer Ejaz, Nirma, Rashid Mehmud, Lateef Arshad.

Alfa Bravo Charlie (1998). Director/script: Shoaib Mansoor. Cast: Captain M. Qasim Khan, Captain Abdullah Mehmood, Faraz Inam, Shahbaz Khan, Farah Moin, Hashmat Sheikh, Malik Ata Muhammad, Shanaz Khawaja, Wiqar Ahmed, Rafay Moin, Brigadier Tahir, Farhat Pasha. This play has been discussed in the text.

Grift (1999) takes up the issue of Indian-sponsored "Hindu" terrorism on Pakistani soil. Director: Syed Qamber Ali Shah. Script: Tariq Ismail Sagar. Other details are not available.

Zameen Badar. Director: Yawar Hayat. Script: Hussain Shad. This 85-minute-long play focuses on the Kashmir struggle. Cast: Aurengzeb Laghari, Naima Khan, Abu Ashrab, Aniq Naji, Zafar Lodhi, Sadaqat Siddiqi, Sohail Asghar, Jamil Fakhri, Asim Bokhari, Khalid Moin Butt, Zara Akbar, Saadat, Khawar Butt, Khurshid Ali, Asghar Masoom. Date of telecast is not available.

Taloh. Script by Iqbal Ahmed Khan. Other details are not available. The theme is Kashmiri "resistance".

Eindhan was a serial scripted by Iqbal Ahmed Khan. Other details are not available. The theme is the Kashmir struggle.

Yatra. Script by Iqbal Ahmed Khan. Other details are not available. The theme is the Kashmir struggle.

Laho Say Kar Kay Wazo. Script by Zahoor Ahmed. Other details are not available. The theme is Kashmir.

Sahar Honay Tak. Directed by Muhammad Azim. Other details are not available. It is based on "resistance" in Kashmir.

References

Ahmed, Aijaz. 1983. "Democracy and dictatorship" in Hassan Gardezi and Jamil Rashid (eds), *Pakistan, the Roots of Dictatorship: The Political Economy of a Praetorian State*. London: Zed Press, 94–172.

Ahmed, Khaled. 2009. *Pakistan and Nature of State: Revisionism, Jihad and Governance*. Karachi: Irtiqa.

Akhtar, Rai S. 2000. *Media, Religion, and Politics in Pakistan*. Karachi: Oxford University Press.

Ali, Tariq. 1983. *Can Pakistan Survive?* London: Penguin Books.

Ali, Tariq. 2002. *Clash of Fundamentalisms*. London: Verso.

Althusser, Louis. 2001. *Lenin and Philosophy and Other Essays*. New York: Monthly Review Press.

Anderson, Benedict. 2006. *Imagined Communities*. London: Verso.

Din, Zia-ul. 2004. *Pakistan Television Drama aur Kashmir. Tehqiqi-o-Tanqeedi Mutalia*. Islamabad: Allama Iqbal Open University.

Gazdar, Mushtaq. 1997. *Pakistan Cinema 1947–1997*. Karachi: Oxford University Press.

Goreja, Yasin. 2003. *Pakistan Millennium Film Directory*. Lahore: Goreja Publications.

Gramsci, Antonio. 1988. *An Antonio Gramsci Reader*. New York: Schocken Books.

Hussain, Zahid. 2007. *Frontline Pakistan*. London: I. B. Tauris.

Imran, Rukhsana. 1984. *Pakistan Television Kay Das Saal*. Lahore: University of Punjab, Department of Mass Communication.

Jalal, Ayesha. 2011. "The past as present", in Maleeha Lodhi (ed), *Pakistan: Beyond the 'Crisis State'*. Karachi: Oxford University Press, 7–20.

Lacy, Robert. 1984. *Saudiernas Rike*. Stockholm: Askild & Kärnekull.

Mir, Amir. 2004. *The True Face of Jehadis*. Lahore: Mashal.

Munawwar, Muhammad. 1993. *Dimensions of Pakistan Movement*. Lahore: WAJIDALIS.

Murad, Tahir. 1990. *Lahore Television dramay ki adbi rawait*. Lahore: FC College.

Nasir, Agha. 2013. *This is PTV: Another Day, Another World*. Lahore: Nisar Art Press.

Niazi, Zamir. 2010. *The Press in Chains*. Karachi: Oxford University Press.

Noman, Omar. 1988. *The Political Economy of Pakistan 1947–85*. London: KPI.

Perlmutter, Amos. 1974. *Egypt: The Praetorian State*. New Brunswick: Transaction Books.

Pervez, Nasreen. 1998. *Pakistan Television Drama and Social Change*. Karachi: University of Karachi, Department of Mass Communication.

Raja, Masood A. 2010. *Constructing Pakistan. Foundational Texts and the Rise of Muslim National Identity 1857–1947*. New York: Oxford University Press.

Rashid, Ahmed. 2002. *Jihad: The Rise of Militant Islam in Central Asia*. New Haven, CT: Yale University Press.
Siddiqa, Ayesha. 2007. *Military Inc. Inside Pakistan's Military Economy*. Karachi: Oxford University Press.
Toor, Saadia. 2011. *The State of Islam: Culture and Cold War Politics in Pakistan*. New York: Pluto.

Articles

Abbas, Akhtar. 1991."Kashmir ka Muqadama: Tareekh ka behtreen post mortem". *Nawa-i-Waqt*, 26 February 1991.
Awan, M.I. 1994. "Mohasra Kashmir kay mozo per kabal-e-qadar series". *Jang*, 7 June 1994.
Behzad, Khalid. 1990a. "Wasal ki pehli do iqsaat ghair mo'asr raheen". *Nawa-i-Waqt*, 12 June 1990.
Behzad, Khalid. 1990b. "Dhop dorr main farsoda andaz-e-mazah". *Nawa-i-Waqt*, 19 June 1990.
Butt, Salah-ud-Din. 1987. "Show Time kay zare'ay tabqati nafrat phail rahi hey". *Nawa-i-Waqt*, 20 January 1987.
Cultural Reporter. 1992. "Sitam sha'ar say tujh ko churain gay aik din". *Nawa-i-Waqt*, 14 July 1992.
Cultural Reporter. 1998. "Laag main masla-e-kashmir ko ujagar karnay ki koshish ke gaye". *Jang*, 26 August 1998.
Frontier Post. 1990. "CNN/PTN: Broadcasting horizons". *The Frontier Post*, 20 August 1990.
Hussain, Nadim. 1985. "Rashid Minhas Shaheed ankhon ko ashkbar kar gaya". *Nawa-i-Waqt*, 7 May 1985.
Jafri, Qaiser M. 1985. "Major Tufail Muhammad Sheheed television ki tareekh main aik or sang-e-meel sabit ho ga". *Jang*, 18 August 1985.
Mirza, Nusrat. 1995. "Angar Wadi bharti fouji general ka bail out". *Nawa-i-Waqt*, 20 May 1995.
Pervez, Saba. 1994. "Wafa main mera kirdar masali tha. Interview with Tayyaba Lodhi". *Jang*, 21 October 1994.
Qureshi, Aftab Z. 1990. "Wasal: Ab tak tehreek-e-azadi drawing room tehreek lag rahi hay". *Jang*, 6 December 1990.
Qureshi, Aftab Z. 1995. "Aag aik alamti or ruhani kisam ki kahani thee". *Jang*, 5 July 1995.
Riaz, Tabinda. 1994. "Mohasra PTV kee nai serial". *Nawa-i-Waqt*, 31 May 1994.
Saghar, Riaz-ur-Rehman. 1994. "Pakistani akhbarat nay her dour main masla-e-kashmir ko zinda rakha". *Nawa-i-Waqt*, 19 July 1994.
Shumar, Akhtar. 1994. "Wafa Kashmir kay hawalay say juratmandana koshish". *Nawa-i-Waqt*, 9 August 1994.
Shumar, Akhtar. 1995a. "Pukar or Angar Wadi ka ikhtatam: duno khail kamyab rahay". *Nawa-i-Waqt*, 9 May 1995.
Shumar, Akhtar. 1995b. "Lahore markaz ka Eindhan kamyabi say agay barh raha hay". *Nawa-i-Waqt*, 21 November 1995.
Shumar, Akhtar. 1995c. "Nishan-e-Haider aik mo'asr or bamaqsad khail". *Nawa-i-Waqt*, 18 September 1995.
Sipra, Saifullah. 1998. "Alfa Bravo Charlie: Awam ko kia dikhaya ja raha hey". *Nawa-i-Waqt*, 23 June 1998.
Sohail, Raza. 1989. "Kisi bhi daur main 'tv Khabarnama' apna aitbar qaim na kar saka". *Jang*, 21 November 1989.
Yazdani, Khalid. 1994. "Kashmir kay mozo per sirf puranay dramay kyon". *Nawa-i-Waqt*, 10 May 1994.

Yazdani, Khalid. 1995. "Aay wade-i-kashmir: drama serial Angar Wadi aaj kay Kashmir ki tasweer". *Nawa-i-Waqt*, 10 March 1995.

Online Sources

Paracha, Nadeem Farooq. 2011. "Meet the ANP". *Dawn* (accessed 6 September 2011), www.dawn.com/2011/09/04/smokerscorner-meet-the-anp.html.

Filmography

AalmiGhunday. Director: Idrees Khan. Butt Productions. 1996.
Changa-te-Manga. Director: Hyder. G & S Co. 1981.
Gandhi. Director: Richard Attenborough. International Film Investors, National Film Development Corporation of India (NFDC), Goldcrest Films International. 1982.
Hum Panch. Director: Haider Sami Warriach. Name of production company not available. 1998.
International Gorillay. Director: Jan Muhammad. Evernew Pictures. 1990.
KhakaurKhoon. Director: Masood Pervez. NEFDEC. 1979.
Mujahid. Director: Zahoor Hussain. Shahnoor Studios. 1995.

Interviews

Aslam Azhar
Agha Nasir
Colonel Mansoor Rashid
Ayesha Siddiqua (via email)
Masood Raja (via email)

4

THE POLITICS OF PITY AND THE INDIVIDUAL HEROINE SYNDROME

Mukhtaran Mai and Malala Yousafzai of Pakistan[1]

Fawzia Afzal-Khan

In this chapter, I argue that the newly refashioned liberal feminism, which privileges individual stories of empowerment and redemption over the collective struggles at the heart of more radical Western and non-Western feminist approaches, is the dominant form of feminism today in the West/global north. It is also the most palatable feminism for our mediatised age and one whose stories are most easily spectacularised for consumption by Western audiences eager to learn about, then pity, the suffering of both geographically remote and internally distanced "others". It is this now neoliberal feminist formation that works in lockstep with Western imperial designs and interventions in the global south (specifically Muslim lands)—to fight for "women's rights". Part of that "fight" takes the form of sensationalising via media spectacularism cases that highlight the "individual heroism" of "feminist voices" such as those of Malala Yousafzai and Mukhtaran Mai of Pakistan, which can be recuperated for pedagogical purposes at the service of Islamophobia. Such recuperative redemption is, I argue, the intent and effect of writers like Phyllis Chesler, whose feminism advances these other, less salubrious agendas of imperialism and neo-colonialism, aided and abetted by the "spectacular rhetoric" of our mediatised age.

Using Lilie Chouliarki's questions regarding the ethical responsibilities of spectators towards visual suffering in our mediatised age as a start-off point, wherein she states, "the mediation between spectator and sufferer is a crucial political space because the relationship between the two of them maps on to distinct geopolitical territories that reflect the global distribution of power", I ask to what degree does the West's obsession with "the cultural politics of recognition", which is based on an "identity-based politics of visibility", and which has dominated Western liberal feminism since the end of the twentieth century, been responsible for directing "public attention away from the regressive politics and growth of global capitalism"—and which in turn is implacably intertwined with the politics of US Empire in the twenty-first century? How do these two performances of individual Pakistani women refusing victimhood feed, nonetheless and paradoxically, into a neoliberal politics of redemption?

Neoliberal feminism

It is my contention that Western liberal feminism serves as a screen masking the reframing of an old colonialist trope, that of "white men saving brown women from brown men"[2]—which, in our contemporary imperialist moment, speaks the language of an individual empowerment and redemption agenda that the West now sells to poor brown women, especially in the Muslim world as part of its "rescue" narrative. Angela McRobbie offers an insightful take on this process and the ways such a narrative affects Western female subjects too in today's European neoliberal states such as her native United Kingdom, in her book, *The Aftermath of Feminism: Gender, Culture, and Social Change*, explaining:

> Elements of feminism have been taken into account and have been absolutely incorporated into political and institutional life. Drawing on a vocabulary that includes words like "empowerment" and "choice", these elements are then converted into a much more individualistic discourse and they are deployed in this new guise, particularly in media and popular culture, but also by agencies of the state, as a kind of substitute for feminism. These new and seemingly modern ideas about women and especially young women are then disseminated more aggressively so as to ensure that a new women's movement will not re-emerge.
>
> (McRobbie 2009: 1)

Indeed, we can trace these ideas and their deployment back to the conception of the "sovereign state" envisioned by Thomas Hobbes back in the seventeenth century, a conception exposed for its depoliticisation of the emerging bourgeois citizen of Western liberal democracies by none other than Hannah Arendt in her books and articles published in the 1950s. She was one of the few thinkers who saw the ways in which a Hobbesian view of absolute state power and concomitant lack of direct political engagement and power by the average bourgeois citizen was intimately linked to the imperialist project of Europe in her time[3]—and which endures up through our time, although ironically, the Western liberal state no longer provides the "security"—from want, or hunger, or violence—that was supposed to be the trade-off for decreased personal liberty and direct political involvement in the Leviathan of Hobbes. Thus, linked to this macho neo-imperialism abroad, is a weakening of the welfare-state apparatus at "home"—which we see in the reduction of individual freedoms such as the freedom to live and work in dignity for those who are not part of the bourgeoisie. But, as a cover for imperialism abroad, white middle-class feminism today continues to direct its appeals to young white women (and women of colour aspiring for white capitalist privilege)—through an economic rhetoric of individual "self-empowerment" that absolves the militaristic state of its responsibility toward its poorer citizens, as well as the citizens of the countries it invades (in cahoots with those countries' rulers of state)—as the capitalist state's search for new markets and territories to bring into its economic and ideological orbit continues unabated.

In such a world, McRobbie contends, "feminism is instrumentalized. It is brought forth and claimed by Western governments, as a signal to the rest of the world that this is a key part of what freedom now means. Freedom is re-vitalized and brought up to date with this faux feminism" (McRobbie 2009: 1). In the US, this is so obviously the strategy Sheryl Sandberg and her supporters have deployed: Sandberg uses feminist rhetoric as a front to cover her commitment to Western cultural imperialism, to white supremacist capitalist patriarchy.[4]

Islamism, Islamophobia and the neoliberal feminist project

I am caught between the Scylla of Islamophobia (*Legislating Fear*) and its resurgent orientalist tropes concerning "brown Muslim women who need saving" by the West (white "feminists" and men) and the Charybdis of Islamism which resurrects the nationalism of early postcolonial history, conflating women with the nation, and hence with a factitious "tradition" of male dominance over "their" women as a prideful response against encroachment of national sovereignty by neo-colonial imperial Western forces (Chowdhury 2011: 157). To get past and beyond this no-woman's land of helplessness, I would like to think through alternative strategies including drawing on work done by scholars on the following:

1. Delinking tradition/woman/nation[5]
2. Challenging the tradition-as-Islam, modernity-as-West binary
3. Most importantly, perhaps, pointing to a different trajectory and understanding of feminism than the one being touted in the centres of Western power as symbolic of Muslim Pakistani feminism, such as comes across in the way the stories of Mukhtaran Mai and Malala Yousafzai have been framed for public consumption. Such representations dovetail all too neatly with various expressions of liberal Western feminism, and contribute to the anxiety I have and share with many other scholars who live and work in the global north regarding Muslim women and the circulation of orientalist tropes about them. The performative—that is to say, iterative—trope of the individual heroine, fighting bravely against a uniformly and always-already patriarchal, oppressive culture coded this way because of its adherence to Islam, thus exemplifies a (faux) feminism that undergirds and contributes to Islamophobia and US military adventurism in Muslim lands such as Pakistan (Bhattacharyya 2008: 10).
4. The "individual heroine" syndrome is problematic for several reasons, not least of all because it aligns too neatly with Western liberal feminism's ideology of individual autonomy and "equality", which has itself undergone scrutiny and critique by other schools of Western feminist theory.

The most pertinent of these critiques for my purposes has to do with this feminist modality's cosy relationship to a patriarchal neoliberal capitalism which is the engine of contemporary globalisation—as I've alluded to in the previous section.

The question, then, that I wish to think through in this paper, is framed around the two "feminist performances" of Mukhtaran Mai and Malala Yousafzai's life-stories circulated, respectively, to the world through, most recently, an opera on the rape of Mukhtaran Mai called *Thumbprint*, and the memoir of Malala, *I Am Malala* subtitled *The Girl Who Was Shot by the Taliban*. It is a question Elora Chowdhury also raises in the final chapter of her important book on the Bangladeshi Women's Movement, *Transnationalism Reversed: Women Organizing against Gendered Violence in Bangladesh*. This is the question of, as she puts it, "feminist complicity in, and mounting dissent against, interlocking hegemonies of neoimperialism, fundamentalism, and patriarchies" (Chowdhury 2011: 157).

Feminist complicity in maintaining "interlocking hegemonies of neoimperialism, fundamentalism, and patriarchies" (Chowdhury 2011: 157) are apparent when self-styled feminist Phyllis Chesler writes uncritically of the opera *Thumbprint* about the life of Mukhtaran Mai, the Pakistani peasant, illiterate woman who was the victim of a gang-rape by men of the powerful Mastoi clan in 2007, and whom Mukhtaran challenged in court, undoubtedly a first in the history of the country. Nevertheless, Chesler's championing of Mukhtaran is not really "feminist" and we see her complicity in maintaining "interlocking hegemonies of neoimperialism, fundamentalism, and patriarchies" when we examine Chesler's other activities that reveal her ideological positioning as a "faux feminist". For example, Chesler was invited to deliver a keynote at the first Muslim Women's Seneca Falls convention in July 2014, an event which set itself up as the Muslim feminist equivalent of the Seneca Falls 1848 convention which is widely considered as setting the stage for the US women's movement. Yet Chesler is also a fervent supporter of Israel, a state whose oppressive policies against Muslim-majority Palestine, including Palestinian women, has made it a bête noir of Muslim countries. Her allegiances to Israeli right-wing military policies that trample the rights of Palestinians, trump/colour her claims to feminism as we see in one of her comments posted on the conservative news and opinion website *Breitbart*, where she castigates the leading academic feminist organisation in the USA, the National Women's Studies Association, for supposedly using feminism as a front for anti-Semitism when she opines:

> The next National Women's Studies Association annual meeting will take place in San Juan, Puerto Rico on November 13–16, 2014 and is aptly named "Feminist Transgressions." Indeed, the conference itself is "transgressive" in that it minimizes the cause of women to focus, yet again, on the cause of Palestine, aka the destruction of Israel.

She continues in the same vein:

> This is only the latest, among many other examples, of the way in which Women's Studies—an idea which I pioneered so long ago—has been Stalinized and Palestinianized [sic]. I wonder whether the forces of evil will try to pass a resolution in favor of boycott, divestment, and sanctions—not against Sudan, Somalia, Syria, Saudi Arabia, Iran, North Korea, or Russia—but against Israel only.
>
> *(Chesler 2014)*

Chesler further goes on to castigate the feminist movement in the United States and elsewhere as "It's almost as if the feminist world has become a wholly owned subsidiary of the PLO!" (Chesler 2014). When a performance such as *Thumbprint*, therefore, gets an enthusiastic thumbs-up from the likes of Phyllis Chesler, we are thick in the midst of a politics of reception and circulation that casts feminists like me into the abyss of the Scylla of an Islamophobia that goes hand in glove with an extreme pro-Zionist agenda that people like Chesler champion, a right-wing agenda that refuses to countenance the Palestinian human and women's rights as worthy of feminist attention! Here are some choice quotes from her review of the opera about Mukhtaran Mai on the web-based magazine, ontheissuesmagazine.com:

> She could have been forced into an unwanted marriage and literally tortured for the rest of her days by her in-laws and husband [after her rape]—but since she was of a lower tribal caste (she is a Gujjar biradiri—*and yes, everyone is Muslim*), they instead decided to shame her, spoil her. What they did to Mukhtar was meant as a prelude to her suicide.
>
> Pakistan, especially the Punjab, is virulently misogynist. Daughter- and wife-beating are normalized as is polygamy, forced child marriage, often to a first cousin, forced veiling, and the honor killing of any girl or woman who is perceived as even slightly disobedient, or who has shamed her family in any way.
>
> *(Chesler 2014: 83)*

After casting Mukhtaran's rape as exemplary of the savagery *specifically* of Muslim men who are representative of *the entire province* of Pakistani Punjab, Chesler then goes on to cast her as the individual heroine par excellence, fitting the syndrome of a feminist exceptionalism once she pushes away the darkness: "Our Mukhtar [sic] is a different kind of heroine. According to librettist, Susan Yankowitz, who interviewed Mukhtar [sic] three times, she tried to kill herself multiple times, failed, and decided that since she was 'as good as dead,' she might as well go to court and demand justice".

Jeff Lunden, another liberal commentator reviewing the opera for NPR, is quoted on the show's website as similarly emphasising the "individual" nature of Mukhtaran Mai's resistance: "One single person: one body, one voice made this enormous change" (Lunden 2014).

That some measure of justice was indeed delivered in her case, with the sentencing to death of six of Mukhtaran's rapists, is, as Chesler describes, "absolutely unprecedented" (Chesler 2014). However, when Chesler then goes on to generalise that "Such justice is an incredible accomplishment *for any woman who lives in Southeast Asia, the Middle East, and Africa*" (emphasis added), we have a problem. Does any and every woman face a lack of justice across the board everywhere, undifferentiatedly across all of "south East Asia, the Middle East and Africa"? Perhaps Chesler should read some Pakistani feminists, such as Zamurrad Awan, who while recognising the courage and tribulations of Mukhtaran Mai, also observes, correctly, that, "The status of women in Pakistan varies considerably across classes, regions and the rural/urban divide due to uneven socioeconomic development and the impact of tribal, feudal and capitalist social formations on women's lives" (Awan 2009).

And as Sehar Mughal, another Pakistani feminist scholar points out in her Master's thesis, *The Fate of Tomorrow is in the Hands of Women: Gender, Social Position, and the Media During Zia-ul-Haq's Islamization Campaign,*

> Even today the image of Mukhtar Mai represents Pakistani women largely as victims of patriarchy—her courage and resolve portrayed as rarely found among other Pakistani women. The same representation of women as oppressed was capitalized on by Western media, and used in Afghanistan to find legitimacy in the ongoing war in order to show Afghani women how to think and act so that they could be "free."
>
> The place that women hold in society in Pakistan, however, is much more complex and multi-faceted than is apparent in media coverage of the case of Mukhtar Mai. The state of women in Pakistan has much to do with economic class, caste, location, and education.
>
> *(Mughal 2011)*

The opera, *Thumbprint*, unfortunately, as Mughal points out regarding other media coverage of Mukhtaran Mai in the West, reworks the same trope of the oppressed Muslim woman, who, unlike the majority of her Pakistani sisters, stands up, alone, against the patriarchal rapists and oppressors who think they can rape her with impunity knowing she will be so devastated and "shamed" that she will either commit suicide or stay silent. The opera focuses on her courage, which appears *sui generis*—and presents her to the audience as an exceptional portrait of courage. After she is gang-raped by some of her village's most powerful feudal lords, heads of the Mastoi clan, we hear a chorus of women singing: "Every girl fears this fate/It is like a vulture flying right above our heads. When we walk or work or play/A man can grab you/take you into darkness, break into your body/take you into darkness/Day and night, night and day/Every girl/Fears this fate will come to her" (*Thumbprint* quoted in Chesler 2014).

But from such "darkness", a great light shines forth in the shape of Mukhtaran Mai. The women express their wish, their desperate hope: "In a dark season,/ Someone must be the first ray of light". To which Mukhtaran replies: "Let it be me, let it begin with me".

And it is true that in the context of this particular village, Meerwala in Southern Punjab, what Mukhtaran Mai did was trailblazing and made her into an icon for women's rights. However, there is a larger context within Pakistan of the women's movement's active championing of women's rights and challenging of misogynistic Islamisation laws such as the Hudood Ordinances since their promulgation by military dictator Zia ul Haq in 1979 that has played a big role in helping Mukhtaran Mai's quest for justice achieve the degree of success it has. As Nadia Tariq Ali, writing for the weekly newsletter of the Asia Foundation on 1 June 2011, says, countering her own question in her article "Does Mukhtaran Mai Verdict Mean Failure for Pakistan's Women's Rights Movement?":

> It is clear that Mai and many other women like her have suffered extreme injustice. But it is not right to assume this verdict is a benchmark to measure overall progress of Pakistan's larger women's movement—a movement that originally emerged in the 1980s to reclaim the rights of millions of women in the face of state oppression and General Zia ul Haq's Islamization program.
>
> *(Ali 2011)*

That movement has come a long way since its beginning. It was launched by a handful of highly qualified and enterprising women who were sometimes misunderstood even by other female members of society. Today, despite setbacks like Mai's horrific case, thousands more women and men continue to become the torchbearers in the women's movement. They have worked on gender issues in Pakistan, fought against discriminatory legislation, advocated for reducing gender-based violence at all levels of society, and pushed for laws that are imperative for the welfare of women in their country.

The recently approved Sexual Harassment Act, the restoration of women's reserved seats in the national and provincial assemblies, and the inclusion of gender issues of vital importance into the manifestos of all leading political parties, are some of the examples where the Pakistani women's movement has generated concrete results. The repeal in 2007 of the controversial Hudood Ordinance, the battles and organising for voting rights of women and for peasant land rights, mobilising other civil society groups to become active on issues related to women's rights, are developments that could not have happened without a collective movement for women's rights in Pakistan. Nadia Ali underscores this point:

> In some ways, one can even sense the progress of these efforts by looking again at the Mukhtaran Mai case: not long ago, sexual assaults of similar nature were most often simply swept under the carpet in Pakistan. But Mai's case was brought dramatically to the forefront and all effort was made to help her get justice. Also, the widespread outrage that followed the court verdict clearly reflected that people were aware of her plight and expected serious punishment for the perpetrators of the crime. This increased awareness around justice is particularly significant, because the women's rights movement in Pakistan

has been primarily about educating the masses on significant gender issues and changing their mindsets over the long term.

(Ali 2011)

Sadly, these very real contributions of the Pakistani Feminist and Women's Rights movement to challenge misogyny of a patriarchal culture and its laws is not what either the mainstream American media has focused on in its coverage of the Mukhtaran Mai case, or what the opera on her life, written by liberettist Susan Yankowitz, with music composed and title role performed by Kamal Sankaram, chose to highlight.

Seher Mughal enumerates various examples of the stereotypes of Pakistan and its women that are endlessly circulated in Western media, and become the performatives of operas like *Thumbprint*:

> A *Washington Post* article published on April 21, 2011 reporting on the Supreme Court ruling of Mai reads "[t]he case exposed to the world a side of Pakistan's tribal culture in which women are often punished harshly for affairs or sold as brides to settle disputes or compensate for the perceived sins of their relatives." Pakistani culture is routinely characterized as "traditional" and Pakistanis are often portrayed as illiterate. Nicholas D. Kristof, a *New York Times* journalist who has written a lot about Mukhtar in his column, routinely points out Mai's illiteracy. Almost all stories from the *New York Times*, refer to the "illiteracy that is rampant in Pakistan," and the *Jirga* or tribunal council is mentioned in all articles. The *Jirga* is seen as a parallel judicial system run by tribal chiefs that operates in contrast to civil laws. "The decision of the *Jirga* which apparently ordered Mai's rape is another instance that directly sheds light on the traditional and savage nature of "Pakistan's rural tribal culture".
>
> *(Mughal 2011)*

Following a similar line of analysis, Madiha Kark writes:

> The *New York Times* also failed to provide reporting on local protests in Pakistan following Mai's case, instead, most of the articles that did mention any form of protest, attributed it to "worldwide outrage" or "international outcry" failing to mention the local sentiments following the rape. By not covering the local sentiments of protestors, the *New York Times* chose to frame the news by portraying an indifferent image of Pakistanis that are mum about injustices on women.
>
> *(Kark 2013)*

What, then, is the way out of this morass of Islamophobia that also would avoid the pitfalls of a knee-jerk nativism that ignores the very real injustices committed against poor illiterate peasant women like Mukhtaran and the immense courage it took her to fight back against a powerful feudal system and an indifferent state apparatus? Mukhtaran herself suggests a solution, which also points to a direction transnational feminist scholarship has begun pursuing in its analyses and activist concerns over recent decades. It is, as both Chowdhury and McRobbie suggest, a direction that warns us of the danger of instrumentalising feminism for the neoliberal ends of globalisation paradigms that tout individualism as a panacea for social and economic ills, and back towards what Nancy Fraser calls the "solidaristic scenario" of a transnational second-wave feminism. Here is Fraser's spot-on analysis of how a white Western liberal feminism has served as a handmaiden to neoliberal capitalism that has not helped, nor ever will, "rescue" the Mukhtarans and Malalas of our unequal world:

> feminism [of the white liberal variety] contributed a third idea to neoliberalism: the critique of welfare-state paternalism. Undeniably progressive in the era of state-organised capitalism, that critique has since converged with neoliberalism's war on "the nanny state" and its more recent cynical embrace of NGOs. A telling example is "microcredit", the programme of small bank loans to poor women in the global south. Cast as an empowering, bottom-up alternative to the top-down, bureaucratic red tape of state projects, microcredit is touted as the feminist antidote for women's poverty and subjection. What has been missed, however, is a disturbing coincidence: microcredit has burgeoned just as states have abandoned macro-structural efforts to fight poverty, efforts that small-scale lending cannot possibly replace. In this case too, then, a feminist idea has been recuperated by neoliberalism. A perspective aimed originally at democratising state power in order to empower citizens is now used to legitimise marketisation and state retrenchment.
>
> *(Fraser 2014)*

Holding Mukhtaran Mai up as the "individual heroine" of Pakistan's uniformly oppressed women serves the ends of (neo) liberal individualism which loves words such as "empowerment", but this does not help her or advance her goals for herself or for other "disempowered" women—and men—of her village. In an interview with Samira Shackle of the *New Statesman*, Mukhtaran says bluntly, in response to a question about the state's responsibility to control extremism and to help women like her achieve justice, "Our laws are made, but they're never acted upon. It is our government's fault, the fault of our legal institutions, the police, that they don't enforce these laws" (Shackle 2014). Here, she is clearly in favour of a strong state, that could—and ought to—enforce laws that are meant to protect women like herself (a state that is strong in terms of protecting its most marginalised citizens, working for and with them—not a militaristic/imperialist state as conceptualised by Hobbes and feared by Arendt).

Mukhtaran also points out, commenting upon the hope she sees for Pakistan and its women, "The future is brighter. Women have a voice. They use it in public to ask for their rights. You see now, even a child like Malala has the courage to speak out. There are dangers—but placed against the need to achieve something, to express yourself, the threat is diminished. We have to keep moving ahead" (Shackle 2014).

She uses "we" in her response to a question about her "individual" vision, a "we" that encompasses other women of Pakistan who feel emboldened to challenge injustice, to fight back against violence in the name of tradition or religion. She links her struggle to that of Malala Yousafzai and elsewhere in the interview says, "There are many more Malalas in this society", thus moving away from the individual heroine syndrome, to recognition of a collectivity. She also acknowledges that she was encouraged in her dream to start local schools for girls—and boys—in her village after her ordeal was publicised, by supporters she met throughout Pakistan, who were "educated people and they agreed with the course I had chosen to take. They encouraged me. It was then it occurred to me that education is important. It brings enlightenment" (Shackle 2014).

Neo-colonial human rights/neoliberal pity politics

Unfortunately, Mukhtaran Mai's acknowledgment of the role of others in her struggle for justice, and the need to articulate this struggle within a broader critique of state obligations to its citizens, is overlooked by the creators of *Thumbprint*, its funders and backers, voices of the "expert panellists" brought in to comment on the opera on its premiere at Baruch College Performing Arts Center on 11 January 2014, commentators like Phyllis Chesler, as well as, finally, Mukhtaran Mai herself who has been mobilised to take her place as witness of a depoliticised neoliberal Western feminism's forward march into a repoliticised neo-colonial regime of power. The "need to achieve something"—in her statement that I cited earlier—is set up against, and diminished by, global attention paid to her second statement, that women like her now have a "voice" and thus access to a means of self-expression, viz "empowerment". But as Spivak so brilliantly asked us to consider long ago, can the subaltern really "speak"? What does her "voice" amount to, what can it actually say in the space that is always and already overdetermined by universalist discourses of women's human rights enabled by the very neoliberal and neo-imperialist regimes of power that continue to practice policies which circumscribe the same lives they claim to be "liberating"?

Put another way, "women's empowerment" narratives—especially in regard to "third world Muslim women" in the post 9/11 world—lend themselves to a spectacular rhetoric of human rights that erases the possibilities for a meaningful transnational feminism that could actually challenge structural causes of global inequality which neoliberal economic models simply have no interest in addressing. This "spectacular rhetoric", according to Wendy Hesford, enacts, through the image of the "suffering other", not so much a politics of the other's recognition through accessing her "voice", as much as it validates the presence and self-recognition of the Western feminist who has rushed to that other's rescue, whether through aid agencies, or through performances in the other's name, or through "activist" writing and publishing acts which are also affective performances meant to connect the Western performative subject to her "other" through shared experiences of suffering (Hesford 2011: 7). Thus, for example, the "staged unveiling" of Zoya, a representative of RAWA (the Revolutionary Association of Women of Afghanistan), at New York City's Madison Square Garden in February 2001, began with Oprah Winfrey reading aloud Eve Ensler's poem, "Under the Burqa", which the latter wrote after travelling to Afghanistan and meeting with women living under Taliban rule, written, much like the opera about Mukhtaran Mai's life, in the voice of one of those suffering women. Later, Winfrey, who had asked Zoya to come on stage wearing a burqa, went and lifted the burqa off her, letting it fall to the ground on the stage. This performance choreographed by Winfrey, as Wesford notes, enacted "a dual rhetoric of recognition" which was "staged between Zoya and the audience [with Winfrey as stage manager], a rhetoric that cast Zoya as a victim 'awaiting liberation' rather than an 'active agent in history'" (Hesford 2011: 6). At the same time, the "solidarity" Eve Ensler laid claim to as a by-product of her own "affective identification" with Zoya's pain at the same event, put Eve centre stage as the benevolent "rescuer", thus validating her own presence: "To allow another's pain to enter us, forces us to examine our own values … insists *that we be responsible for others*, [and] compels *us* to act" (Ensler quoted in Hesford 2011: 6, emphasis added). As Hesford quite correctly stipulates, "In this way, Ensler's imaginative identifications are a form of self-recognition" (Hesford 2011: 6).

Such a cultural politics of recognition, resting as it does on an "identity-based politics of visibility"—or "voicing"—which, to recall Nancy Fraser once again, has been the cornerstone of Western liberal feminism at the end of the twentieth century and into the first decades of the new millennium—has indeed served to direct "public attention away from the regressive politics and growth of global capitalism" (Fraser 2014). Such a regressive politics, which is occluded in the human rights spectacle which the performances of Zoya, Mukhtaran Mai, and Malala are made to enact on the global (read Western) stage, underwrites, in fact, the very discourse of universal human rights. Hesford's term, "human rights spectacle" thus "encompasses appropriations of human suffering in activist, cultural, and legal contexts, as well as Western democratic nations'" use of images to deflect attention away from their own human rights violations by turning other nations into spectacles of violence (Chow 1991: 81–100). And it further instantiates the regressive politics at the heart of global capitalism by "mapping the world in terms of spectator zones and sufferer zones" (Chouliarki 2008: 4), without analysing how such "zones" might in fact be linked through the inequalities exacerbated by current economic systems and policies of neoliberalism.

These mediatised zones, as Lilie Chouliarki describes them in her book *The Spectatorship of Suffering*,

> embed new transnational technologies of communication in existing and relatively stable transnational relationships of power and these map out an asymmetrical and unjust landscape of news flows. The consequence is new divisions rather than simply new unifications ["affective identification" in Ensler's words]. The parallel to the digital divide in new media is the satellite divide in global news flows … The division between safety and suffering

captures a fundamental aspect of this asymmetry in the viewing relationships of television. This is the asymmetry of power between the comfort of spectators in their living rooms and the vulnerability of sufferers on the spectators' television screens.

(Chouliarki 2008: 4)

Of course, the "safe spectators" whether they be consumers of news flows or of news stories of suffering others represented in plays, operas, books, etc, are elite Western audiences, and the sufferers are the poverty-stricken illiterate "others". Said would call this viewing asymmetry "a contemporary mutation of the old divide between the West and the 'orient'" (quoted in Chouliarki 2008: 5).

Such a "viewing asymmetry" is constitutive of the visual field of human rights discourse which is the subject of Wendy Hesford's study in *Spectacular Rhetorics: Human Rights Visions, Recognitions, Feminisms*. Using the term "spectacular rhetoric" to draw attention to the visual rhetoric embedded in human rights discourse, Hesford alerts us to the visual economy that undergirds the distribution of visual capital in human rights politics (Hesford 2011: 8). Such an understanding of human rights discourse is dependent upon and constituted by a visual rights economy—wherein pity (and even its superior cousin, empathy) at the image of the other's spectacularised suffering is "made possible by and productive of relations of power, and that these power relations bear at least some relationship to wider social and political structures which are themselves associated with transnational relations of exchange in which images are commodities" (Hesford 2011: 8).

Such an analytic frame allows me to read the production of *Thumbprint*, as well as the memoir *I Am Malala*, as two related instantiations of the visual performance of asymmetrical power relations between the Western world and its Muslim Others that arises out of and reconfirms those relations within the neoliberal world order *in the guise of empowering Muslim women*. As Hesford clarifies, "to focus on the visual economy of human rights is to examine the potential of neoliberal politics and human rights politics to jointly incorporate victim subjects into social relations that support the logic of a global morality market that privileges Westerners as world citizens" (Hesford 2011: 9).

By highlighting the performances of Mukhtaran Mai and Malala Yousafzai as represented through the visually discursive field of human rights, we can indeed see how, as Hesford claims, "Spectacular rhetoric activates certain cultural and national narratives and social and political relations, consolidates identities through the politics of recognition and configures material relations of power and difference to produce and *ultimately to govern human rights subjects*" (Hesford 2011: 9, emphasis added).

Or, as Moon Charania argues in *Spectacular Subjects: The Violent Erotics of Imperial Visual Culture*:

> I also use this description of Mai, as a brown woman in which a white audience takes interest, to make clear an insidious investment on the part of human rights regimes. As an apparatus of neoliberal, neocolonial and the war

on terror's machinery, human rights in its (over)use of such visual tropes and imagery to paint a picture of brown oppression, demonstrates a simultaneous allegiance to whiten the brownness of these women's lives while using that same brownness to mobilize a narrative of the *other*.

(Charania 2011: 67)

Following the money

It is unsurprising then, to learn that this activation of the performative spectacle of "women's rights as human rights" in *Thumbprint* was initially funded as a monologue written by Susan Yankowitz for a production called *Seven*, by the nonprofit Vital Voices Global Partnership, which in turn grew out of the US government's successful Vital Voices Democracy Initiative. The Vital Voices Democracy Initiative was established in 1997 by then First Lady Hillary Rodham Clinton and former Secretary of State Madeleine Albright after the United Nations Fourth World Conference on Women in Beijing to promote the advancement of women as a US foreign policy goal. According to the Vital Voices website, we are told that:

> Under the leadership of the Vital Voices Democracy Initiative, the US government, in partnership with the Inter-American Development Bank, the United Nations, the World Bank, the Nordic Council of Ministers, the European Union and other governments coordinated Vital Voices conferences throughout the world, bringing together thousands of emerging women leaders from over 80 countries.
>
> These conferences launched regional Vital Voices initiatives that continue to give women the skills and resources they need to lift up themselves, their communities and their countries.
>
> The overwhelmingly positive response to the Vital Voices Democracy Initiative led to the creation of Vital Voices Global Partnership as a nonprofit non-governmental organization (NGO) in June 2000. Vital Voices is now continuing the work of advancing women's economic, political and social status around the world, by providing skills, networking and other support to women around the world, whether they are working to increase women's political participation in Latin America or to promote women's entrepreneurship in the Middle East.

(*Vital Voices* 2014)

The cosy partnership of the United States government with the NGO called Vital Voices should alert us to the neo-imperial agenda that props up the narrative of women's empowerment which is this NGO's main goal. Promoting democracy becomes similarly suspect when it suppresses people's grassroots resistance initiatives in favour of a one-size-fits-all idea of democracy fashioned on a Western liberal economic model.

Malala Yousafzai: Performing a different narrative?

Malala's memoir of growing up in Pakistan's Swat region in the 1990s, written with British journalist Christina Lamb, is yet another iterative performance of the Muslim female subject of oppression, who casts off her yoke to become the voice of the empowered Muslim woman with the help of her British interlocutors—both Lamb and the British imperial state, her saviours. The fact that her memoir remained on the *New York Times* best seller list for 25 weeks straight after its publication in 2013 underlines the appeal the particular performance that her narrative of individual self-empowerment and courage holds for her largely Western audiences. One could argue that Malala Yousafzai has become a household name in the West—a brand of sorts.

What makes her narrative "brand" somewhat different from that of Mukhtaran Mai's, and perhaps surprising for Western audiences more familiar with images of fathers and brothers as oppressors, is that she has a strong male figure—her father—who protects and encourages her on her path of self-discovery, learning, and empowerment in the heavily patriarchal Pathan culture of Pakistan's north-west regions where tribal norms circumscribe the lives of women to domestic arenas.

In his essay "Brand, Citationality, Performativity", Constantine Nakassis explains:

> I have suggested that the brand, in all its complexity, can only be clearly apprehended, and thus theorized, once we begin to account for the moments when brands are de- natured, when brands begin to shade off into that which they are not. Such an approach requires us to be committed, on the one hand, to the empirical [and I would suggest, ethnographic] study of the actual social lives of brands [here, Malala]—in their historical and cultural contexts and, on the other, to the ways in which such social lives always spill outside of the intelligibilities and performativities that (attempt to) normatively regiment them.
> *(Nakassis 2012: 624)*

What is of interest to me in Malala's performative memoir, then, is the question of the degree of agency she exerts over her own "branding" as the individual Muslim Pakistani heroine, an agency that I do think allows her—up to a point—to de-naturalise the performative normativity that seeks to regiment her and to render her otherness intelligible within the interpretive frame of the bourgeois liberal subject of secular democracy, which is a normativising frame that wants to construct her as an empowered woman in charge of her own destiny, who can then be trotted out to serve as a role model to inspire other individual girls and women around the world to become good female citizens of neoliberal states. The question to ask, then, is to what extent Malala, as a ward now of the British state, has been co-opted by the "new sexual contract" that Angela McRobbie claims is being currently made available to young women and girls in the West (I would argue everywhere) in lieu of feminism, interpellating them in the name of women's rights "to come forward to make good use of the opportunity to work, to gain qualifications, to control fertility, and to earn enough money to participate in the consumer culture which in turn will become a defining feature of contemporary modes of feminine citizenship" (McRobbie 2009: 54).

Such a "contract" is based on the understanding that feminism (understood narrowly as a fight for women's "equality" with men)—has won its battles, hence causing feminism to give way to a discourse of women's rights, with women's rights now largely integrated into the vocabulary of human rights. The problem with this shift, as Chandra Talpede Mohanty has also pointed out, is that "it coincides with the general shift in global politics towards the right, and the concomitant decline of social welfarist models coincides with processes that recolonise the culture and identity of people" (Mohanty quoted in McRobbie 2009: 55).

To what extent, then, have Malala and her father, Ziauddin Yousafzai, been "recolonised" by the neoliberal capitalist paradigm that speaks in the name of individual human and women's rights?

Agency: Slipping out of normative boxes

A little more than halfway through her memoir, *I Am Malala: The Girl Who Stood Up for Education and Was Shot by the Taliban*, in Chapter 15 entitled, "Leaving the Valley", the then 13-year-old Malala bemoans the loss of her peaceful homeland of the Swat valley, which she and her family must leave in the wake of the Taliban takeover. There are a few key statements that need to be analysed to understand both her future "branding" as well as the ways in which her social life escapes such branding by spilling outside of the normative frames that seek to hegemonise her narrative into one that fits that of individual women's and human rights which lead to the creation of an educated, empowered feminine consumer citizen at the service of neoliberal regimes of power.

She begins by sharing part of a native folk song for us, called a *"tapa"* which her grandmother used to recite to them: "No Pashtun leaves his land of his own free will. Either he leaves from poverty or he leaves for love" (Yousafzai and Lamb 2013: 88). Malala then goes on to add a third reason—a reason the original writer of the song could never have imagined, which is causing her family to abandon their homeland: the Taliban.

The mention of poverty as a main cause of exodus from native lands hints at the "spilling over" effect that can help us theorise the limits and extent of the "branding" process of young girls like Malala. Poverty is a structural consequence of the global capitalist economic system which enables governing elites of different countries to band together in their oppression of external and internal "others" in their societies. That the young Malala is aware of this collusion between the governing elites of Pakistan and the West—specifically the USA and Britain—comes out in several instances, as for example, when she describes her and her father's friends' disgust at the corrupt ways of General Musharraf, who is being kept in power by the USA and being coddled by the British government as well. She explains:

> Anyone could see that Musharraf was double-dealing, taking American money while still helping the jihadis—"strategic assets", as the ISI calls them.
> The Americans say they gave Pakistan billions of dollars to help their campaign against Al-Qaeda, *but we didn't see a single cent*. Musharraf built a mansion near Rawal Lake in Islamabad and bought an apartment in London. Every so often an important American official would complain that we weren't doing enough ... But *President Bush would keep praising Musharraf, inviting him to Washington and calling him his buddy*. My father and his friends were disgusted. They said the Americans always preferred dealing with dictators in Pakistan.
> *(Yousafzai and Lamb 2013: 88, emphasis added)*

What her memoir doesn't state is what are the alternatives to dictators in Pakistan that she and her father, as well as the writer of the *"tapas"* which her grandmother was so fond of singing, might have been aware of? What inspires her father to stay back in Swat after he sends his family to the safety of Islamabad in Chapter 15? Malala tells us,

> My mother tried very hard to persuade him to come with us, but he refused. He wanted the people of Peshawar and Islamabad to be aware of the terrible conditions in which IDPs [internally displaced persons] were living [due to the mass exodus of Swati people from the valley] and that the military was doing nothing.
> *(Yousafzai and Lamb 2013: 181)*

Clearly, Ziauddin and his famous daughter are critics of the Pakistani military and government, both of which are seen as corrupt and unhelpful to the citizens they are supposed to be serving. At several points in the memoir, the collusion between a weak and corrupt civilian state, and the strong military elite of Pakistan as well as Western leaders—again at the expense of the people—is also noted. Unfortunately, what we don't get from this narrative is a true picture of the leftist activism of the father or the fact that Malala for several summers attended the Young Marxists camp in Swat as a way of countering this neoliberal tripartite Leviathan structure.

A report from the National Marxist Youth School in July of 2012 reveals the leftist activist roots of father and daughter in a way that the memoir published in the centre of neoliberal capitalism conceals. For instance, we realise that Malala's father's zeal and commitment to stay back in dangerous conditions in Swat is prompted by his work as an activist in the International Marxist Tendency, a worldwide organisation of Marxist activists. As the report states,

> Swat is a place known for religious extremism and the Taliban. A war has been going on between the Pakistan Army and the draconian religious fanatics it itself created and nourished just two years ago. During all those months of war the Marxists not only exposed the reality of the Islamic fundamentalists and their connections with the Pakistani state but also organized the local masses against this evil nexus.
> *(Kamyana 2012)*

Here the Taliban, who are causing the mass exodus of Swatis, are seen to be creations of/nurtured by the same state and military nexus that purports to be against them! And as seen in the earlier quote, vested foreign powers (Bush et al.) don't stop funding the military dictators like Musharraf even when the latter does little to contain the jihadists and Taliban. It is precisely to educate and thus hopefully to inspire his fellow citizens to challenge such harmful power interests that leads Ziauddin Yousafzai to do the activist work he does and which inspires his daughter. In an article written by Imran Kamyana describing the third session of the Marxist School that took place in Swat in the summer of 2012, we learn that

> [the session] started with the topic "Pakistan Perspectives." It was chaired by Comrade Shehryar Zauq. Comrade Vinod in his lead off analyzed the economic, political and social conditions in Pakistan. He said the Pakistani State is facing its worst crisis today and running the whole country on internal and external debt. *Neo Liberal policies as dictated by imperialist institutions are being imposed on the Pakistani working class. Privatization, downsizing and restructuring are throwing millions of people below the poverty line every year.* Capital is being shifted abroad due to the energy crisis thus creating massive unemployment. In this scenario the ruling classes are creating non issues to divert popular attention from the real issues but all this won't last for a very long time ... Comrade Rehana from Kashmir, Comrade Zubair from North Punjab, *Malala Yousafzai from Swat*, Comrade Mahblos from Multan, Comrade Razzaq from Peshawar, Comrade Rashid Khalid from Lahore, Comrade Atif Javed from Rajanpur, Comrade Khalil from Kashmir, Comrade Safdar from Faisalabad, Comrade Hosho from Dadu and Comrade Adam Pal made their contributions in the light of questions asked by the audience.
>
> *(Kamyana 2012: n.p., emphasis added)*

Here we learn about the budding socialist training of Malala, who is beginning to realise the nexus of capitalism, religious fundamentalism, and imperialism which works to keep the people down. Yet, this is not the Malala—by and large—that we meet when we read her memoir, because of the normative framework of "individual voicing as empowerment" that she is being made to fit into by her publisher (and co-writer?). As Jawed Naqvi, an Indian journalist writing for the *Dawn* newspaper observes,

> there is evidence of a Marxist underpinning that runs the risk of being overlooked in the teenaged girl's ideological shaping.
>
> A picture in which she is seen with a poster of Lenin and Trotsky should indicate her proximity to some of the most ideologically groomed bunch of men and women in Swat. They are members of the International Marxist Tendency (IMT), which condemns religious extremism and imperialism equally.

> We have been told of Malala's blogs and interviews with global news groups, but her involvement with the Marxists of Swat (of all the places) tends to be ignored.
>
> *(Naqvi 2012: n.p.)*

There is certainly no such evidence of Malala's Marxism presented or discussed in the memoir; the only hints we have are those spaces where "spillage" occurs, and we read between the lines the implicit challenge to unholy alliances between all these power groups that her narrative at times poses. The ultimate effect of this "spillage", however, is allow us to theorise the efficacy of the Malala brand, which builds on the previous neoliberal branding of Mukhtaran Mai. Malala's memoir, and her co-optation by former British Prime Minister Gordon Brown, much like the opera on Mukhtaran Mai's life, become, unfortunately, examples of performatives that produce the neoliberal figure of the "Can Do" girl—which of course begs the question, "what is at stake in this process of endowing the new female subject with capacity?" (McRobbie 2009: 58).

Education as empowerment

The DIY approach that has increasingly dominated liberal discourse and policy-making in the last decade of the twentieth century and into current times permeates Malala's memoir and helps explain her lionisation in Western media, much as it did for Mukhtaran Mai. For both Mukhtaran and Malala, education—especially for women—equals "voice", or "freedom", which becomes a tool for "empowerment", that is to say, allows them, and other women like them, access to jobs and goods and the dignity such gainful employment and ability to become a "good" consumer confers on their status as "capable citizens" (or as McRobbie has referred to it, endowing "the new female subject with capacity"). Neither asks what the quality of this "freedom" really is—or where the kind of education they are seeking might lead, what kind of "capacity" is being formed. Indeed, in Malala's case, she *does* want all children in Pakistan to have access to education so that they can lead better, more informed lives—but *how*, precisely, would it solve the problem of the children living on rubbish mountains, scavenging on rotting food for survival? Commenting despairingly on the breakdown of law and order in Swat which she realises is connected to the corruption of Pakistan's rulers, she seems to think she, as an individual heroine, could solve these endemic problems by becoming a politician herself—"We felt frustrated and scared once again. When we were IDPs [internally displaced persons] I had thought about becoming a politician and now I knew that was the right choice. Our country had so many crises and no real leaders to tackle them" (Yousafzai and Lamb 2013: 204).

Becoming a "leading politician" in the mode of her icon Benazir Bhutto is not a fate that most women who could become workers as a result of some educational opportunities would be able to claim. As McRobbie reminds us, for the "global girl working 18 hours a day in a clothing factory in an Export Processing Zone and sending most of her wages home", surely independence or "freedom" is a very different beast (McRobbie 2009: 61)? In other words, it is fair to say that what Malala and Mukhtaran have succumbed to is a certain "luminosity". The theatrical effect of this luminosity, of being put under a spotlight, "softens, dramatizes and disguises the regulative dynamics" (McRobbie 2009: 54) at play in the discourse of empowerment, which has at this point in history become utterly instrumentalised in the service of neoliberal ideologies. As Srilatha Batliwala, writing about the history of this concept (with a particular focus on India), poignantly observes, "[the discourse of] Empowerment was hijacked in the 1990s … converted from a collective to an individualistic process, and skillfully co-opted by conservative and even reactionary political ideologies in pursuit of their agenda of divesting the 'big government' [for which, read the welfare state] of its purported power and control by 'empowering' communities to look after their own affairs" (Batliwala 2013: 81).

Indeed, Malala, her father, and Mukhtaran Mai, whilst cognisant and disgusted by the Pakistani state's and military's failure to protect its citizens from all manner of depredations including the Talibanisation of society and endemic poverty and lack of education and employment opportunities, nevertheless adopt the neoliberal dogma of self-empowerment. At the end of the opera *Thumbprint*, on its opening night, the producers of the show had Mukhtaran beamed up over Skype for a Q and A session with the audience. Via a translator, Mukhtaran Mai kept begging us to send money to help her keep her children's school running, as the funds she had won as an award for her courage from the government after her case came to light were now used up. Similarly, Malala notes that during the exodus of Swati people when almost 2 million of them fled their homes escaping the Taliban takeover, it was the hospitality of the Pashtun people of Mardan and Swabi (towns across the mountain pass of Malakand) that really helped ease the suffering of the refugees. She writes, "We were convinced that if the exodus had been managed by the government many more would have died of hunger and illness" (Yousafzai and Lamb 2013: 180). In both cases, the government of Pakistan (along with foreign governments that prop it up) is let off the hook, advertently or not, by our two heroines.

While the idea of self-empowerment appears attractive in the face of intransigent, corrupt state apparatuses, its instrumentalisation (like that of human rights and women's rights) in the service of neoliberal ideologies of privatisation and retrenchment of social services that shift the spotlight from addressing the root causes of structural inequalities to a can-do ethic of individual success, is what needs debunking. And this is where Brand Malala (like Brand Mukhataran), far from debunking this individualist worldview and politics, ends up becoming its handmaiden.

Let me conclude by quoting a passage from *The Socialist Appeal: The Marxist Voice of Labor and Youth* website. After duly noting the suffering of Malala as well as her courage, the article, attributed to a collective called "The Struggle", reminds us of Gordon Brown's regressive politics, who now has become the standard bearer of female education and major supporter of the Malala Fund for Girls' Education; it is with him that Malala travelled to New York City to address the United Nations

General Assembly on her sixteenth birthday, a speech that made her a darling to the world, and propelled her to frontrunner status for the Nobel Peace Prize in 2013. Here is the passage from the article entitled, "Malala's Ordeal":

> Gordon Brown, the former British Prime Minister, has become the cheer leader of the campaign for educating girls in Pakistan and for so-called Millennium Development goals of providing education to girls in the developing world. This right-wing Labour politician is someone who not only voted to invade Iraq but provided a massive influx of emergency funds for this illegal war and endorsed crimes against humanity committed by Bush and Blair.
>
> There are vested interests behind Brown's manoeuvres. He is an arch-supporter of capitalism and an economist who was ignominiously claiming in 2007 that capitalism had overcome its cycle of booms and slums [sic] and was treading on a path of permanent growth. This was just about a year before the greatest crash of capitalism in its history in 2008, forcing this prophet of never ending capitalist boom to even contemplate sending British troops onto British streets to control the anger of workers and youth and provide protection to international finance capital and capitalism. Brown's policies both as a Chancellor and Prime Minister on health and education were based on trickledown economics, which means that the state's role in education and other social sectors should be seriously diminished.
>
> Western imperialist nations have all gone into full gear in capitalizing on Malala's tragedy to camouflage the campaign of mass killing of children, women and the elderly in illegal wars and the use of illegal drones across the world or, to be more precise, in Iraq, Yemen, Libya, Syria, Pakistan, etc. This is a deliberate and calculated strategy on the one hand to dupe the working masses in the western world and on the other to enhance their policies of privatization and promotion of NGO's and other reformist organizations in Pakistan and the developing world to foster a culture of acceptance of capitalism—a system that is devastating society as a whole.
>
> (Khan 2013: n.p.)

The reformist drama continues to be enacted on the world's stages. Or as Wendy Hesford encapsulated it so cogently, "spectacular rhetoric unleashes a politics of pity"—which allows audiences to both pity and then admire the objects of their pity, as long as the latter can be (re) constructed in the image of the "ideal" citizens for our neoliberal times (Hesford 2011: 8).

Notes

1 A version of this chapter was published in *Performing Islam*, 4(2), 2015 and is published here with permission.
2 This by now eponymous phrase was used by Gayatri C. Spivak in her article, "Can the Subaltern Speak?: Speculations on Widow Sacrifice" which was first published in the journal *Wedge* in 1985; reprinted in 1988 as "Can the Subaltern Speak?" in Cary Nelson

and Larry Grossberg's edited collection, *Marxism and the Interpretation of Culture*, Urbana: University of Illinois Press.
3   See particularly Hannah Arendt's book *The Origins of Totalitarianism*, 1958.
4   See for instance, trenchant intersectional critiques of Sandberg by bell hooks and others on *The Feminist Wire*: www.thefeministwire.com/2013/10/17973/.
5   See Afzal-Khan, Fawzia. 2007. "Betwixt and Between? Women, the Nation and Islamization in Pakistan." *Social Identities* 13(1), 19–29.

References

Afzal-Khan, Fawzia. 2007. "Betwixt and between? Women, the nation and Islamization in Pakistan". *Social Identities*, 13(1): 19–29.

Ali, Nadia Tariq. 2011. "Does Mukhtaran Mai verdict mean failure for Pakistan's Women's Rights Movement?" *In Asia*, June 1 (accessed 15 July 2014), http://asiafoundation.org/in-asia/2011/06/01/does-mukhtaran-mai-verdict-mean-failure-for-pakistans-womens-rights-movement/.

Arendt, Hannah. 1994. *The Origins of Totalitarianism*. San Diego: Harcourt.

Awan, Zamurrad. 2009. "Gender biased society of Pakistan: A case-study of Mukhtaran Mai." *Pakistan Concerns*, April 16 (accessed 30 Aug 2015), https://zamurrad.wordpress.com/2009/04/16/gender-biased-society-of-pakistan-a-case-study-of-mukhtaran-mai-by-zamurrad-awan/.

Batliwala, Srilatha. 2013. *Engaging with Empowerment*. New Delhi: Women Unlimited.

Bhattacharyya, Gargi. 2008. *Dangerous Brown Men: Exploiting Sex, Violence and Feminism in the War on Terror*. London: Zed Books.

Charania, Moon. 2011. *Spectacular Subjects: The Violent Erotics of Imperial Visual Culture*. PhD dissertation, Georgia State University.

Chesler, Phyllis. 2014. "Activists hijacking feminism to attack Israel at Women's Studies Association meeting." *Breitbart*, June 6 (accessed 2 July 2014), www.breitbart.com/national-security/2014/06/06/hijacking-of-feminism/.

Chow, Rey. 1991. "Violence in the other country: China as crisis, spectacle, and woman", in Chandra Talpede Mohanty, Lourdes Torres, and Ann Russo(eds) *Third World Women and the Politics of Feminism*. Bloomington: Indiana University Press, 81–100.

Chowdhury, Elora. 2011. *Transnationalism Reversed: Women Organizing against Gendered Violence in Bangladesh*. New York: SUNY Press.

Chouliarki, Lilie. 2008. *The Spectatorship of Suffering*. Thousand Oaks, CA: Sage.

Fraser, Nancy. 2014. "How feminism became capitalism's handmaiden—and how to reclaim it." *The Guardian*, 14 October 2014 (accessed 2 July 2014), www.theguardian.com/commentisfree/2013/oct/14/feminism-capitalist-handmaiden-neoliberal.

Hesford, Wendy. 2011. *Spectacular Rhetorics: Human Rights Visions, Recognitions Feminisms*. Durham: Duke University Press.

Kamyana, Imran. 2012. "Pakistan: National Marxist Youth School Summer 2012—Red flags in Taliban Country" *International Marxist Tendency*, October 10 (accessed 2 July 2014), www.marxist.com/pakistan-national-marxist-youth-school-in-swat.htm.

Kark, Madiha. 2013. *Understanding Indian and Pakistani Cultural Perspectives and Analyzing U.S. News Coverage of Mukhtar Mai and Jyoti Singh Pandey*. MA Thesis. University of North Texas (accessed 2 July 2014), http://digital.library.unt.edu/ark:/67531/metadc271840/.

Khan, Lal. 2013. "Malala's ordeal." *Socialist Appeal*, October 15 (accessed 20 August 2014), www.socialist.net/malala-s-ordeal.htm.

Lunden, Jeff. 2014. "Oppression to opera: Could a woman's courage change Pakistan?" *NPR Weekend Edition*, January 11 (accessed 13 June 2014), www.npr.org/sections/deceptivecadence/2014/01/11/261433890/from-oppression-to-opera-could-one-woman-s-courage-change-pakistan.

McRobbie, Angela. 2009. *The Aftermath of Feminism: Gender, Culture, and Social Change.* Thousand Oaks, CA: Sage.

Mughal, Sehar. 2011. *The Fate of Tomorrow is in the Hands of Women: Gender, Social Position, and the Media During Zia-ul-Haq's Islamization Campaign.* Honors Thesis, Rutgers University, New Brunswick (accessed 2 July 2014), http://history.rutgers.edu/honors-papers-2011/289-the-fate-of-tomorrow-is-in-the-hands-of-women/file.

Nakassis, Constantine. 2012. "Brand, citationality, performativity." *American. Anthropologist,* 114(4): 624–638.

Naqvi, Jawed. 2012. "A flag and a battle plan." *Dawn,* October 25 (accessed 15 April 2020), www.dawn.com/news/759230.

Shackle, Samira. 2014. "Mukhtar Mai gang-rape victim who defied her attackers." *New Statesman,* October 19 (accessed10 July 2014), www.newstatesman.com/world-affairs/2012/10/mukhtar-mai-gang-rape-victim-who-defied-her-attackers.

Vital Voices Global Partnership (accessed 2 July 2014), www.vitalvoices.org/.

Yousafzai, Malala and Christina Lamb. 2013. *I Am Malala: The Girl Who Stood Up for Education and Was Shot by the Taliban.* London: Orion.

5

TV NEWS AS MERCHANT OF WAR HYSTERIA

Framing the Kashmir conflict in India and Pakistan

Qaisar Abbas

> One may have doubts about the media's de-escalating or peacemaking potential, but at the same time, it can be demonstrated that news media can make matters a lot worse and can certainly contribute to the escalation of group conflicts into mass killing. This is especially so when media workers become agents for the dissemination of the "elimination belief" and when media are internationally used as weapons to incite people to commit crimes against humanity.
>
> *(Hamelink 2008: 79)*

As Hamelink argues here, when mass media tend to create an image of "others" as the enemy, they also perceive a group or nation as harmful to their ethnic, cultural, or national identities. In doing so, media outlets promote violence rather than strengthening the peace process. It is also true of the media coverage of conflicts between the two nuclear powers in South Asia, India and Pakistan, especially when both countries are engaged in a military clash on the territory of Kashmir, which they both consider their territory.

It is because of this colonial mindset and media hype that the Kashmir dispute between India and Pakistan has not been resolved yet, besides other geopolitical and security-related reasons. Both nations have fought three wars and engaged in numerous border clashes which have claimed thousands of lives, mostly of Kashmiris who are caught between the two countries. During the five years of insurgencies, 13,000 Kashmiris were killed from 1990 to 1995 according to the official data. The Kashmiri resistance groups, however, claim that 50,000 were killed during the same period (Wolpert 2010: 69). This mindset seems to be as active in the media in Pakistan and India as in any other institution in both countries.

Manifesting this mindset, public and private media outlets in India and Pakistan serve the nationalistic, official, and popular discourse. The mainstream media content in both countries promotes the discourse that Kashmir, a disputed region occupied by the two nuclear powers, is their colony. Although a strong movement is underway in Kashmir to get independence from both countries, the TV news coverage is one-sided and biased, rarely reflecting this struggle.

This study compares TV talk shows in India and Pakistan, one from each country, to assess how they offer similar or divergent patterns of coverage on the Kashmir dispute. Positioning the research within the theoretical notion of news frames and proposing a conceptual model, it provides a historical context of the Kashmir conflict in post-colonial South Asia. The next section analyses two talk shows, "The Buck Stops Here" of NDTV in India and "Capital Talk" of GEO TV in Pakistan, aired on 29 September 2016. These news and current affairs programmes discussed the surgical strikes of Indian forces into Pakistani-controlled Kashmir. Finally, the study concludes by evaluating the dominant frames revealed as part of the textual analysis.

News frames as theoretical framework

Mass media tend to cover national affairs with a substantial degree of objectivity in Western democracies, but they support a patriotic and nationalistic worldview most of the time in international relations. A study confirmed that the American press framed the shooting of an Iranian airliner by a US warship and a similar shooting of a Korean plane by the Soviets differently. Although the shooting incidents killed passengers in both cases, the press termed the Soviet attack as cold murders of passengers and downplayed the American strike as a technical mistake (Entman 1991: 11). Additionally, an unpublished doctoral thesis concludes that editorials of the American press, supporting US foreign policy, sided with the Indian position on the Kashmir conflict (Umber 2014: 111).

Similarly, when it comes to regional conflicts and war involving developing countries, the media tend to support the official and security positions in the name of patriotism and national unity. Some studies also confirmed this pattern. Lee and Maslog (2005: 311–329), for example, found in their research that the coverage of Kashmir by Indian and Pakistani newspapers and news agencies had more war-related stories as compared to other conflicts in Asia. They concluded that war, rather than peace journalism, was dominant in newspapers of both countries, but the war perspective got more coverage in the Pakistani newspapers. But how do the media mould news stories into their desired frames? The theoretical construct of news frames further elaborates this phenomenon, discussing the process of news making.

Researchers have taken different approaches to elaborate and define news frames. The process of framing involves a preferable interpretation of news stories where the media use a chosen worldview based on semantic, visual, and symbolic frames. In this sense, "News frames are constructed from and embodied in the keywords, metaphors, concepts, symbols, and visual images emphasized in a news narrative" (Entman 1991: 7).

For Auerbach and Bloch-Elkon (2005: 83–99), "On the whole, frames are conceived as fixed patterns for presenting and commenting on the news that organise the political debate in a way that is comprehensible to the public". They also talk about meta-frames, which are broad-based frameworks used for an analytical purpose such as security and world order, while frames are specific themes under these broad categories. For example, the American role in the "Vietnam war" (meta-frame) was invariably seen by the US government as a strategy to introduce "democracy" (frame).

Speculating that mass media are not a mirror of society, but they frame news stories to mould public opinion, Gitlin offers a broad-based definition of frames: "media frames are persistent patterns of cognition, interpretation, and presentation, of selection, emphasis, and exclusion, by which symbol-handlers routinely organize discourse, whether verbal or visual" (Gitlin 1980: 7). In his seminal work *The Whole World is Watching*, Gitlin analysed how media covered the American student movement against the Vietnam war in the 1960s, proposing that the media of mass communication tended to construct news frames to present a different picture of the protest campaign. In doing so, the press used innovative devices such as depreciating the size and significance of the movement, marginalising it, trivialising it by excluding events, polarising it, and recreating the agitation as a generational issue. These news frames also serve to conform to the dominant ideologies of society by supporting the state ideological positions.

More recently, Scheufele (1999: 103–122), discussing the theory of frames as part of media effects, emphasises the social constructivist function of frames in political communication where the media reconstruct a social reality as opposed to the existing conditions. The concept is highly relevant to the Kashmir issue as the mass media in India and Pakistan try to create a social reality very different from the objective truth. Interestingly, receivers of news stories are not aware of these induced frames because they perceive them as reality.

Some researchers also see parallels between framing and other theoretical notions of agenda setting, priming, and peace journalism. McCombs, Shaw, and Weaver (1997) consider framing as an extension of agenda setting, while peace journalism (Galtung 2004) is also recognised as news framing as part of peace- or war-related reporting.

Although the above definitions elaborate a range of varied dimensions on media frames, Gitlin's notion of framing appears to be more relevant to the Kashmir conflict. Expanding on Gitlin's theory of news frames, this study proposes the following model of the framing process.

The proposed model of news frames (Fig 5.1) represents the framing process at the field, media, and audience level. At the field level, events or statements provide raw knowledge for journalists as ground reality who then create news frames using this knowledge. This framing, at the media level, is accomplished following the news writing routines of the organisation, its institutional values, market conditions, and journalists' cognitive predispositions. Media audiences process these news frames to reconstruct their reality based on their cognitive preferences and experiences. This perceived reality might be similar or different from the news frames shaped by media outlets.

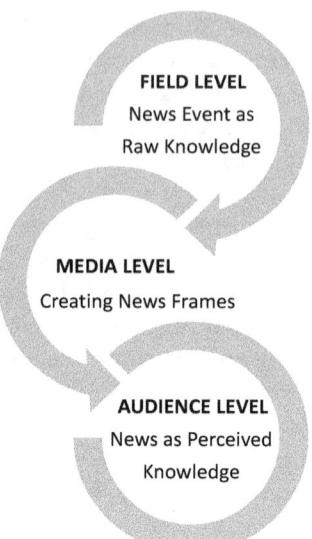

FIGURE 5.1 Proposed model of news frames
Source: Author

Kashmir as a colonialised territory

Not too many people outside South Asia know that three nuclear powers are occupying a stunningly scenic territory in the region. India, Pakistan, and China have chalked out parts of Kashmir among themselves and claim these areas as an integral part of their states.

Kashmir remains a colonial legacy of British rulers who left India in a hasty withdrawal and finally ended up carving out the two countries of India and Pakistan, but no decision on the future status of Kashmir, a princely state with a Muslim majority population. In the early post-colonial period, both nations tried to annex the area belligerently—armed forces in the case of India and tribal warriors in the case of Pakistan—and ended up dividing it into two parts between them. After three major wars, numerous border conflicts, and sacrificing thousands of lives over the last 70 years, both countries still claim Kashmir as an integral part of their national boundaries with no resolution in sight. The Indian and Pakistani governments are using draconian administrative mechanisms in Kashmir through legal provisions, security forces, as well as intelligence agencies. As a result, the region has practically become a colony of India and Pakistan.

Pakistani-controlled Kashmir comprises two separate areas: Azad Jammu and Kashmir (AJK) and Gilgit-Baltistan (GB). The Pakistani-administered AJK has an assembly with a combination of elected members from Kashmir, Kashmiri refugees in Pakistan, and appointed members from the federal government in Islamabad. Although elections are free, candidates are legally bound to support accession with

Pakistan and those who do not endorse it are not allowed to participate in elections. The overall control and legal framework, however, lies in the AJK Council (AJKC) which is presided over by the prime minister of Pakistan. This council has judicial, legislative, and executive powers and appoints judges in the territory. Gilgit-Baltistan also has a legislative assembly, but the GB Council practically controls the territory, headed by the prime minister in Islamabad. Security and intelligence organisations are very active in both areas to check resistance groups. A Freedom House report in 2018 demonstrates that although a variety of media outlets operate in AJK, "coverage of news and politics does not diverge from official Pakistani narrative, including that India's hold over the Kashmir Valley is illegitimate and all Kashmiris aspire to Pakistan accession" (Freedom House 2018).

Until recently, Indian-administered Kashmir was being governed through a parliamentary system with the status of an autonomous state governed by an elected chief minister and a powerful governor who represented the federal government. The territory had a special status for a specified period under Article 370 of the Indian constitution which gave the state an autonomous status with a limited federal domain to defence, foreign affairs, and communications. Additionally, it also restricted applicability of the Indian constitution in Kashmir. On 5 August 2019, however, this status was revoked by a presidential order which was duly endorsed by parliament. The new arrangement divided Kashmir into two federal territories: Kashmir Valley with a legislature and Ladakh without any legislative body. Before this action, India at least had a moral upper hand over Pakistan by giving special status to Kashmir, but both countries are now on a par in colonising the territory in a real sense.

The territory has growing media outlets, with a limited degree of freedom of expression as "threats of government reprisal, including the detention of journalists under the Public Safety Act, continue to intimidate the media" (Freedom House 2018).

Amid continued insurgencies and unrest, the territory has a heavy presence of security forces who maintain law and order with a heavy hand. There are 250,000 security forces in the Indian side of Kashmir, including the Central Reserve Police Force (CRPF), a paramilitary force deployed in the territory, making it one of the most militarised zones in the world (Habib, Yasir, and Kumar 2019: A8). Courts in the area are politicised, and the powerful security forces usually ignore their decisions. With limited freedom of expression and freedom to assemble, "Indian security forces have continued to carry out arbitrary arrests and detentions, torture, forced disappearance, and custodial killings of suspected militants and their alleged civilian sympathizers" (Freedom House 2018).

These groups and political parties can be divided along three ideological lines: pro-India, pro-Pakistan, and independence from either country (Abbas 2016). From the Pakistani-supported groups to the domestically grown youth movement, insurgencies in the Indian-administered Kashmir have many faces. Frustrated by the Indian mismanagement in Kashmir and vested interests of Pakistani-sponsored groups, the Kashmiri youth have embarked upon the third option of self-determination since 1989 (Cohen 2002: 32–60).

Sulehria (2018) argues that neither India nor Pakistan is interested in addressing the Kashmir issue as they are pressured by their domestic political environments to keep the status quo in the Valley. On the other hand, disunity among the political parties and factions in Kashmir further diminishes the possibility of an acceptable resolution soon. Additionally, as the ground realities have changed during the last 70 years, "Neither India nor Pakistan wants plebiscite simply because neither party is sure to win" (Sulehria 2018: 204). Probably that's why scholars and writers on both sides have been insisting on a political solution, not security-oriented short-term measures: "What is needed in Kashmir to retrieve the situation is political intervention and diplomatic outreach. That is one of the reasons why engaging with Imran is key" (Chengappa 2018: 35).

As the ongoing fiasco continues, both nuclear powers rule Kashmir with an iron fist as their colony. If, for India, the whole issue is confined to the infiltrating terrorists from across the border, for Pakistan it is the atrocities and human rights violations of the Indian forces that incite resistance. As it is, the unfortunate but most beautiful terrain of South Asia seems to be a victim of its geostrategic location, colonial legacies, and natural resources.

Framing the Kashmir conflict: Textual analysis

Despite the prevailing status quo on the Kashmir issue, "The LoC is the only place on earth where two nuclear-armed countries routinely shoot at each other", (Unnithan 2018: 39). Starting from the death of Hizbul Mujahideen commander Burhan Wani on 8 July, a wave of bloody protests swept through the Valley which entangled India and Pakistan in cross-border shootings by September 2016.

Against this backdrop, four insurgents attacked the Uri military base in Indian-administered Kashmir on 18 September 2016, killing 19 soldiers. The Indian government announced it would respond, and surgical strikes were conducted to destroy several "launchpads" on the Pakistani side within ten days on 29 September. While India claimed that it destroyed several launchpads two kilometres inside Pakistani-administered Kashmir, Pakistan denied any surgical strikes, but accepted two casualties in the cross-border firing. The BBC, however, reported that Indian soldiers attacked in Mundakali, Dudhnial, Poonch, Kotli, Bhimbher, and other sectors (Ilyas 2016). Reportedly, Pakistani soldiers repulsed some of these attacks.

Since then, incidents of cross-border firing have increased to an unprecedented level. *India Today* reported 1,300 violations of ceasefire by India in 2017 and 980 by Pakistan. In 2018, these violations from the Indian side were 70 and 244 by Pakistan (Chengappa 2018: 38). With this historical context, this study evaluates TV talk shows in both countries to see if they covered the dispute with a preferred frame on retaliatory surgical strikes by the Indian forces inside Pakistani-administered Kashmir on 29 September.

The NDTV talk show in India, "The Buck Stops Here", discusses significant socio-political issues in English with Barkha Dutt as its anchor. She is a respected and well-trained journalist with a Master's degree in journalism from Columbia

University, New York. With over 20 years' experience as a reporter and anchor, Dutt is known for the coverage of the Kargil war between India and Pakistan. NDTV panellists on the talk show included former Chief of Army Staff General Deepak Kapoor, Air Chief Marshal Fali H. Major, BJP leader Rajeev Chandrasekhar, another BJP representative Nalin Kohli, the Ministry of External Affairs (MEA) official Ambassador K. C. Singh, and senior journalist Ashok Malik. In introducing the show, the anchor also showed a clip of Lt. Gen. Ranbir Singh, Director General of Military Operations (DGMO), addressing a press conference after the surgical strikes, a recorded interview with Minister of State Col. Rajyavardhan Singh Rathore, and an on-camera live report by Sudhi Ranjan Sen (NDTV 2016).

The Pakistani programme "Capital Talk" on GEO TV also discusses national and international themes in Urdu with Hamid Mir as its host. A known journalist, renowned for his reporting on the Taliban and Osama bin Laden, he has a Master's in Mass Communication from the University of the Punjab, Lahore. He has worked as a journalist and broadcaster for the last 30 years. GEO TV panellists as part of the programme were Retired Major General Ejaz Awan, Pakistan Muslim League, Nawaz (PML-N) leader Talal Choudhry, and Pakistan Tehrik-e Insaf (PTI) representative Shahryar Afridi (GEO TV 2016).

These shows, accessed online, were transcribed and analysed within the context of the recorded discussion. The textual analysis revealed four frames in both talks shows: Kashmir as a colonialised territory, warmongering, construction of social reality, and subscribing to a patriotic ideology. The following section analyses these frames.

Both anchors introduced their talk shows setting a clear pitch for the discussion. From the beginning, they created a highly charged and emotional mood for panellists with their nationalistic angle on the conflict. Mir introduced the show casting doubts on the Indian claim that it had conducted surgical strikes into Pakistani-controlled Kashmir, which was also the official position:

> You know that India has claimed that it has launched a surgical strike against militants in Azad Kashmir from the other side of Line of Control. But Pakistan's military says there was no such strike. And all over the world, this debate goes on if there was a surgical strike. What does it mean actually? So let's talk about what the surgical strike is and, as a result of Pakistan's response, what was the Indian loss. There was no claim from the Pakistani side, but the information we have been receiving from different sources say there was a full-scale response from Pakistan inflicting a tremendous loss on the Indian forces.
>
> *(GEO TV 2016)*

From the outset, he established two clear directions for the talk show: there were no surgical strikes, and the Pakistani forces retaliated with a full force inflicting heavy losses on Indians. Both claims were unauthenticated but deeply rooted in state and military positions.

Dutt also introduced her talk show subscribing to nationalistic and official narratives:

> India has conducted surgical strikes in multiple sectors along and across the LOC attacking seven terror launchpads going deep inside Pakistan-occupied Kashmir. One highly placed source confirming to me that this was the special forces going at least two kilometres deep. All day long we have been reporting this. The big story, this is a paradigm shift in India's response to Pakistan-supported terrorism. A clear response that Pakistan-backed cross-border terrorism will come at a price.
>
> *(NDTV 2016)*

She announced that conducting the surgical strikes deep inside the Pakistani side of Kashmir was a paradigm shift in Indian policy. Also, by saying that the strikes gave a clear message to Pakistan that terrorist attacks will come with a price, she created an emotional atmosphere supporting the nationalist and patriotic positions. After both anchors established a high ground for their side based on unconfirmed information, they created a proper ambiance for the panellists.

The NDTV panellists claimed the Valley of Kashmir as their territory directly and aggressively. On the other hand, the GEO panellists indirectly implied that the Valley is under their jurisdiction. The colonial mindset was at work in both cases. When Dutt promptly reminded a panellist of an earlier comment by a participant, "Col Rathore says it is our territory", Ashok Malik responded affirmatively, "That is true. Even the PM has said that Gilgit, Baltistan, POK is our territory".

When Nalin Kohli stressed that the Indian strike was against terrorism and "it is a pre-emptive strike against terrorists, that's what the government is saying, that's what we are saying", Dutt reiterated the claim that Pakistani-occupied Kashmir is Indian territory: "This is an anti-terror operation. This is done to stop terrorists who will be pushed across the LOC and any terror attack. But this is no violation of anything because this is taking place in Pakistan-occupied Kashmir which India has always considered a part of India".

Indian DGMO Gen. Ranbir Singh, addressing a press conference after the surgical strikes, discussed in detail why the operation was carried out. Throughout his statement, however, he referred to Kashmir as part of the country:

> Based on very specific and credible information which we received yesterday, that some terrorist teams had positioned themselves at launchpads along the line of control with an aim to carry out infiltration and terrorist strikes in Jammu and Kashmir and various other metros in our country, the Indian army conducted surgical strikes last night at these launchpads. The operations basically focused on ensuring that these terrorists do not succeed in their design of infiltration and carrying out destruction and endangering the lives of citizens of our country. During these counter-terrorist operations, significant casualties have been caused to the terrorists and those who support them.

Here the army General was using the semantics of "our country" and "citizens of our country" to imply that Kashmir is not a disputed area but an Indian territory.

Following the official line, as "Capital Talk" was trying to downplay the strikes, their claim over the territory was not as direct as it was in the Indian program. Coloniality over Kashmir, however, was all over the Pakistani media after the incident. The nation also observes 5 January as "Kashmir Solidarity Day" with the theme "Kashmir banayga Pakistan", meaning Kashmir will become part of Pakistan. Not only media outlets play this theme; rallies and statements of political leaders tend to proclaim that the territory is part of the nation based on religious affinity. *Dawn*, the respected English newspaper reported in an opinion piece that slogans such as "Kashmir is Pakistan's jugular vein" and "Kashmir and Pakistan are like one soul in two hearts" were repeated as part of the rhetoric throughout the day (Zakaria 2019).

Warmongering became the mantra on both talk shows as participants were busy criticising the rival country and justifying the claims of their forces. Journalists, analysts, diplomats, and political leaders chose the path of brinkmanship, intimidation, and framing the conflict in their favour throughout the discussion. Amazingly, none of the participants and anchors, who were well-respected professionals and intellectuals, tried to talk peace and analyse the conflict with a rational approach.

Talal Choudhry, a leader of the party in power in Pakistan, responding to a question elucidated, "our response has all the things you just mentioned. It has the maturity, restraint, patience, and no panic. Not because we are not wrong, but because we are confident, because of our nuclear capability, our forces, and our people. We didn't start it, we responded". As if India does not have a nuclear arsenal, he went on to boast on the nuclear capability of Pakistan in a threatening posture.

Underlining the Muslim factor, GEO panellist Afridi was trying to stress the religious divide between India and Pakistan:

> We are a nation and might have political differences among our self, but we will be united if there is a need and we will sacrifice our lives if needed. And this message should be loud and clear to Modi. And he should know the nation he is challenging has just one slogan: "God is great", and we don't look back after that.

Gen. Awan also reminded the Indian forces of Pakistan's retaliation in response to their strikes, "In Samahni, Tatta Pani, and Bandala where we had an exchange of fire, for sure they had casualties". "And when these (dead bodies) will go home", he warned the Indians of public outcry, "there will be a public and media pressure".

On the other hand, NDTV tried to boost the strategic superiority of their armed forces when BJP leader Chandrasekhar observed,

> It has put Pakistan on notice that we opened all kinds of tools that we have, the Indus Water Treaty, the most favoured status, diplomatic isolation, and the military option. And this is the only language that Pakistan will understand because for years this doctrine of strategic restraint has led Indians and

Pakistanis to believe that we don't have the capability militarily to respond to Pakistan and its terrorism. And today they have demonstrated that not only we are diplomatically capable, but we also are economically capable, we are militarily capable of demonstrating to Pakistan that what they are doing will be registered and responded to.

Speaking of war and revenge, the politician also reminded the viewers that Pakistan only understands the language of a strong military response. While the Pakistani discussants were trying to downplay the surgical strikes, the Indian panellists were boasting about their strategy to strike the enemy inside its territory.

To focus on their strategic superiority over the enemy, both sides were also constructing the social reality that suited their nationalistic goals. While Pakistan admitted that they lost two soldiers in the cross-border firing, they denied any surgical strike on its side of the border. Mir also told the viewers that there had been casualties on the other side: "According to my sources in one sector, they had eight dead bodies of Indian soldiers and six on the other. In Tatta Pani eight dead bodies of Indian soldiers were seen across the LOC until 4 or 5 p.m., not removed".

Confirming the information, Maj. Gen. Awan, announced, "That's right. I have discussed it with an eye-witness; these dead bodies were still there, not removed". He also tried to assert that these Indian attacks were part of a diversionary tactic from increasing human rights violations when he said, "Two things. First, they achieved their objective. They had the drama of Uri attack to avoid responding at the UN Security Council on human rights violations in Kashmir. And now they had started another issue of external intervention, and they have achieved that objective. Now the world attention has been diverted".

Dutt, refuting this claim, was insisting there were no casualties on their side: "In fact, we are told that massive casualties have been inflicted on terrorists and maybe those details will be revealed as and when, but certainly DGMO confirming those massive casualties, no casualty at all to Indians".

As the two sides were manipulating the information coming from the LOC, they framed news stories in line with the military establishment position. For the NDTV reporter Sudhi Ranjan Sen, "The troops were given very clear instructions that you don't leave any bodies or your body behind. Go strike and carry everyone back and that is exactly what has happened". And based on his assertions, he concluded, "The terror launchpads are struck, heavy casualties, the DGMO says, are inflicted, and they came back".

Choudhry even went further in speculating that RAW might interfere with their sit-in planned for the next day: "If there are indications that RAW might have a terrorist attack on the Dharna of Imran Khan, the government should provide full security by the Punjab or federal government. We should arrest these terrorists and unveil them to the world".

The world probably will never know what happened during the surgical strikes that night as both TV channels were presenting their versions of the encounters to establish their supremacy. Although the panellists on both channels also included military experts and seasoned journalists, they were creating their social reality ignoring the truth out there. Either they were trying to influence the audience, or they were pressured by viewers and media owners not to bring forth the alternative discourse.

In the wake of conflict and war, the nationality of journalists and editors affect the coverage and "this assertion is even stronger when the coverage is of a conflict in which the journalist's nation is involved" (Ginosar and Cohen 2019: 16). The nationality issue becomes so vital that journalists cover conflicts with a patriotic lens, disregarding the traditional notions of objectivity and balance in covering news. This trend also became obvious in both talk shows as, following the anchors' set tone, the panellists continued supporting the nationalistic positions subscribing to a patriotic ideological thrust throughout their discussions.

For Air Chief Marshal Major, surgical strikes were the result of a planned strategy: "There is no doubt that what happened last night is a wonderfully planned and executed operation to take across Pakistan that our age-old restraint doctrine is now history and we mean business. It's as simple as that". Former Army Chief of India Gen. Kapoor was further elaborating and supporting Fali's point of view: "Let me first begin by congratulating and complimenting the Indian Military for the surgical strike, very well calculated, very well calibrated, well planned, and well-executed strikes carried out by them".

Gen. Awan of Pakistan remarked, following the official line, that the real issue was human rights of Kashmiris:

> Second, the real Issue of Kashmir is human rights violations and brutality. We should start our efforts diplomatically not to divert attention from the real issue. We must reveal the brutalities in Kashmir. The opposition should continue its role; the government should do its role; it does not make any difference. When all the political parties and people support the military, we don't have to worry.

Col. Rathore appeared to be more diplomatic on NDTV when he tried to isolate the military establishment in Pakistan from the masses at large:

> I think the larger message here is India always wanted, we will continue to want that peace and will continue to have peace, however, Pakistan must realise that a large number of Pakistanis want peace but a smaller, a handful of people are taking us to that ride, and that smaller number of Pakistanis need to be isolated.

Pakistan's opposition party (PTI) leader Afridi looked like a government representative when he said, "we will go to any limit for the security of Pakistan. There are no two opinions on that".

In an environment full of patriotic zeal, participants on both sides were demonstrating their nationalistic loyalties. Gen. Kapoor criticised Pakistan's efforts to exaggerate the ongoing chaos in the Indian side of Kashmir: "firstly, by doing what they did in Uri, Pakistani deep state was also trying to create a situation where in addition to what is happening within the Valley, they were trying to depict a picture of total chaos and mayhem within the Valley, therefore, inviting international attention".

Mir concluded the program with highly charged and emotional remarks, jeopardising the credibility of his show as well as his impartiality as a journalist: "in 1996 Benazir Bhutto's speech at the UN General Assembly and Nawaz Sharif's speech this year, both were excellent. I was in the gallery, and I heard it. Although we can assess, who did better or worse, we can say whoever is talking in the interest of Pakistan is correct".

Overall, the Indian participants discussed the conflict with an antagonistic posture. The Pakistani panellists, on the other hand, trying to downplay the strategic strikes, kept a low profile throughout the program. Also, to show business as usual, GEO had a smaller number of panellists as they devoted only a part of the talk show to the Indo-Pak conflict and reserved the rest of the time for domestic politics. On the other hand, the Indian show devoted the whole program (60 minutes) to the strategic strikes with a larger panel. The role of the anchors appeared to be partial when they made comments loaded with patriotic bias, something not expected from hosts and panellists of this high calibre; their views were not so different from patriotic citizens at large.

As this textual analysis demonstrates, GEO and NDTV covered Kashmir with paradoxically opposed as well as similar dimensions. While the Pakistani channel considered insurgents as Kashmiris fighting for their human rights, Indian TV called them terrorists or infiltrators from Pakistan. Both panels claimed heavy casualties on the enemy and limited or no losses on their side. Both tried to blame the enemy for interfering in their domestic affairs. Both talk shows were also very similar in creating media hype over the conflict and contributing to war hysteria.

Table 5.1 includes the semantic game both talk shows played to thrust their worldview on the interstate conflict. It identifies predominant themes, words, and phrases used as part of the four frames discussed. Coloniality was a potent symbol for NDTV, whereas GEO did not invoke it directly as part of the discussion. Kashmir was an integral part of India for the NDTV panellists, and they meant the whole Valley, not just the Indian-administered territory. Phrases such as "Kashmir is Indian territory" and referring to Kashmiris as "Indian citizens" they established their jurisdiction and moral authority over the Valley.

Warmongering as another frame also became the overall agenda for both channels rather than discussing relevant issues seriously. While the Indian programme used threats such as "Pakistan will pay a heavy price" and "we mean business", the GEO panellists, knowing Pakistan's vulnerabilities, were using the nuclear card saying "we have the nuclear capability".

TABLE 5.1 News frames and themes

TV channel	Coloniality	Warmongering	Construction of reality	Patriotic thrust
NDTV	Pakistani administered Kashmir is our territory. Kashmir is Indian territory. Kashmiris are Indian citizens.	Pakistan will pay a heavy price. We will fight terrorism. The military option is open. We will use water as a weapon. Pakistan is a deep state. Paradigm shifts to attack the enemy. We mean business.	Seven launch-pads destroyed. No Indian casualty. Heavy Pakistani casualties. Pakistan as a terrorist state. Terrorists infiltrate in Kashmir from Pakistan.	Our operation was well planned. Well executed plan. We are superior. India is peaceful. National security is vital for India.
GEO TV	Implied religious affinity with Kashmiris.	We have a nuclear capability. Religious divide. We will retaliate. "God is great" is our slogan.	Uri attack was a drama created by India. There were no surgical strikes. Chaos and brutalities in Indian Kashmir. Heavy Indian casualties in border firing. RAW interferes in Pakistan.	We are united, mature, and patient. We are peaceful. We will retaliate if attacked.

Source: Author

As we have seen, both programmes also constructed a social reality, based on inauthentic information as opposed to the objective truth, on the LOC. The participating "experts" tried to create reality by mutilating, denying, or manipulating the information coming from the LOC. This newly constructed reality became a hallmark of both channels which presented a preferred frame for the conflict. While the Pakistani panellists denied the Ori attack as an Indian-created "drama", they also denied that surgical strikes were conducted. On the other hand, the Indian participants claimed "heavy Pakistani casualties" denying any casualties on the Indian side.

Finally, a voluntary subscription to the nationalistic/patriotic ideology also became a significant frame for both shows. Amazingly, discussants and anchors became patriotic opinion leaders who looked like state agents on TV screens. When GEO declared "we are united" and "we are patient and peaceful" it was reflecting a nationalistic position for presenting a positive image of the nation. For the Indian programme, "the operation was well planned" and "national security was important" were the main symbolic gestures to prove their superiority.

Discussion

When Noam Chomsky says, "But it is entirely typical for major media, and the intellectual classes generally, to line up in support of power at a time of crisis and try to mobilize the population for the same cause" (Chomsky 2001: 30), it explains why media outlets in India and Pakistan voluntarily subscribe to state and defence policies. This partiality, however, is opposed to peace efforts and creates nationalistic frames with little room for alternative viewpoints.

We can also comprehend this phenomenon through the framing model discussed earlier in Figure 5.1. The framing process began with the field level, getting the raw information from the LOC. At this level, NDTV and GEO received information from their reporters, security agencies, or government sources. Instead of confirming this information through journalistic investigations, both anchors transformed the raw knowledge into their desired frames. They actively managed their talk shows, setting the discussion agenda early on. Taking directions from the hosts, participants then completed the framing process with their statements which were further reinforced by the anchors' questions and continued interpretations.

At the audience level, viewers reframe the information with three possible kinds of responses: they accept the news story, reject, or modify it with their interpretation. Stuart Hall, in his encoding-decoding model for TV contents, explains the same process with three types of audience readings: dominant-hegemonic, negotiated, and oppositional. The audience tends to accept the proposed coding, they accept it with some reservations, or reject it altogether (Storey 2003: 12–13). Although the print media and some TV channels in India and Pakistan do offer in-depth and impartial coverage of the conflict, most of the time, the mainstream TV outlets remain one-sided and biased.

With these dimensions of coverage, the question remains whether the media tried to influence the audience or framed the information as a result of the emotionally charged national environment. The whole process of creating news frames by both outlets seems to be reciprocal. While the talk shows created frames, they were also influenced by public opinion over the claimed surgical strikes.

Overall, the analysed talk shows were a classic example of how TV as an organisation frames news with the art of exclusion and inclusion. None of the discussants raised the issues of human rights, poverty, violence, and the daily hardships the Kashmiris go through on either side of the border.

With these frames in mind, what contributions do these talk shows make towards the long-term peace process? Galtung's theory of peace journalism can be helpful here in understanding the long-term impact of this framing process when he proposes three major dimensions in covering war and peace. For him, while direct violence is visible, cultural and structural violence is invisible. Usually, peace efforts are focused on the apparent violence, ignoring the hidden causes built into cultural and structural dynamics of societies (Galtung 2004). This model is also highly relevant to the Kashmir issue where policymakers and the mainstream media in India and Pakistan concentrate on the apparent conflict but ignore the hidden subtleties of the problem. Consequently, the conflict subsides for some time only to re-emerge with a stronger force later.

Media organisations, as a result of government pressure, market dynamics, or public opinion, tend to focus only on the visible aspects of the conflict which ultimately serve their purpose, and consequently develop a warmongering hysteria among the audience in an already charged environment. Within the context of regional hostilities, the process of framing news becomes comparatively more comfortable for the media as the narrow nationalistic ideology is already there, created by the politicians or the military establishment to serve their vested interests.

TV news generally contributes a great deal to ideologically biased coverage, which further increases the enormous gulf of mistrust between the countries in conflict. Not only do the mainstream TV channels follow the official and popular narrative, but they also fail to explore the truth behind interstate conflicts. Following the pattern, as demonstrated by this study, most of the coverage of Kashmir in India and Pakistan was biased, aligned with a nationalistic and patriotic ideological thrust. As truth became the first casualty of the conflict, the so-called experts of NDTV and GEO contributed to a great extent to the process of creating news frames based on partiality and mendacity.

References

Abbas, Q. 2016. "Is Kashmir ready for independence from India and Pakistan? Interview with senior Kashmiri leader Raja Muzaffar". *Pakistan Link*, January 16 (accessed 21 September 2019), http://pakistanlink.org/Commentary/2016/Jan16/22/01.HTM.

Auerbach, Y. and Bloch-Elkon, Y. 2005. "Media framing and foreign policy: The elite press vis-à-vis US policy in Bosnia, 1992–95". *Journal of Peace Research*, 42(1), 83–99.

Chengappa, R. 2018. "Imran's googly". *India Today*, December 17.

Chomsky, N. 2001. *September 11*. Crows Nest, NSW: Allen & Unwin.

Cohen, S. 2002. "India, Pakistan, and Kashmir". *Journal of Strategic Studies*, 25(4).

Entman, R.M. 1991. "Framing U.S. coverage of international news: Contrasts in narratives of the KAL and Iran Air incidents". *Journal of Communication*, 42(4).

Freedom House. 2018. "Reports on Pakistani Kashmir & Indian Kashmir" (accessed 21 September 2019), https://freedomhouse.org.

Galtung, J. 2004. "Violence, war and their impact on visible and invisible effects of violence" accessed 21 September 2019), http://them.polylog.org/5/fgj-en.htm.

GEO TV. 2016. "Capital Talk" (accessed 21 September 2019), http://geovideos.tv/2016/09/29/capital-talk-29-september-2016/.

Gitlin, T. 1980. *The Whole World is Watching*. Berkeley and Los Angeles: University of California Press.

Ginosar, A. and Cohen, I. 2019. "Patriotic journalism: An appeal to emotion and cognition". *Media, War, and Conflict*, 12(1).

Habib, M., Yasir, S. and Kumar, H. 2019. "India accuses Pakistan in deadly Kashmir attack". *New York Times*, February 6, A8.

Hamelink, C.J. 2008. "Media between warmongers and peacemakers". *Media, War, and Conflict*, 1(1).

Ilays, K. 2016. "India's surgical strikes in Kashmir: Truth or illusion?" *BBC News*, 23 October (accessed 21 September 2019), www.bbc.com/news/world-asia-india-37702790.
Lee, S.T. and Maslog, C.C. 2005. "War or peace journalism? Asian newspapers coverage of the conflict". *Journal of Communication*, 55(2).
McCombs, M., Shaw, D.L. and Weaver, D. 1997. *Communication and Democracy: Exploring the Intellectual Frontiers in Agenda-setting Theory*. Mahwah, NJ: Erlbaum.
NDTV. 2016. "The Buck Stops Here" (accessed 21 September 2019), www.youtube.com/watch?v=EgcoDjO49GM.
Scheufele, D.A. 1999. "Framing as a theory of media effects". *Journal of Communication*, Winter.
Storey, J. 2003. *Cultural Studies and the Study of Popular Culture*. Athens: The University of Georgia Press.
Sulehria, F. 2018. "Kashmir as partition's unfinished business", in A. Ranjan (ed), *Partition of India*. New Delhi: Routledge.
Umber, S. 2014. *Media and Conflict Resolution: Portrayal of Kashmir in the Editorials of US Press 1998–2008*. Unpublished Doctoral thesis, University of the Punjab, Lahore.
Unnithan, S. 2018. "No war no peace". *India Today*. February 26.
Wolpert, S. 2010. *Continued Conflict or Cooperation: India and Pakistan*. Berkeley: University of California Press.
Zakaria, A. 2019. February 5. "This Kashmir Day who will stand up for Azad Kashmiris?" *Dawn* (accessed 21 September 2019), www.dawn.com/news/1387465.

6
PERFORMING PIETY AND SEXUALITY IN PAKISTAN

Afiya Shehrbano Zia

Karin van Nieuwkerk (2011: 10) finds through some Middle Eastern case studies that there may be an emergence of a "post-Islamist cultural sphere" in which younger generations of Muslims are creating pious art that turns away from rigid doctrinal views. She states that more liberal attitudes towards art, the development of a middle- and upper-middle-class market-oriented Islam, moderate religious ideologies, and the influence of media and the global transnational sphere indicate the emergence of this post-Islamist cultural sphere. A body of post-secular scholars have made a similar case for Pakistan in relation to Muslim women's piety and subjectivities and their politics, performances, writings, production, and consumption of Islamic religiosity via the media and markets. This includes predominantly diasporic Pakistani scholars such as Masooda Bano (2012), Humeira Iqtidar (2011), Sadaf Aziz (2011), and Ammara Maqsood (2017), and several others (including men) who regularly comment on such issues online and in blogs.

Even with the development of a market-oriented Islam that now includes the framing and funding of women's social development within a religious ethos (Zia 2018), and the fuelling of orthopraxy through media, Pakistani Muslim attitudes towards art, women's sexualities, and religious ideologies remain firmly conservative. Moreover, as Daniels (2013: 107) observes about Malaysia, "the Islamic TV dramas and film, and the emergent Muslim cultural sphere they participate in, do not counter or oppose the state ... [but] ... contest religious pluralism and liberal Islam". He observes how this reinforces "a 'postdivision' cultural sphere, one in which Muslims, united in their piety, maintain dominance, uphold the faith, and solve social problems" (Daniels 2013: 108). Associated with the hope of syncretic possibilities in such performative politics, the question of gender identities is a crucial consideration. Below, some examples in Pakistan's context are discussed with reference to how pious and reformist Islam, as projected through media forms, restrict women's empowerment and freedoms within a prescribed and patriarchal gendered order while their sexual performativity and autonomy are direct threats to the same.

The journey of piety

The unresolved place of religion in Pakistan dates from its genesis in 1947 and no meaningful secular alternative discourse has been allowed to evolve. Historically in South Asia, the responsibility of redeeming women of their ignorance always has been undertaken by men (just as civilising the native was invariably the white man's burden). The zeal with which the cause of Muslim women's acculturation has been championed reveals a patriarchal view of this project of cultural and religious literacy. There were several such sources of prescriptive (male) literature for Muslim women that emerged with the nineteenth-century Islamic reform movements, but it is encapsulated most comprehensively in the advice literature of the early twentieth-century magnum opus *Bihishti Zewar* (*Heavenly Ornaments*) authored in India in 1905–6 by Ashraf Ali Thanawi. The clear bent of these was to assign the responsibility of Muslim women's lagging status to polluting culture over Islamic textual authenticity and so most male reform literature paves the way for a reversal to a more rigid interpretation and exegesis.

Included in the domestic guidance in Book Ten of *Bihishti Zewar* are 38 suitable activities for women, two-thirds of which involve sewing (Metcalf 1990: 320). There are several pages of recipes and instructions for saleable products (some with diagrammatic aids). Advice against the excess of eating and talking are replete with repeated reminders for curbing one's tongue throughout the books, especially "informal conversation with anyone with a marriageable degree" (Metcalf 1990: 202). Thanawi cautions against anger and desire for material goods and even prescribes the order in which women should dress: "begin dressing from the right side of the body and undressing from the left" (Book Seven). Thanawi covers all imaginable codes of daily conduct related to the private realm.

The advice on sex is not dealt with in any detail by Metcalf but the books are unabashed about various directions including the circumstances and details of (il)licit intercourse. In Book Four, a prayer couplet is recommended prior to sex, which Thanawi suggests will lend the added benefit of protecting any child who may be conceived out of that intercourse from *Shaitan* (devil/evil). Thanawi includes the rules for intercourse in polygamous circumstances too. Interestingly, and for all the hand-wringing explanations among progressive interpretations of this Islamic provision about how all polygamous wives must be treated equally, Thanawi repeatedly clarifies that multiple wives do not need to be loved equally nor receive equal sexual attention. Optimistically, Thanawi suggests that "Equality is not *wajb* (an Islamic requirement) when embarking on a journey. The husband can take whichever wife he wishes. However, it is preferable to cast a lot and to take the wife in whose favour the lot was drawn. In this way there will be no unhappiness or disgruntlement" (Book Four, *Bihishti Zewar*).

Modernity and celebritisation of piety

The pietist proselytisation movement in post-partition Pakistan after 1947 continued in a quietist mode in Pakistan (Metcalf 1990; Robinson 2008). The influential religious scholarship in the early years was spearheaded by the prolific political Islamist Abul Ala Maududi who founded Jamaat-e-Islami Pakistan (the leading religious party of Pakistan) and his writings echo Thanawi's advice for women in the new Muslim nation. Maududi focused on education and training a Muslim woman to become a "good wife, good mother and good housekeeper" (Maududi 2010: 152).

They should not be provided the same education designed for men but rather with that designed to correlate with the demand of private spaces. Moreover, they should not be educated in a co-educational system and every effort should be made to procure women teachers for them (Maududi 2000: 208; 2002: 163–164; 2003: 209–210). Maududi justified his stance on limiting women's sphere of activity to the domestic by relying on the *hadith* that "the woman is not allowed to go on a journey except in company of a *mahram*" (a male member of the family with whom sexual relationship is forbidden) (Maududi 2010: 148). The contribution of women members of the Jamaat to the gender discourse through its women's magazine (*Batool*) makes for fascinating textual analysis since such critical engagement is sometimes set up through fictionalised narratives and circumstances to which members respond.

Cheema notes that this is not "carried out by women of the JI for the purpose of acquiring more freedom in the sense it is understood in liberal philosophy (Mahmood 2005). Rather, the entire exercise has been undertaken for the purpose of thorough internalization and embodiment of coercion [of the male discourse] itself" (Cheema 2013: 86).

It was during Zia-ul-Haq's (1977–1988) dictatorship, which purported to turn Pakistan into a true Islamic Republic, that male clergy were empowered to control the narrative of social discourse and it was dominated by uber conservatives such as Dr Israr Ahmed who devoted his daily TV evangelism to the importance of confining women to the *char devari* (four walls of a house) and domesticity and piety. The pioneering theocratic TV game show, *Neelam Ghar* (*Auction House*) was hosted by Tariq Aziz. Despite its ironic name, which aptly identified the state as a brokerage house for peddling religion, it was more of an ascetic, cold-war era, dry religious quiz show (with questions to which hardly anyone had the answers), rather than an entertaining pietist performance. The popularity of the religious trivia game-show trend became far more compelling in the post-9/11 period.

One exemplary bridge of this populist turn was the pop musician Junaid Jamshed, who was a true example of the pietist conversion of a celebrity who rechannelled his musical talent from profane entertainment in the 1990s to Islamic proselytisation (*dawa* or invitation) in the post-9/11 period. His required repentance enabled him to become a virtuous subject and use his talent to become a preacher himself, but who directed his musical talent for evangelical ends and sustained a profitable career and achieved fame in the process.

After the events of 9/11, a clear pietist turn could be observed across the social spectrum, including within the Pakistan cricket team under the captaincy of Inzama-mul Haq and the publicised performances of piety and collective prayer congregations by its team members. Similarly, the re-veiling of one of the first fashion models, Atiya Khan, signalled the rise of the debate around veiling practices in Pakistan that continue to rage today, now including debates over the full veil as observed by the spiritual leader (pirni) and current first lady of Pakistan, Bushra Imran.

The Al-Huda pietist women's movement founded in the 1990s peaked in its influence and institutionalised *dawa* by establishing a base in the public sphere across the country and was particularly strong among the Pakistani diaspora. Media is an instrumental factor in the propagation of Al-Huda's programmes. It gathered a cult-like following under the leadership of its founder Dr Farhat Hashmi, and considerable academic work by and on gendered identities in Pakistan in the post-9/11 period focuses on the subjectivities and self-accounts of women members of pietist and Islamist movements. The core theses of such scholarship fall within a post-secular framing and argue that pietist/Islamist women's politics are not sourced in false consciousness but are agentive in their docility or may be seen as sharia-minded activists. However, these arguments stop short of specifying that such activism opposes women's legal and constitutional equality, promotes anti-women and anti-minorities policies, and stabilises patriarchy and conservatism.

Faiza Mushtaq argues against the finding that Farhat Hashmi's ideas and authority are due to her sophisticated use of electronic media. Instead, Mushtaq suggests that Hashmi's "television appearances or tapes and CDs have a limited transformative impact on their own" and it is "ties of fellowship and loyalty to a group through which women can sustain their moral commitments, and feel themselves to be part of an authoritative consensus" (Mushtaq 2010: 39). Over the last decade, however, Pakistan has seen the palimpsest of religious orthopraxy and spread of pietist performativity in the media increase multi-fold and become so influential that, in one case, the pietist movement of Tehreek-e-Labaik YaRasoolallah was formed almost overnight and a few months later converted into a political party that went on to win a few parliamentary seats and a considerable vote share in the general elections of 2018.

To underestimate the nexus of the media, piety, and gender in aesthetic forms of religious practices is to deny their interconnectedness and how these embody everyday religious life. Hashmi's comments denying the very concept of marital rape in Islamic marriage simply revealed the seamlessness between Islamist and pietist views (Hashmi 2019). In the clip, Hashmi insists that the concept of rape in a Muslim marriage is a misnomer and wives should exercise their "docile agency" and willingly consent and submit to, not resist, the sexual demands of their husbands.

According to social media commentary, Hashmi has received mass support from viewers for her bold clarification on the sexual rights of a Muslim husband over his wife's body, against a smaller number of viewers who are offended by her interpretation of religious duty. However, in this section of the video, Hashmi does not offer any justifications for violence, as has been misinterpreted by some outraged members of the Twitter community.

Oddly enough, Hashmi and her fare of piety have always upheld and supported the regular patriarchal religious status quo that depends on the pious woman as the obedient subject, but such criticism was dismissed by defenders as binary setting and even Islamophobic. Such selective reactions have meant that after years of theological exegesis, discussion, and research, core issues around the issue of women's rights within Islam are left unsettled and repeatedly return as topics for public and social media debates.

Interestingly, Hashmi opposes the concept of marital rape due to the belief that lay law cannot supersede the Islamic sexual order in which the duty-bound wife holds subordinate sexual status. Regardless of the insistence on finding scriptural justifications for sexual equality, religious prescriptions restrict sexual conduct within the bounds of a patriarchal gendered order. Muslim marriage is a contract that is literally defined by the clause of the (male) *force majeure* (superior force) by way of the husband's unilateral right to polygamy, divorce, and, significantly, payment of the *haqmeher* (dowry) on consummation.

The persistence of this pietist discourse is situated in a time when a new wave of the anti-sexual harassment and #MeToo movements in Pakistan are struggling to do the opposite—that is, to expand the definition of sexual freedoms and of violence to include all forms and sites, including verbal and mental abuse, in marriage and even in illicit consensual relations. New players in this mix include a frequent morning show guest, "Mrs. Khan", who runs a marriage bureau service and who opined on one programme that divorce rates were spiking because Pakistani women refused to adequately conduct their domesticated duties or curb their sharp tongues (Khan 2019). The considerable backlash to such masculinist apologia led to an on-air apology by Mrs. Khan but echoes the pervasive notions around women's responsibilities in marriage, piety, domesticity, and Thanawi's early twentieth-century reformist instructions against women's excessive talking in order to preserve the Islamic gendered order.

Celebritisation of piety

During General Musharraf's "Enlightened Moderation" attempts, scholar Dr Khalid Masud, as chair of the Council of Islamic Ideology, and jurisconsult Javed Ahmed Ghamdi attempted to rearticulate an inclusive role/place of women in society. In the same time period between 1999 and 2008, the expanse of private television channels in Pakistan were all competing for high ratings, and so televangelism, piety programming, and Ramadan game shows became regular and lucrative fare. This relinquished the narrative of state-led religious "capture" and allowed the segmentation of religious power by way of TV cleric-scholars and created a subculture of televangelism for the first time in Pakistan.

The encounters between the "wayward" and religious erudite became a regular media-staged performance, serving as entertainment that combined spectacle and religious aesthetics. TV *fatwas* (edicts) could be purchased via cell phone technology, Islamic portals expanded, and incalculable international funds streamed in for social and cultural development, including animated documentaries and TV serials which stressed reformist (or deradicalising) religious content (Zia 2018). There was even an online cleric who called his programme *Aalim Online* (*Online Scholar*). As an example of the importance of this interactivity, the most popular leader of the Tableeghi movement in Pakistan, who mentored the late Junaid Jamshed and is a supporter of the current Prime Minister, Imran Khan, Tariq Jameel, was recently awarded YouTube's Golden Play Button Award after hitting one million subscribers on his channel. His channel is, apparently, Pakistan's first Islamic online streaming content provider to receive this award.

TV evangelism spread and peaked during these years with overnight clerics turning into experts (including women) who dedicated their programmes to a wide range of religio-political debates—from the concept of jihad and suicide bombings, to the recommendation that the Prophet's reportedly favourite vegetable must be referred to with veneration and not dislike. Pop-Islam call-in shows for Islamic rulings were led by men and women anchors who were pious celebrity-scholars and who opined on anything from hair removal to halal banking. Controversy followed when some TV anchors and hosts violated journalistic restraint and incited hate, which led to the murders of members of the Ahmedi[1] community (Shahid 2015). One woman anchor, Mehr Bokhari, opined that the Governor of Punjab was in fact, a heretic, adding to general suspicions that this state officer was a blasphemer for attempting to help a poor Christian woman against the accusation of blasphemy and for which he was, soon after, assassinated by his guard. In one case, a popular morning show host, Maya Khan, was fired after she sparked controversy for conducting vigilante-style shows in public parks trying to expose young, unmarried couples for their "unIslamic" dating (Dawn 2012).

Even sartorial fashion for Muslims became a niche market that catered to so-called "Muslim sensibilities" with hijab fashion and even shampoos, halal vaccines, and women's dresses advertised by images of female models with veiled faces or decapitated images on billboards.[2] Clearly, the religio-conservative male heads of such fashion houses (including Junaid Jamshed and Shahid Afridi, another cricketer who ventured into fashion) can exploit women's biologies and consumer habits, but with the power to completely erase women's minds, individual identities, and their physical worth and contributions in the process.

This control is not just through exaggeration or amputations of women's images in public visuals. It is also through the spoken advice and wisdom of the self-acclaimed authoritative holy man, even if he is unelected and unaccountable. The bulk of such guidance is reserved for women out of fear of their permanent *fitna* (disruption/chaos) potential or due to Muslim men's own insecurities. Jamshed even reiterated the common advice to Pakistani men to not allow their women to drive, reflecting the popular sentiment that infantilises Muslim women as those who need protection rather than recognising their pursuits for individual identities unless they are serving the Muslim man's or Islam's larger cause.

Feminine aesthetics and the performativity of their pieties remained central themes through this decade, with plenty of liberal-versus-religious views clashing on TV programmes. Even models and actresses appeared on prime-time TV programmes to defend their careers and wardrobe choices against the condemnation of clerics. The "Veena vs the Mullah" incident symbolised this growing tension of women's sexual freedoms against theocratic prescriptions and controls over women's bodily choices (Malik 2011).

It was as if the flux between syncretic and hard-line Pakistani Islam under these embattled War on Terror years was being fought out on Pakistani TV screens each day. There were casualties among Islamic scholars too, and to complicate matters, orthodox and jihadist leaders reversed their stance on an aniconism and decided to propagate their views through regular mainstream media too.

The politics of piety

Politically, the translation of Islamist women's pietist ideologies into pragmatic politics were demonstrated through their governance in the national and provincial legislative assemblies in the War on Terror years. In 2002, an alliance of religious parties, the MuthaidaMajlis-e-Amal (MMA), agreed to support the coup-maker General Pervez Musharraf, which led to their victory in the northern province, Khyber Pukhtunkhwa, which neighbours Afghanistan. Once in power, these religious parties worked towards actively subverting all constitutional women's rights, including the right to vote, legislating for a vice and virtue police to restrain women's mobility in public spaces (Hisba Bill), which essentially attempted to legalise gender apartheid, and to appoint a culture police for the "Promotion of Virtue and Prevention of Vice". It was ultimately disallowed by the Supreme Court in 2006 as a contravention of the Constitution. The campaigns against theatre, films, music, Indian TV/films, and family planning messages were led by women leaders and activists of the Islamist parties who supported such oppressive campaigns and policies. Women's shelters were shut down and participants in sporting activities were harassed and attacked (Brohi 2006). The most symbolic act was the provincial government's order that all mannequins must be removed from shops as they represented the (disembodied) female form in public. All forms of femaleness had to be relegated to the private, domestic realm of the family.

This was the time that the anti-Valentine's Day campaign resurged in Pakistan, but the trenchant sentiment of celebrating love with hearts and cards has been hard to prohibit. It has taken the president of the country and the courts to weigh in with their disapproval and even impose legal bans against its observance in recent time. Realising the futility of state-led attempts at forbidding love, one university decided recently to consecrate the observation by declaring it "Sisters' Day" (Hussain 2019).

Valentine's Day politics is not simply about disapproval of Western practices—it has become a direct religious issue. In 2015, a young woman, Sabeen Mahmud, who had opened a communal space for cultural exchanges and concerts, discussions, and for expanding civic spaces, was assassinated on the streets of Karachi. The assassin, Saad Aziz, was a university graduate who confessed several motivating factors in an interview: "There wasn't one particular reason to target her: she was generally promoting liberal, secular values. There were those campaigns of hers, the demonstration outside Lal Masjid [in Islamabad], *Pyaar ho jaane do* (let there be love) on Valentine's Day and so on. He laughs softly, almost bashfully, as he mentions the last" (Syed Ali and Zaman 2016). Kamila Shamsie (2015) notes that Sabeen's death was "the latest in a series of high-profile assassination attempts (most of them tragically successful) of women in Pakistan who fearlessly take on one group or another that seeks to terrify its opponents into silence".

In 2007, the tipping point of the politics of piety was revealed in the form of the rise of the women of the Jamia Hafsa—the seminary associated with the Lal Masjid (Red Mosque) which had illegally occupied the premises adjoining the mosque land and which Sabeen's assassin mentioned in his confession (above). Their protest was against the government's threat to demolish and reclaim this property (and other illegally constructed mosques in the city) because it was suspected to have become a hotbed for terrorist indoctrination. The madrassa women wore complete black veils, carried banners in English and Urdu, and wore headbands declaring *Sharia ya Shahadat* (Sharia or martyrdom). They carried bamboo sticks and kidnapped a woman from the neighbourhood whom they accused of running a prostitution enterprise. For years following, the head of the institute, Umme Hassan, and her students continued to narrate graphic stories about the atmosphere of death and destruction inside the mosque during the state siege titled, "Operation Silence". Many have appeared on television to mobilise sympathy and support through their stories of grief. This strategy of "truth-telling" and invocation of gendered tropes to counter the official state narrative surrounding the operation has been immensely successful (Yusuf 2011).

In a booklet entitled *Saniha Lal Masjid: Hum Par Kya Guzri* (*The Tragedy of Lal Masjid: What We Suffered*) that was later published by the mosque administration, Umme Hassan narrates the horrors of the siege and cites last wills posted by the residents on the inside walls and pillars of the mosque as the young women allegedly prepared themselves for the possibility of "martyrdom". The two strongest emotions invoked in such textual confessions/narrations are of grief and forfeiture of feminine desires for the larger political cause.

A strategic difference between this more radical group and the other more pietist women of the Al-Huda is that the latter emphasise religious education so that women can raise pious children and families and build more Islamically aligned nations (Ahmad 2009). On the other hand, for mothers of the definitive militant group, Lashkar-e-Tayyaba, their cause is the willingness to sacrifice their sons to become martyrs for the movement and Islamic nation (Haq 2007). The state's perceived willingness to compromise sovereignty to infidels' interests motivated the women of Jamia Hafsa to break out of the private, domestic, and protective sphere, discard their invisibility, and engage in an aggressive moral-cleansing campaign in order to rebuild an Islamic nation state themselves.

Liberal commentators disparagingly viewed these "ninjas", "burqa brigades" and "chicks with sticks" (see Shamsie 2007), commenting on their appearance, and accused them of being mere pawns in the hands of the Red Mosque's male leadership. They cited their impoverished class backgrounds as the reason behind their susceptibility to manipulation by a powerful leadership seeking a popular base. On the other hand, sympathetic scholars (Bano 2012) sanitised altogether the politics of the Lal Masjid by denying its historical role with state-sponsored jihadist strategies (Hussain 2013; Ahmed 2016) and glorifying the social significance that the women disciples of the Jamia Hafsa derive in their roles as mothers, sisters, wives, and daughters as they spread their Islamic learnings. Bano (2012: 146) argues madrassa education and learned piety "empower[s] the girls to deal with material scarcity" and cope with peer pressure against observing Valentine's Day and fashion trends. Such scholars advocate support for Islamic female leadership as a viable alternative to Western feminism.

The important point here is that agentive embodied performances are not always docile but rely on self-construction as authentic moral actors who oppose a supposedly secular state and sexually compromised society. The cultural purity claimed by the Jamia Hafsa women is invested in rigidly patriarchal constructions of gender and sexuality. Their narrative of *Sharia ya Shahdat* (Sharia or martyrdom) supports the discipline and purpose of gendered bodies and prescribes asexual roles and representations in public spaces. The common charge against Islamic militants is that they simply deny women's agency. This was progressively challenged as militants recognised the potential in offering women temporal roles in the insurgency and immortality as martyrs and even at one point, as suicide bombers (Zia 2018).

In retrospect, the post-9/11 decade entrenched piety as a clear political and alternative occupation which included Muslim women authorities and followers. Some sceptics scoff at visions and dreams such as the one claimed by Khan's third and current wife and which reportedly carried the divine instruction for their marriage as part of a condition for his becoming prime minister.[3] But oneirocentrism is an integral part of Islam, including the original revelation. Connecting visions/revelations to the social or political is at the heart of the piety experience and another example of the fusing of the personal with the political. Once repentant, to stop pursuing piety would only result in a lapsed soul. No political leader or born-again celebrity can afford that without risking redundancy.

Although piety is compatible with modern urban life, the beauty of piety is that it can serve as an effective decoy, shield, firewall that deflects from material-based responsibilities. The right to veil as an Islamic obligation or desire distracts from the hard fact that due to the lack of basic rights, women's status in Pakistan remains second from last in global indices. Pietist celebrities cleanse their historical slates of polygamy, divorce, or transgressive sexual behaviour by acquiring a pietist persona and pursuits. This is clear in the case of Veena Malik (mentioned above) who after her encounter with the cleric on TV, responded to the constant pressure of disapproval for her sexually seductive performances by succumbing to male-defined rules. She chose to be rescued by the religio-nationalist model of redemption that demands conformity, straightness, and domesticated sexuality. She married, covered her head, and redirected her seductive skills to lure men towards religious practice.

Veena's case represents a peculiarly Pakistani version of the Madonna-whore complex—one which accepts seductive performances, capitalist enterprises, game shows, and other profane ventures as long as these promise to entice audiences towards piety rather than self-gratifying pleasure. Such performative piety is simply part of the market that offers Islamic consumerism but depends on the same gender dynamics where the male gaze dominates and objectifies women. Repentance turns the subject into a virtuous one even if s/he may be abusive, misogynistic, racist, bigoted, sexually transgressive, a cheater, or a blasphemer. Piety wins votes and has a market share, but the piety industry is not a gender-equal playing field. The patronage of saints or political Islamists is competitive and upper-class patrons monopolise its political value.[4]

On the eve of Pakistan's national election in 2018, two significant events signalled the shifting place of religion in the post-War on Terror period. First, the candidate most favoured by Pakistan's military establishment, Imran Khan, contracted a quick marriage for the third time with his spiritual guide or *Pirni*. She observed the full veil as a departure from the trend of partial or comprehensive unveiling in Pakistan's mainstream politics. There was considerable speculation that their marriage was due to her dream revelation which made their nuptial a condition to his success at the polls. Soon after, a video of the Oxford-educated urbane Khan prostrating and praying at a famed Sufi[5] shrine, as guided by Bushra, went viral and took many liberal supporters by surprise.

Veiling by politically elite women has always been a significant way of capturing and influencing the bourgeois imagination and a relevant signal of the policies of various governments. By definition, an Islamic republic is not a neutral state and so what women wear is always conformist or resistant to religious policy prescription. In an Islamic republic, signifiers like the veil are neither insignificant nor incidental, but have always been a thermometer to measure the cultural milieu and have always held a political role. Khan's announcement of converting Pakistan into a *Riyasat-e-Medina* (a purported welfare state as governed by the Prophet of Islam) confirms how pietist politics is likely to become a serious political project under the schematics of the country's contemporary governance.

Scripts of piety

The well-received and influential work of Saba Mahmood (2005) on Muslim women's piety confirms the politics of this piety and argues how the hijab and other Islamic signifiers are not insignificant or incidental but part of the vocation/career/ aspiration that is piety. Piety is also performance. Mahmood calls it "performance of Islamic gendered virtue" and since performances require props, it is simply a liberal squeamishness that urges restraint from commentary about these props or religious accessories (such as veils, rosary beads, amulets). These are certainly not irrelevant to the practitioners themselves—personally and politically observing women are claiming the choice to veil and acknowledging that they are empowered in their pursuit of piety. The practices of purdah and piety are not one-dimensional but interrelated, and while these are not exclusively restricted to Islamic modesty there is a fundamental, historic, and identifiable gender politics associated with it.

In Pakistan, following the events of 9/11, piety, propriety, and patriarchal traditions are the favoured sites that are being promoted as more culturally and religiously relevant for Muslim women. These are deemed as appropriate replacements to the denouement of Western modernity, secularism, and sexual freedoms in Pakistan. One such site is popular Urdu-language pulp fiction authored by women, and TV programming which thematically promotes the "docile agency" of pious Muslim women who need to be rescued (by Islam). These have print runs of hundreds of thousands and outsell those of "higher" literature. These stand in contrast to feminist poetry of the past that has challenged military dictatorship and religious politics. It is not just vernacular literature; a fair share of post-9/11 English-language fiction has also peddled the leitmotif of Islamic identity for literary profit (Naqvi 2018).

Women's novel-scripts for TV in the 1980s and 1990s carried strains of resistance under the stringent censorious policies of state-owned media and, while not championing feminist causes, managed to open up the contradictions of the prevailing patriarchal ideologies (Kothari 2005). In the millennial pietist novels, the good Muslim woman is more aligned with one who fits into the patriarchal frame of the nation—Muslim, obedient, who accepts her lesser inheritance, opposes Western values, rejects Indian culture, is submissive in an agentive manner, virtuous, sexually abstaining, or active only in the service of her lawful husband, not self-pleasure. In all of this, piety offers a substitute or replacement for material needs, sexual desire, or political rights.

Umera Ahmed is a prolific female writer of Urdu-language pulp fiction, best known for her female-oriented novels that are often compiled from stories that first appear in "digest" or magazine forms. Along with Farhat Ishtiaq and many other contemporary women authors, Ahmed's work comprises a genre of spiritual or contemporary reformist literature (aimed at women's readership) that falls within the broader culture of Islamic hagiography described above. Ahmed is best known for her popular Urdu best-selling story carried in *Shuua Digest, Pir-e-Kamil* (*The Perfect Mentor*, 2003–2004). Ahmed and Ishtiaq's stories/novels have been turned into TV screenplays that have not just been hugely successful in Pakistan but captured hundreds of thousands of Urdu-speaking Muslims in the diaspora.

The recurring plot of these stories involves the trials faced by the Muslim woman protagonist, usually in the form of failures in marriages due to lapsed spiritual self-awareness. The protagonist atypically lives a cycle demonstrating patience, suffering, and resistance as a penalty that is often greater than her sin and which usually involves false aspersions or suspicion around her lapsed sexuality or generally due to the prevailing patriarchal system. Rather than challenging the unjust male dominant societal system, this can be overcome through religious education, pietist practice, and eventually, by forgiveness for those who have been unjust to the unwitting woman. In *Pir-e-Kamil*, redemption and male piety is linked to the rejection of un-Islamic secular careers, such as interest-based banking, and morality in the novel is linked to geopolitics.

In another digest story by Ahmed, *Shehr-e-Zaat* (*A City of the Self*, 2012),[6] the female protagonist is devoid of religious knowledge and it is only after she aspires to self-realisation which leads her to the path of religious knowledge and where *salat* or supplication becomes her priority, that resolution is possible. In the process, she must lose her elite privilege and refute her outward beauty which have not been able to triumph or gain her the fidelity of her husband. Instead, her salvation lies in aspiring to Mahmood's (2005) description of pietist women as those who must cultivate virtuous selves. The lesson is that a woman remains submissive and subservient in a male-dominated society like Pakistan, but her religious knowledge can make her gain some kind of alter-parity over the male gender.

Amjad and Khushi (2017: 37) summarise the metaphor Ahmed deploys in *Shehr-e-Zaat* to explain gender relations in the novel as follows:

> A woman is like a creeper and a man is like a wall. The creeper is always in search of a wall to creep up and gets noticed. The creeper remains in debt to the wall as it assumes that without its support it could not have existed. Hence, it provides shade to the wall and decorates it with its flowers, gives fragrance and even when it dries away it remains glued to the wall. In this relationship the wall gets equally benefitted but it never admits. The wall gets covered, ornamented and protected because of the creeper but it never exhibits its gratitude to the wall because it feels that it was its right to get all those benefits. The relationship between husband and wife is based on same parameters in Pakistan.

The hope in such textual piety that is regularly transcribed for television and which makes it accessible to millions of (unlettered) viewers is that "this process would sooner or later contribute to shifts in the very structures of authority, opening the path for women to become authorized interpreters of religious sources" (Amjad and Khushi 2017: 39). However, the more direct resistance to "structures of authority" that is currently being observed in Pakistan is offered via a very different form of transgressive politics—one that challenges the very cause and expectations of piety, virtuosity, and modesty from women.

Resisting piety

Sexual rights have never been discussed openly in Pakistan. The Zina Ordinance imposed by General Zia in 1979 became a discriminatory and dangerous tool of control over women's sexualities and autonomies and many thousands of women were persecuted under this law for the crime of suspected adultery and non-marital consensual sex (Jahangir and Jilani 1990). The subsequent rise of women's movements challenging this law marked the most serious confrontation against the patriarchal use of religion against sexual autonomy. The activism of women's movements over the next 27 years points to the importance of secular resistance against such religious politics (Zia 2018). However, sex still remains a taboo subject and sexual freedoms is a highly stigmatised concern. Sexual rights remain disguised under the rationale of "reproductive health", or as "life skills" education.

In cases of zina/illicit sex and honour crimes, women's rights activists have always focused on the wrongful accusations against the woman, and the victim narrative dominates the pursuit of justice for accused women even though some women may very well have been "guilty" of sexual transgressions. The reason for this is that acknowledging a woman's sexual transgression makes it impossible to get her justice because of the criminalisation of adultery and consensual sex under Islamic law. So since 1979, activists argued for the repeal of the Zina laws on the principle that the state must not interfere in private matters and demanded courageously that the state should be a secular or neutral entity, but even after the reform of the Zina laws in 2006, they have made no overt demand for sexual freedoms or equality for women.

It took nearly 30 years of lobbying by secular women's movements to reform the Zina laws with the passing of the Protection of Women Act in 2006. This has reportedly resulted in a drastic drop in adultery accusations and prosecutions but is still used as a tool to threaten women if they show signs of any form of transgression. However, the issue of crimes committed in the name of honour remained unresolved due to the framing of a *Qisas and Diyat* Law that permits "forgiveness" of the crime by members of the victim's family.

In 2016, the murder of the risqué social media celebrity Fouzia Azeem (famed under her screen name Qandeel Baloch) reignited consideration of how propriety, secular resistance, and non-traditional sexual expressions represent disruptive, risk-laden, and subversive politics. Unlike Veena Malik, who was also a working-class woman making her way up in the entertainment business, Qandeel Baloch refused to conform to the rules of modesty, piety, or even normative routes to media success. Her provocative online posts began to gain notoriety and curiosity and became political when she included a promise of a strip dance if the Islamic Republic of Pakistan were to win a cricket match against arch-enemy India. In one deft pledge, Qandeel subverted the traditional notion of national honour and also redefined the South Asian practice of forced naked parades of women to shame or disgrace them for alleged sexual transgressions. Pakistani puritans could not make out how to tame this woman who flaunted her body in the Islamic Republic and offered her sexuality as a national duty.

Qandeel's pre-emptive threat-promise sabotaged the male gaze and destabilised sexual politics in the Islamic Republic. Before her murder, she posted on her Facebook account, which was reported to have had nearly 800,000 followers, "I am trying to change the typical orthodox mindset of people who don't wanna come out of their shells of false beliefs and old practices" (Kanj 2016). She had released a music video on YouTube called "Ban", which was a critique of the two-year YouTube ban in Pakistan due to blasphemous content, but which resonated with her own experience of criticism for her performances. She claimed a feminist politics in one post saying, "I am a modern day feminist. I believe in equality. I need not to choose what type of women should be. I don't think there is any need to label ourselves just for sake of society" (Kanj 2016).

But this genius impropriety provoked political tension for pious conservatives, as was clear in the formula confrontation that found Qandeel on a TV programme with the same populist cleric, Mufti Qavi, who had harangued Veena Malik some years earlier. This national broadcast and her subsequent postings of selfies with the cleric at a hotel meeting were said to have been the final provocation for her brother who decided to murder her, abetted by other men, for her cultural and religious irreverence, which apparently shamed him/them.

The passing of the Protection against Harassment at the Workplace Act in 2010 by Pakistan's legislature predated the global #MeToo movement which has recently gathered momentum in Pakistan, but it was the murder of Qandeel Baloch that led to the pragmatic step of finally pushing through the amended Anti-Honour Killing Laws (Criminal Amendment Bill) 2015 which was shelved due to resistance by the religious parties in the national Parliament (Zaidi 2016). The very recent verdict in Qandeel's murder case where the court has indicted her brother for the crime after denying his recourse to "forgiveness" by her parents is a signifier of the potential turn in the legal and social narrative around sexuality, honour crimes, the state's responsibility, and gender normativity.

The first *Aurat March* (Women's March) as a protest movement inspired by the global #MeToo movement was organised by young feminists in 2018, but by the following year activism against sexual harassment had increased in numbers and geographical spread, and was amplifying the anxiety of the gatekeepers of patriarchy. This was evident in the severe backlash from conservative and even some like-minded quarters in reaction to the provocative slogans and hard-hitting jabs at masculinist norms carried by the marchers in their street gatherings across several cities (Nizam 2019). These were powerful reminders of a deeply entrenched religio-cultural patriarchal privilege that is jealously guarded in Pakistan. Most of these objectionable posters were challenging male norms of propriety and sexual harassment and some even carried refrains of LGBTQ+ politics, unprecedented in Pakistan's public sphere. Consistent with their record, the women of religious organisations of the Minhajul Quran and the Jamaat-e-Islami outright condemned and despaired at the International Women's Day *Aurat March*—an event that otherwise the women's wing of the Jamaat has historically supported and celebrated in its own framing of women's rights. Under the false objections to impropriety, the far more serious hostility to the *Aurat March* was because it staged sex and sexual rights on to the public agenda.

In a recent study of women audiences' reception of TV religious shows in Karachi, Kazj (2018) finds dissenting women viewers deem many of these prescriptions "out of sync with the values of human rights, individual autonomy, and citizen equality. These values are not only guaranteed under Pakistan's Constitution but also constitute the basis for organizing urban, middle-class life in Pakistan". This is an important departure from previous studies that present Muslim women's piety as a form of dissonance based on rejection of liberal or secular alternatives, careers, or imaginings altogether.[7]

One such TV show is hosted by the conservative commentator Orya Maqbool Jan, who dedicated an entire programme to castigating the *Aurat March* for its obscenity. For days and weeks, the women organisers of the March were trolled, abused, and even threatened with violence for daring to publicise the cause of normative sexual violence. Many of these regular conscientious objectors of feminist protests are not just clerics but male celebrities, including popular actors such as Shaan and Hamza Ali Abbasi, who sermonise on religious prescriptions on women's propriety on social media. The twining of religio-entertainment is laced with a patriarchal populist force that is sometimes challenged by a feminist consciousness from within and outside the industry, but the pietist bent serves less as some interrupter or challenger to authority and more as a prop and facilitator to the male-defined Islamic gendered order.

Conclusion

Pakistani women's sexual defiance as an expression of avoiding or resisting conformance to male-prescribed piety and the more impious challenges to the authoritative monopoly of traditional male scholars are likely to prove more confrontational in Pakistan in the coming years. All those who had invested in piety as the antidote to militant or political forms of religion will have to revisit their theories of how there is some mild, apolitical, and benign alternative to religious politics that can be found within the realm of Islam. The hope invested in the emergence of "divergent rationalities" emerging from Islamist competitiveness has failed in repeated examples of the emergence of unlikely pietist leaders launching new religio-political movements, sometimes sectarian, and, more recently, to safeguard any perceived effort to reform Pakistan's rigid blasphemy laws.

Joan W. Scott has challenged the conventional understanding that secular arrangements and sexual freedoms are guarantors of tolerant practices in Western countries. Redefined as the sexular, Scott argues that religion is seen as a powerful counterforce to a favoured way of thinking about sexuality. In Western states and within their policies on migration and national identity, sexuality has replaced religion as the body-politics and even Muslims in those contexts depend on this notion by their defiant insistence on wearing a headscarf as a sign of a "sexy", transgressive authentic identity. As Verkaaik and Spronk (2011: 86) summarise this shifting relationship, "Another way to put it is that sexuality is now as holy as religion is sexy".

However, in Pakistan's Muslim majority context, the veil, piety, sexual modesty, and an overall adherence to the Islamic gendered order are the props of performativity associated with social, legal, and political conformity for the female body-politic. Here, Muslim men remain custodians and spokesmen of theology, while Muslim women are the ecclesiastical icons who are tasked to promote its politics by wearing (or removing) its symbols or jostling for some share within the politics of this piety discourse. There is no equation of sexuality or sexual freedoms as a fundamental right and the price for transgression and claims to sexual autonomies remain risky and sometimes deadly when publicised across the range of media expressions discussed earlier.

Notes

1 Declared a heretic community in Pakistan.
2 Figurative imagery is considered to be prohibited in Islam; however, the place of art and figures within Islamic history is so diverse that this is more of a common-sensical practice to refute idolatry rather than a fixed legal or cultural policy.
3 In a TV interview that followed the appointment of Imran Khan as Prime Minister, Bushra Imran denied any such divine revelation and stressed how she waited for the mandatory three-month time lag required in Islam after divorce from her previous husband and before marrying Imran Khan.
4 The murders of reformist Islamic scholars and Junaid Jamshed's "forgiveness" for blasphemous comments are just a few examples. A progressive scholar is murdered for no proven accusation while a self-confessed blasphemer gets welcomed back into the Islamists' fold. The privilege of blasphemy lies clearly between and among Islamists who wield it as a power tool.
5 Mystical Islamic belief popular in South Asia.
6 *Shehr-e-Zaat* was first published in *Khawateen Digest*. It, along with five other unrelated stories, was then compiled and published in book form as a collection under the title *Main Ne Khuwabon Ka Shajar Dekha Hai*.
7 It should be noted, though, that the bulk of studies on women's piety have focused on the province of Punjab, which has a history of social and political religious conservativism, while Kazi's study is on the cosmopolitan and multi-ethnic and pluralistic city of Karachi.

References

Ahmad, Sadaf. 2009. *Transforming Faith; The Story of Al-Huda and Islamic Revivalism Among Urban Pakistani Women*. New York: Syracuse University Press.
Ahmad, Umera. 2000. *Meri Zaat Zar-e-Benishan*. Lahore: Ilam-o-Irfan Publishers.
Ahmad, Umera. 2003–2004. *Pir e Kamil*. Shuua Digest.
Ahmad, Umera. 2012. *Shehr e Zaat*. Khawateen Digest.
Ahmed, Khaled. 2016. *Sleepwalking to Surrender: Dealing with Terrorism in Pakistan*. Penguin/Viking.
Amjad, Heena and Khushi, Qamar. 2017. "Islamic path to self-realization: Application of feminist poststructuralist discourse analysis to 'Shehr-e-Zaat'". *Pakistan Journal of Islamic Research*, 18(1).
Aziz, Sadaf. 2005. "Beyond petition and redress: Mixed legality and consent in marriage in Pakistan". *Bayan; Bi-Annual Socio-Legal Journal. Marital Law and Customary Practices*, 4: 58.
Aziz, Sadaf. 2011. "Making a sovereign state: Javed Ghamidi and 'enlightened moderation'," *Modern Asian Studies* 45(3): 597–629.
Bano, Masooda. 2012. *The Rational Believer; Choices and Decisions in the Madrasas of Pakistan*. Ithaca: Cornell University Press.
Brohi, Nazish. 2006. "*The MMA Offensive; Three Years in Power 2003–2005*." Monograph. Islamabad: Action Aid.
Cheema, Shahbaz A. 2013. "An analysis of women's contribution to the gender discourse of Jamaat-i-Islami of Pakistan". *Wagadu: A Journal of Transnational Women's and Gender Studies*, No 11, 79–90.
Daniels, Timothy P. 2013. "'Islamic' TV dramas, Malay youth, and pious visions for Malaysia", in T.P. Daniels (ed) *Performance, Popular Culture, and Piety in Muslim Southeast Asia*. New York: Palgrave Macmillan.
Dawn. 2012. "Firing of TV host a victory for Pakistani liberals". *Dawn*, 29 January (accessed 6 October 2019), www.dawn.com/news/691699.

Hashmi, Farhat. 2019. "Kya Shohar Zabardasti Hambistri Kar Sakta Hay" (accessed 7 October 2019), www.youtube.com/watch?v=wUefgcrXIQs&feature=youtu.be&t=25.
Haq, Farhat. 2007. "Militarism and motherhood: The women of the Lashkar-i-Tayyabia in Pakistan." *Signs: Journal of Women in Culture and Society*, 32: 4.
Hussain, Kashif. 2019. "Valentine's Day now Sisters' Day: Faisalabad varsity to 'promote Islamic traditions' on Feb 14". *Dawn*, January 13 (accessed 6 October 2019), www.dawn.com/news/1457290.
Hussain, Zahid. 2013. *The Scorpion's Tail: The Relentless Rise of Islamic Militants in Pakistan–And How It Threatens America*. New York: Free Press.
Jahangir, Asma and Jilani, Hina. 1990. *The Hudood Ordinances: A Divine Sanction?* Lahore: Rohtas Books.
Iqtidar, Humeria. 2011. *Secularizing Islamists? Jama'at-e-Islami and Jama'at-ud-Da'wa in Urban Pakistan*. Chicago: Chicago University Press.
Kanj, Tala. 2016. "Qandeel Baloch died a feminist hero". *Global Comment*, July 21 (accessed 6 October 2019), http://globalcomment.com/qandeel-baloch-died-a-feminist-hero/.
Khan, Mrs. 2019. "Mrs. Khan blasts on newly married girls". *Subh Saveray Pakistan* (accessed 7 October 2019), www.youtube.com/watch?v=gSuvByFd02c.
Kothari, Suchi. 2005. "From genre to *Zanaana*: Urdu television drama serials and women's culture in Pakistan". *Contemporary South Asia*, 14(3), 289–305.
Mahmood, Saba. 2005. *Politics of Piety; The Islamic Revival and the Feminist Subject*. Princeton: Princeton University Press.
Maqsood, Ammara. 2017. *The New Pakistani Middle Class*. Cambridge, MA: Harvard University Press.
Maududi, SyedAbul Ala. 2000. *Khawateen aur deenimasayl*. Lahore: Islamic Publications.
Maududi, SyedAbul Ala. 2002. *Taleemat*. Lahore: Islamic Publications.
Maududi, SyedAbul Ala. 2003. *Purdah*. Lahore: Islamic Publications.
Maududi, SyedAbul Ala. 2010. First published 1940. *Purdah and the Status of Woman in Islam*. Translated from Urdu and edited by Al-Ash'ari. Lahore: Mohit Publications.
Malik, Veena. 2011. "Pakistani actress Veena Malik defies Mullah accusing her of immoral behaviour" (accessed 7 October 2019), www.youtube.com/watch?v=qi945O_F5Jk.
Metcalf, Barbara D. 1990. *Perfecting Women: Maulana Ashraf Ali Thanawi's Bihishti Zewar* (a partial translation with commentary). New Delhi: Oxford University Press.
Mushtaq, Faiza. 2010. "A controversial role model for Pakistani women". *South Asia Multidisciplinary Academic Journal*, 4 (accessed 7 October 2019), http://samaj.revues.org/index3030.html.
Naqvi, Maniza. 2018. "Pakistani English fiction's search for approval and recognition". *Monthly Herald*, March (accessed 6 October 2019), https://herald.dawn.com/news/1154041/pakistani-english-fictions-search-for-approval-and-recognition.
Nizam, Maadiha. 2019. "Aurat March 2019: When the streets of Karachi thumped with the echoes of 'azaadi'". *The News*, March 8 (accessed 6 October 2019), www.thenews.com.pk/latest/441327-aurat-march-2019-when-the-streets-of-karachi-thumped-with-the-echoes-of-azaadi.
Robinson, Francis. 2008. "Islamic reform and modernities in South Asia". *Modern Asian Studies*, 42, 259–281.
Shahid, Kunwar K. 2015. "Murderous televangelism". *The Friday Times* (accessed 6 October 2019), www.thefridaytimes.com/murderous-televangelism/.
Shamsie, Kamila. 2007. "Misguided women". *New Statesman*, April 30 (accessed 6 October 2019), www.newstatesman.com/middle-east/2007/04/female-students-women-pakistan.

Shamsie, Kamila. 2015. "Murdered on the streets of Karachi: My friend who dared to believe in free speech". *The Guardian*, April 27 (accessed 6 October 2019), www.theguardian.com/commentisfree/2015/apr/27/murdered-karachi-free-speech-sabeen-mahmud.

Syed Ali, N. and Zaman, Fahim. 2016. "Anatomy of a murder". *Herald*, September (accessed 6 October 2019), http://herald.dawn.com/news/1153209.

Thanawi, Muhammad A.A. 1999. Original 1905–6. *Bihisthi Zevar*. Karachi: Zam Zam Publishers.

Van Nieuwkerk, Karin (ed) 2011. *Muslim Rap, Halal Soaps, and Revolutionary Theater. Artistic Developments in the Muslim World*. Austin, TX: University of Texas Press.

Verkaaik, Oskar and Rachel Spronk. 2011. "Sexular practice: Notes on an ethnography of secularism". *Focaal: Journal of Global and Historical Anthropology*, 59, 83–88.

Yusuf, Huma. 2011. "The future of Pakistan". *U.S. Institute for Peace*, January 31 (accessed 6 October 2019), www.c-spanvideo.org/program/297769-1.

Zaidi, Hassan B. 2016. "Anti-honour killing, anti-rape bills finally passed". *Dawn*, October 7 (accessed 6 October 2019), www.dawn.com/news/1288569.

Zia, Afiya Shehrbano. 2018. *Faith and Feminism in Pakistan: Religious Agency or Secular Autonomy?* Brighton: Sussex Academic Press.

7

THE COST OF DOING THEIR JOB ONLINE

Harassment of women journalists

Ayesha Khan

Online harassment or trolling of women journalists is a pernicious problem the world over. However, its scope is hard to quantify owing to unreported cases. Though trolling goes beyond gender, these technological attacks are assuming a uniquely gendered dimension (Citron 2009: 374) because of their profound effect on targeted women. Trolling of women manifests in many forms, such as name-calling, shaming, embarrassing publicly, blackmailing, intimidation, belittling their work, cyberstalking, and rape and murder threats.

In this chapter, I present the case of Pakistani women journalists aggressively trolled for their professional work. I anchor my work around women journalists within a constructivist approach through semi-structured interviews taking, alongside, theoretical considerations of the overlapping liberal feminism and post-feminist theories.

I argue that the primary reason these women receive more threats and abuse online than their male counterparts is that their work is either considered by the trolling armies as the "male domain" (such as politics and terrorism) or is challenging prevalent normative societal attitudes (for instance coverage of minorities and LGBTI&Q communities).

The purpose of this chapter is not to invalidate the abuse or threats male journalists in Pakistan may face, but to explore the nature of abuse and threats to women journalists, and analyse their response mechanism.

In making this argument, I have two goals. First, to present an agentic view in which these women journalists operate and struggle to have human agency to make choices that can impact the world. My second goal is to explore the nature and frequency of this harassment for understanding and combating the harm inflicted by this abuse and threats. These goals, in turn, provide the basis for the three research questions this study endeavours to answer: (1) What kind of online abuse and threats do women journalists face in Pakistan? (2) What are their response mechanisms to combat online abuse and threats? (3) What support, if any, is available/offered from their employer media organisations?

I start with sketching a theoretical framework with the help of the fundamental assumptions of liberal feminism and post-feminism to address the issue. I then explain my methodological approach, which is based on semi-structured interviews. Later, I support my argument with literature and scholarship in the field before I present my findings and analysis of the participants' responses during the interviews. In the last section, I document and analyse major trends in the participants' responses to show that online harassment is like street harassment that aims to restrict women's speech and movement and debase their agency. Lastly, I conclude with some suggestions.

Theoretical underpinnings

This chapter empirically focuses on the online environment in which women journalists in Pakistani media organisations operate and struggle, and on examining and determining the gender predisposition, in the online sphere, as a reaction to their work.

It will be a truism to state that women journalists, with their increased presence in the media industries, continue to change the shape of the media sector, both in Pakistan and globally. Thus the acknowledgment of their individualistic right to create a public domain in mainstream media through their actions and choices is central to understanding the theoretical underpinning of this study. This position focuses on the core issue of "the removal of barriers to the achievement of equality with men" (Bruce et al. 2010: 20). These women will not be accepted and abuse-free in the blogosphere unless their voices and opinions are taken as seriously as those of men. Theoretically, the fundamental assumptions of liberal feminism and post-feminism address the conundrums around these issues—their rights to equality in free speech and online safety from oppression through online harassment—and are the driving force behind the conduct of this study.

Fundamentally, liberal feminist thinking argues that women have the equal right to visibility and acknowledgement as their male counterparts within the existing structures of the media (MacKinnon 1987; Cudd 2006; Sommers 1994; Kian and Hardin 2009). It resonates with the ideology behind post-feminism that speaks to women in contemporary public society where they are free, safe, empowered, acknowledged for the universality of their experiences, and not misappropriated or commodified. It holds the position that (women in media) must "catch up with their actual social position" and provide "a more accurate view" of their struggles and experiences (Bruce et al. 2010: 20). In the context of my study, this approach significantly helps in characterising the online abuse and threats to women journalists in Pakistan, and in creating awareness among media organisations and the audience about the scope of exploitation of women journalists with both visible and light online presence.

Methodology

The prime objective of this study is to map and examine the online gendered harassment directed at women journalists in Pakistani media. The identification of the existence of the problem is the foremost step in examining the dominant narratives in online misogyny. Only then can the next level of examining the language be achieved. The fundamental question that kick-starts the discourse around online gendered harassment is: Do women journalists in Pakistan face online threats, abuse, and harassment?

The answer to this question not only forms the basis of my research but also serves as a starting point for future research. Based on semi-structured interviews with 17 women journalists in Lahore, Karachi, and Islamabad, conducted May 2016–October 2016, I explore this question to analyse the nature and consequences of the practice of online abuse as well as the threats targeted at these women for their work.

These 17 women journalists were part of an earlier cohort of 53 women journalists surveyed between May 2015 and August 2015 for a similar study for a paper presented at a global media conference at the University of Oslo. These 17 participants were selected using a non-probability (purposive) sampling strategy—the snowballing technique—based on their availability and consent to participate in the semi-structured interviews for this research. They served as what Lindlof and Shatzer (1998) refer to as "informants" to generate data in information-rich cases.

One of the participants was affiliated with a Pashto-language newspaper, three with Urdu-language media outlets, and 13 of them with English-language publications. Only 2 of the 17 interviewees were affiliated with state-run media, while the rest worked for privately owned media houses with a visible online presence and following.

I contacted respondents through the press clubs, Women Journalists Pakistan, a national body of active women journalists; the Women Media Centre, a not-for-profit organisation working for the rights of women in the Pakistani media; and Digital Journalists of Pakistan, a closed Facebook group for journalists.

The questions were straightforward, mostly open-ended, to solicit relatively subjective responses from the participants. The aim was to ensure that the participants open up at their convenience to tell their stories and experiences—something Hocking et al. (2003) refer to as "the text in their story". They claim "in-depth interview provides understanding [and allows] the researcher to move in different directions, take time to see that all approaches, theories/ideas have been explored. It also allows interviewees to tell …; the text is their story" (Lindlof and Shatzer 1998: 211).

While the participants who wished to remain anonymous are referred to as participant A, B, C, and so on, others have been named. I have analysed participants' responses and the significant trends emerging from these responses below. However, before furthering my argument and presenting the findings, it is essential here to have a clearer picture of the use of technological spaces for harassment of these women, both globally and in Pakistan.

Global and Pakistani background

Interrogating the online media sphere in Pakistan concerning lexicons of gendered harassment does not only elucidate the links between women journalists and the use of online media spaces for voicing their opinion, it additionally helps map the intersections between feminism and dominant discourses in technological spaces in the country. Therefore, to explore these links and the issue in a holistic manner and to understand the complexities and rationale of this study, it is crucial to first establish an understanding of the role of women journalists in the Pakistani media sphere. It will further help dissect the intent behind the trollers' exploitation of the public and media sphere against these women with a voice.

Notably, Pakistan is the home country of Nobel-laureate Malala Yousafzai, the world's youngest women blogger from a conflict-ridden zone, targeted for raising her voice through writing and advocating regional peace by campaigning for girls' education. Unfortunately, Malala is not alone. According to the International Federation of Journalists' 24th annual country list published in 2014, Pakistan was termed as the world's most dangerous country for journalists.[1] Three years earlier, in 2011, a Thomson Reuters Foundation expert poll put Pakistan third on the list of most dangerous countries for women.[2]

Wrestling between their identities as women and journalists in Pakistan has exposed them to many facets of the multi-dimensional picture of abuse and threats during their work, both offline and online. The same multi-dimensional facets of this issue further serve as a theoretical eclecticism informing this work, which is both an advantage and a disadvantage in terms of understanding and assessing the scope and range of the issue. It is also because of the increasing number of women journalists in the Pakistani media.

Less than a decade ago, there were very few women in journalism in Pakistan. The advent of the age of online journalism and the ever-increasing number of television channels in Pakistan has nurtured the number of women journalists in the profession. However, women journalists are still a limited number in Pakistan—only 5% of the journalism industry in the country (Nusrat 2018). Those working in the country's conflict zones and covering hard issues are even fewer. In 2015, the International Federation of Journalists (IFJ) published a special report on media and gender in Pakistan, *Country Report: Media and Gender in Pakistan*. According to this report, there were only 20 women journalists in the northwestern province of Khyber Pakhtunkhwa compared to an overwhelming 380 of their male counterparts. Between 2012 and 2015, the province welcomed only 4 women journalists, whereas another study of women journalists in Khyber Pakhtunkhwa revealed that there were 16 women journalists in the province (Shabir 2012: 299). The IFJ (2015) study revealed that in Balochistan, geographically Pakistan's largest province, there were only 2 women journalists, compared to at least 133 male counterparts.

According to the study, there are no women journalists in the Federally Administered Tribal Areas (FATA), a region merged into Khyber Pakhtunkhwa in 2019. No women journalists work in the other major cities of Khyber Pakhtunkhwa, which include Swat, Hangu, Bannu, and Dera Ismail Khan. Those covering news and writing about issues such as war and conflict and blasphemy in these regions are mostly based in the country's bigger metropolitan areas, where they work from the media organisations' head offices, which are primarily based in Lahore, Karachi, and the capital, Islamabad.

The IFJ report further suggests that over half of Pakistan's women journalists work for publications that also publish online editions (53.16%); another 18% work exclusively for online media. These statistics show a growing volume of online media content produced by women reporters. But with an increasing online presence, women in media industries are also facing myriad new challenges, particularly since 2014–15.

In Pakistan, online trolling of women journalists accelerated in 2016 following the murder of Pakistani social media celebrity Qandeel Baloch. In the name of honour, she was strangulated to death by her brother in July 2016. In her brief career, Baloch had received rape and murder threats multiple times. She would share these threats on her social media accounts. Baloch's assassination sparked a debate on social media on women's rights to safety. Feminists were calling for country-wide public sit-ins to register their repudiation of violence against women. Mural artists were painting Baloch on public walls. Social media users were changing their profile pictures to express solidarity with Baloch and condemn "honour" crimes against women.

On the other hand, women journalists were vigorously using their voice to condemn Baloch's murder and the inefficiency of the state and social media platforms to stop the abuse and threats and provide her safety in her lifetime. They were questioning the safety and the rights of women in Pakistan, and calling for the government to introduce an anti-"honour" killing bill. In Pakistan, feminism, both online and offline, was finally entering a new wave,[3] and online, women journalists were the easiest targets. There were two primary reasons. First, because they were publicly challenging patriarchy, and second, they were demanding an equitable balance of power in free speech. This takes us back to my point made earlier about the core issue of the barriers to the achievement of equality, where I argue that society failed to acknowledge these women's individual right to create a public domain in mainstream media because their voices and opinions are not taken as seriously as those of men.

To further understand the dynamics of these reasons, it would be useful to note that Pakistan is a patriarchal society with phenomenal gender inequalities (Ali et al. 2011; Shaheed 1986). Women's subordination continues to be preserved, and they are traditionally excluded from the decision-making process (Khawaja 2017: 99; Mahmood et al. 2012). The media industries are no exception, as I have shown above.

Online spaces such as Facebook and Twitter give these women agency to speak and create discourses of individualism and (liberal) feminism. Unsurprisingly, all this is seen as a threat to deeply entrenched patriarchy. It can be done by concealing one's identity. However, online spaces can make personal identities vulnerable to exposure, consequently making social media a volatile space for users, especially women journalists whose identities are seldom kept hidden due to public exposure.

When these women perpetuate ideas in their capacity as journalists, they are met with resistance that can sometimes take an ugly form of abuse, threats, and harassment. One such women journalist is Amber Shamsi, who, in a BBC report, shared her story of online harassment: "Popular insults include 'slut', 'prostitutes', or worse ... These can range from invitations for sex to descriptions of rape fantasies to graphic images".

For Saba Eitizaz, a BBC staff reporter based in Pakistan, the threats came after she covered a story on acid attack victims in the country. In one case, her harasser had called her on the phone, recited her address and went on to say, "You report on acid attacks on women. Let's give you a first-hand taste of what it's like". In 2018, Asma Shirazi, a senior Pakistani journalist, became the target of harsh online hate and abuse after her interview with the former prime minister, Nawaz Sharif. Mr Sharif was going to a Supreme Court trial at the time. She was called "whore", "slut", and a "western agent".

But is there anyone who is listening to these women journalists and documenting their experiences? Apparently, not many.

The missing literature

In Pakistan, the challenges faced by journalists such as safety issues and threats have captured the attention of both practitioners and scholars across disciplines (Ricchiardi 2012; Yusuf et al. 2013; Aslam 2015). However, analysing the gendered experiences of journalists, especially online, largely remains an underexplored area in media scholarship. There is some scholarship that helps understand the problem, find its solution, or analyse the nature of the online blitzkrieg of abuse and threats confronting women journalists globally.

The Organization for Security and Co-operation in Europe, a European security body, has been among the first few to identify, highlight, and warn against the growing number of online threats faced by women journalists. Several studies (Perrin 2015; Hess 2017) suggest that it is enough to be a woman to be the biggest reason for being trolled online. This is referred to as gendered harassment and forms the basis of online misogyny, which, according to Chemaly (2014) has steadily increased since 2013. She writes that harassment is basically "men asserting dominance, silencing, and frequently, scaring and punishing them". This type of harassment also includes rape and death threats. It is evident through research that some situations, for instance, war and conflict, leave women journalists more vulnerable to abuse and threats than some other cases (Ghaffar 2005; Steiner 2017). However, it is equally crucial to comprehend that it doesn't always have to be a war zone for a woman journalist to be exposed to risks and threats such as abuse and harassment. Sometimes these risks creep into their inboxes, Facebook pages, Instagram accounts, Twitter feeds, and other public or personal social media accounts.

The missing literature in academia demonstrates the need for growing scholarly attention on the subject both globally and in Pakistan, where research on the issue is explicitly missing. The question here arises that if this issue has not received adequate scholarly or media attention in Pakistan, then what avenues are available to document this abuse faced by women journalists in the country? In the following section, I examine the relevant law and services offered by the not-for-profit organisations in the country and assess whether or not these have helped women journalists facing online abuse and threats in the country.

Cyber Crime Law 2016 and the hopes beyond

Before furthering my research, it is at this point crucial to examine any public and private intervention in combating the growing trend of online abuse against women journalists in Pakistan. It will help conceptualise their experiences in digital spaces vis-à-vis reliable state-level and non-governmental support available to them.

State-level legal intervention was initiated in 2016 in the form of the Cyber Crime Law. When I first started conducting interviews for this study, the Cyber Crime Law 2016 was not yet promulgated. Arguably, what eventually led to the promulgation of the Law was that Pakistani women journalists had started to come out with their accounts of online abuse and threats hurled at them for their work and voicing their opinion, especially about "honour" killing and feminism. The way to the Law had first started with The Prevention of Electronic Crimes Act, 2015, finally leading to the passing of the Law in August 2016. The Law has been widely criticised for being controversial and draconian. Digital rights activists, members of the opposition, and lawyers pointed out that it only focused on online criticism of religion, the country, its courts, and the armed forces, and completely ignored the digital safety of the people at large, including journalists as well as other professional writers. Since its passing, not a single case has been filed by a journalist (male or female) in four years, raising concerns about the victims' decision to remain silent due to external pressure.

However, grappling with the trivialisation of this online gendered harassment and the inefficiency of the under-resourced state-run National Response Center for Cyber Crime, there is some hope on a private level.

In March 2017, a Pakistani journalist founded the Pakistani chapter of the Coalition for Women in Journalism, which offers mentorship to women journalists subjected to abuse and harassment. Separately, in August 2015, a digital safety helpdesk had been set up at Media Matters for Democracy, a local media development organisation, in the capital city of Islamabad. The helpdesk, set up in collaboration with UNESCO Islamabad, aims to assist women journalists with issues related to digital security such as online harassment, abuse, and threats. The Digital Rights Foundation was another initiative, set up in 2012 by a lawyer/activist. The Foundation focuses on many issues of digital space, including online free speech, privacy, and online violence against women journalists. While these organisations continue to work in major cities of the country, at the same time, this fosters a particular concern about the productivity of these organisations, which can be looked into separately.

Evidence/findings

In this section, I have documented the main findings of this study (which answer the first research question), before moving on to the empirical manifestations and analysis of the interviews (which further explore question 1, and also answer the second and the third research questions). Here, I have also documented the responses to questions about the lexical choices of trollers asked as core indicator for exploring the nature and frequency of online abuse and threats received by these women journalists in Pakistan (Table 7.1). Five main themes surfaced during the participatory interviews with the 17 women journalists, after the prevalence of online threats and abuse was established through their responses:

1. These women journalists received rampant online hate and abuse, irrespective of their religious/ethnic and organisational background and affiliation;
2. The abuse invoked their expertise, sexuality, and gender in ways that interfered with their self-worth, identity, social status, agency, livelihood, productivity, and mental wellbeing;

TABLE 7.1 Nature and frequency of threats and abuse received by women journalists in the Pakistani media, May–October 2016

Participant	Threats/abuse received via:				
	Facebook	Twitter	Email	Website/blog comment	Rape/murder threat
1	Yes	Yes	Yes	Yes	Yes
2	Yes	Yes	No	Yes	No
3	No	No	Yes	Yes	No
4	Yes	No	Yes	Yes	Yes
5	Yes	No	Yes	Yes	No
6	Yes	No	Yes	Yes	No
7	Yes	Yes	No	Yes	No
8	Yes	Yes	Yes	Yes	No
9	Yes	Yes	No	Yes	No
10	Yes	Yes	Yes	Yes	No
11	Yes	Yes	Yes	Yes	No
12	Yes	Yes	No	Yes	No
13	Yes	Yes	Yes	Yes	Yes
14	Yes	No	Yes	N/A	No
15	Yes	Yes	No	Yes	No
16	Yes	Yes	Yes	Yes	Yes
17	Yes	No	Yes	Yes	No
Total: 17	16 (94%)	11 (65%)	12 (71%)	16 (94%)	4 (24%)

Source: Author

3. There is no record of cases that went unreported, where victims had preferred silence over reporting the incident;
4. Participants had been subjected to online harassment, abuse, and threats mostly by email and on social networking sites such as Facebook and Twitter;
5. Most trollers resorted to sexually and racially charged abuse and insults immersed in patronising misogyny.

A common trend that appeared in their responses was the mention of lewd curse words that were sexually and racially charged. These included words such as "whore", "*gashti/randi*" (the Urdu-language word for a sex worker), "need a big dick", "*kaalamoun*" (meaning blackface in the Urdu-language), "*kaaliphuddi*" (meaning dark/black women genitalia), "*lunkibhook*" (meaning hungry for a dick in the Urdu-language), "sexually frustrated", "lesbian", "bitch", "desperate for attention", "focus on getting laid", "quit reporting", and "Indian or American agents". Such forms of lingual exchange among internet users demonstrates misogynistic behaviour patterns online.

Four of the total 17 participants revealed that they had received emails with rape threats (24%), while 16 of them (94%) said trollers had made inappropriate, abusive, or threating comments either on the official websites of their media organisations or their blogs. Four women revealed that two or more commenters had at least once made fun of them as a pair or a group on public pages where their work had been shared. For 16 of these 17 women (94%), the abuse landed in their Facebook messenger inbox, 11 of them (65%) received it via Twitter, and 12 (71%) through direct emails. Six of them said they had received abuse on each of these platforms. None of the participants had been safe from online abuse/threats, with its intensity and frequency varying from participant to participant. For instance, the abuse coupled with death and rape threats were received where women journalists were accused of being "Indian or American" agents. It was more common when they were reporting for international media or working as freelance journalists for American or Indian media organisations.

Analysis: Mapping empirical manifestations

As discussed earlier, this chapter primarily focuses on the exploration of the language of abuse and threats received by women journalists in Pakistan. The additional focus is on their coping mechanisms and the organisational and state response. In this section, I have analysed the participants' responses during the interviews, documented significant trends, and argued, with supporting literature, that online harassment parallels street harassment, which is in general aimed at women to restrict their speech and movement with explicit intentions to debase their agency. Such contentious voices stem from socially and culturally patriarchal and misogynist depictions of public space, such as cyberspace, that is perpetuated as a manifestation of male dominance and control.

From offers of sex to rape and death threats

I observed during the interviews that for some of the participants, the sexist and misogynistic language of the abuse intersected with other forms of oppression that included homophobic and racist comments. For instance, in participant A's case, in May 2016 her blog and her stories on two other websites were attacked by an anonymous individual who commented with the pen name "Me007", and suggested that she should be "taught a lesson" for demanding equal rights for the Ahmadiyya community in Pakistan. The comment read: "Teri jaisigashti … Tujhay tab hi sabak mile ga" ("A whore like you needs a dick, not journalism reporting. You will only learn a lesson then").

She said the same comment was copied and pasted on all three websites and appeared with the same name. She requested her editors to remove the comments, which appeared again two days after they removed the first set. As she explained, "This showed that the person was frequently checking my stories online. I felt like I was watched every time I took public transport to and from work". If read carefully, this comment was an ugly, euphemistic rape threat.

Another participant (P) also shared that an anonymous person kept sending her the same content via different email addresses for three weeks. These emails carried the same "offers for sex" and graphic pornographic images of men and woman. The message read: *"i f**k ur … like man in picture this is fun to your silly reporting of no use!!! U wnt sex with me i give u fun* [sic]".

She further explained: "For the first time, I received the email twice a week; then the next week only once. In the third week, it was sent on three consecutive days. I kept blocking the email address, but the same content was sent from a different email address every time, until it stopped one day". The question here arises: why are some trolls so persistent?

One argument can be intentional, regular intimidation to frighten these women. Herring et al. (2002: 152) write that harassers online necessarily rely on language and actions that intimidate and silence and particularly scare women. The reoccurrence of abusive and threating messages, emails, or comments tend to do that. If participant A or P had not received these threats and abuse repetitively, they might not have been as affected and scared as they said they got when it kept coming back in the same form. These behaviour patterns are fundamentals of patriarchy, and media scholars have long been troubled by violence against women journalists—defining it as the use of patriarchal force against their gender and free speech to intimidate and silence their [feminist] voices and participation in political and social discourse.

However, since the turn of the century, this intimidation and threat have taken a new form and have moved to online spaces in addition to offline, making it harder to detect its source. This online abuse and intimidation varies from abusive DMs (direct messages) in their social media inboxes and comments on their online work to threatening emails sent to their work or personal email accounts. It includes, but is not limited to, slut-shaming, name-calling, stalking, dishonouring their work and effort, intimidation, sexual references, and in most cases outright sexual harassment, and rape and death threats. Another participant, Luavut Zahid, a Lahore-based freelance journalist who works for several English-language print and online newspapers, said she was also targeted by a "regular commenter" specifically for her work around missing persons in Balochistan and LGBTI&Q rights. She said: "I received rape and death threats, which were later extended to my family, too. On several occasion, a regular commenter, but anonymous, has called me a 'whore'. Someone also created a fake account with my name and shared obnoxious content. I got to know about it through a friend".

Xari Jalil, yet another participant of this study, who at the time of this interview worked for *Dawn*, Pakistan's largest English-language broadsheet, said she had faced online abuse and hate "off and on". The most notable incident she recounted was in connection with her coverage of the March 2015 twin bomb blasts in a Christian neighbourhood in Lahore. At least 15 people were killed, and 70 sustained severe injuries in the incidents near a church. She said her reports on the blasts and later pointing out that intelligence and security agency personnel were picking up Christian men from the area attracted a backlash towards her. She said: "Someone sent me a message full of abuse and threat on Facebook. I had never been abused like that before. On Twitter, an unknown user continued to intimidate me by calling me 'anti-Pakistan Army' and a 'RAW agent'. I assume it was a male user, who blamed me for promoting a negative image of Pakistan and Muslims in the country".

Jalil explained that online haters (of women journalists) had increased over the years and tolerance and patience for free speech and thought were declining. "Anything can attract online abuse—from a story as simple as a politician's profile to more controversial topics such as the Blasphemy Law. Nothing deters them [internet trolls]", she told me.

According to participant D, she had to delete all her social media accounts because an anonymous person inundated her social media accounts with abusive posts daily. She said the troll was angry at a feature she wrote on sexual exploitation of internally displaced women. These women were forced to flee their homes, along with their families, in the wake of military operations against the Taliban in Khyber Pakhtunkhwa. The message sent to her Facebook messenger read: "You need an Indian dick, you Indian-ass licking whore. Bitch!"

She later narrated:

> I think this was a man. He accused me of fabricating the story to malign Pakistan's image and wrote that he lived close to my house and knew my work timings and places and that he will "rape me the same way I said the women were being sexually exploited". He accused me of working for Indian media, since I sometimes freelance for a few Indian newspapers and that I had deliberately written the article to please Indians. He wrote disgusting things.

In some cases, trolling forced these women to go underground temporarily or quit altogether; for instance, participants D and E said they were left with no other option but to either go offline for some time or completely delete all their social media profiles.

One of the participants (F) said the threats assumed such severity that she had to report it to the police and hire a private security guard. Three others (G, H, and I) were circumstantially forced to quit their jobs as press reporters after they received threats of rape. One of them left the profession altogether and joined a school as a creative writing teacher after staying unemployed for six months.

Silence: The price to pay

Targeted women journalists demonstrate a broad range of behaviours in response to these threats and abuse. Although significant discussions with the participants evolved around response mechanisms to counter and combat only threats and abuse, some conceptual ambiguities remain regarding the contours of this phenomenon. The biggest of them all was about deciding whether to speak up or go silent. One of the significant trends in participants' responses was resorting to silence or being advised by their seniors to do so. There was a consensus across the participants about choosing to stay silent. For instance, Noor Mehtab, who worked briefly for a television news channel's website, said: "When you stay quiet, the troller is discouraged or ends up believing, in some cases, that the message was never received. Like playing dead in front of a wild bear, you know. I was called a whore, a randi. What can I possibly write back to them?"

Eraj Atiq, who worked for the Women Media Center Pakistan at the time, said her work around peace journalism and women's issues had encountered the most harassment online. One of her important stories about empowering women in conflict zones received comments from people "who apparently seemed to be male users", who told her to "shut-up". The comment read: "Journalism is not for you. The best place for you is the kitchen. Why the hell do women always try to be equal to men? To men, they are meant to be slaves only".

She said such comments left her unnerved for weeks owing to the intensity of hate they carried. In certain other instances, participants O, P, and Q said that they had stopped quoting controversial or outspoken sources in their feature stories. Participant Q explained: "I started toning down my story angles and refrained from quoting sources that were either already targeted for their outspokenness or were in the news for one reason or the other. I later started self-censoring".

These responses echo Deborah Tuerkheimer's (1997: 192) argument that women go silent because they know that if they respond to the perpetrator "with counter aggression, the violence and abuse often escalate". This fear kept my participants from responding to online abuse and threats and continues to silence thousands of women in the digital media sphere in and beyond Pakistan. It also cultivates self-censorship.

The findings of my study reveal that by targeting these women, the abusers were successful in first affecting them in making choices about their stories and sources, and later forcing them to filter information and choose to stay low-profile. Such abuse and the response mechanism feed the structural origins of excluding women from mainstream socio-political and media discourses. These, indubitably, stem from the ancient and modern political theories associating men with the public sphere and women with the private (Okin 1979)—an argument I have reiterated throughout this chapter to highlight the role of patriarchy in "legitimising" the online abuse of these women.

Abandoned to abuse: Weak support systems

Another significant take-away from the responses of the participants was that despite the law and, in some cases, organisational anti-sexual harassment policies, the authorities and the state provided minimum safety to these women journalists. Their role in the detection and accountability of trolls harassing their employees was also unquantifiable. Of the 17 participants, 16 said their employers had wanted them to continue working without providing them safer conditions online after they reported online abuse formally or informally. The one organisation that took action on the complaint was approving one week off from reporting and deleting the abusive comments posted on her online report. To present a holistic picture, in Table 7.2 I have listed the prevalence of online abuse hurled at these women journalists, whether they reported it to the organisation or not, and finally if action by the employer was taken.

TABLE 7.2 Prevalence, reporting, and action taken

Participant	Threats/abuse received	Reported to management	Action taken by management
1	Yes	Yes	No
2	Yes	Yes	No
3	Yes	No	No
4	Yes	Yes	No
5	Yes	Yes	No
6	Yes	Yes	Yes
7	Yes	No	No
8	Yes	No	No
9	Yes	No	No
10	Yes	No	No
11	Yes	No	No
12	Yes	No	No
13	Yes	No	No
14	Yes	Yes	No
15	Yes	Yes	No
16	Yes	No	No
17	Yes	No	No
Total: 17	**17 (100%)**	**7 (41%)**	**1 (6%)**

Source: Author

These figures pose a serious question. Why does such a culture that abandons its women employees prevail in the Pakistani media? Answers to such questions lie in the behaviours that spring from the societal and corporate trivialisation of gendered cyber harassment. It is damaging to both these women journalists and the journalism profession and brings me to a very crucial aspect of online hate and intimidation towards journalists: editorial intervention. Schultz (2003) argues that despite the presence of laws that help prevent this online abuse and threats, it is the "larger institutional and cultural forces" that make a difference, because "these two actually practice laws in daily life". For women journalists, this makes a potent combination: A digital space that invites harassment, a misogynist culture that patronises such behaviour, and an unsupportive or dormant institutional management. No wonder their responses reflected the hopelessness and distrust in the available "support".

Journalists generally trust their editors, bureau chiefs, and news organisations to be helpful in such circumstances, but only to the extent that their beats are changed or to report without a by-line until the troller calms down. Participants K, L, and M expressed their concerns, saying the support available to women journalists in terms of online safety was appalling. Participant L said the situation was hopeless. She observed: "What a joke! Even male reporters covering beats such as terrorism and political corruption are on their own, let alone women reporters, covering human rights and women's issues".

Another participant (N) said she was told by her editor to stay silent and "brush the dust under the carpet if she wanted to survive in the field". Such responses call for making the need for an analysis of Pakistani newsrooms essential, especially in the context of combating sexual harassment both online and offline. The desperation of these women journalists is given backbone by research beyond this study. For instance, McAdams and Beasly (1994), in their study on sexual harassment of Washington women journalists, concluded that most women victims were either left on their own or counselled in a way that they either chose to or were advised to remain silent. They write: "For example, one said, 'I went to my editor and explained the situation. He told me he would stand behind me whatever I chose to do, but told me things might get ugly, and there might be a day when I regretted publicizing the harassment.' I decided to drop the complaint" (McAdams and Beasly 1994:137).

Some participants of my study also reported a similar experience about their respective managements. Participant L stated that her editor was very supportive verbally, but "nothing was said or done officially". She said, he kept telling her how it could hurt her image online as "it is the age of the viral". Cases such as this call for a need to restructure our arguments around the importance of reporting abuse to management (editors/producers, etc.). These cases demand to be highlighted through the media themselves if media organisations are keen on retaining women journalists.

Conclusion: The quest for safe journalism

The findings of this study are themselves a damning indictment of the organised and systematic threats and abuse towards women journalists in Pakistani digital space. The results establish the argument that online trolling of women is primarily used as a way to silence them through intimidation and gives them a message that their opinion is worth nothing. The lack of support from organisations, and dormant state policies, only aggravate the already complicated situation. Participants' responses have strongly suggested that most of them attach multiple fears and insecurities to online abuse and threats, the primary being online becoming a reality offline. It significantly affects a woman's agency in her personal life as well. Not much is being done to combat it. According to Bruce et al. (2010), once discrimination against women has been highlighted, the only logical step is to ensure that it is eliminated. The steps might include government and legal intervention, affirmative action plans for digital safety, and equal opportunity to safety and free speech through fair organisational policies—all three of which seem to lack the trust of the participants. And the findings of this study have only demonstrated my argument made early on in this chapter that the issue of abuse and threats to women journalists has received a more normative and circumstantial discussion than an operational one. At this juncture, it is essential to acknowledge these issues as an increasing challenge for women journalists, and one that needs practical measures towards digital and physical security.

In addition to mapping the online abuse and threats to women journalists in Pakistan, this study also offers a vast leeway for further research in areas related to the safety of women journalists in Pakistan, the psychological implications of work-related challenges, and, most importantly, organisational intervention and support. The findings can help Pakistani media organisations identify the issue as a substantial problem faced by women journalists and to build a case for them to consider developing policies to provide adequate digital safety to the victims. Also, research on these challenges can be incorporated into journalistic pedagogy to help young women journalists in training identify the core issue at hand and equip themselves with proper coping mechanisms to combat the ever-growing online threats and abuse.

It is also evident from the responses of the participants that online harassment of women journalists is a growing issue that is facing two serious challenges: (1) underreporting and (2) trivialisation when reported. While online misogyny towards women writers, particularly women journalists, is embroiled in the male chauvinistic-ridden attitudes in Pakistani society, what makes it worse is first the inaction by targeted women, and then by organisations that employ them. Based on the responses of the participants in this research study, this inaction is because of their lack of faith in the justice system practiced both within the walls of law enforcement agency offices and their newsrooms. The responses received from the participants answered my research questions and strengthened the argument that women journalists in Pakistan are increasingly exposed to more and more serious online threats and abuse. These acts target women journalists performing their journalistic roles and, as such, ultimately violate their socio-political and free speech rights. This study also adds to the existing body of knowledge in media scholarship that identifies harassment and abuse of women journalists as a long-time current parasite for their careers. Also, it draws attention to the case of Pakistani women journalists, who are already struggling to increase their numbers and mark in the profession. It is a bitter truth that needs to be accepted by journalists, media organisations, and law enforcement agencies in Pakistan because it has been pushing women journalists out of the profession and many to the verge of doing so, as some of the participants explained in the interviews. Although, it was a coincidence that all of the participants of this study covered hard issues such as war and conflict, religion, extremism, and other culturally and socially sensitive subjects, the findings can also be applied to women journalists covering different beats such as sports, fashion, and lifestyle.

However, the most crucial argument lies in the conclusion that a solution cannot be found unless we recognise the problem and its intensity. According to Oberoi (2013), "while the stories of attacks on women journalists are proliferating, the documenting of these safety breaches is missing". It speaks volumes about the need for such studies. When I first carried out this study in 2015 as a survey, and later in 2016 as semi-structured interviews, I was hoping to study the issue and identify it for the authorities to take notice and action in providing women journalists a safe space online. However, unfortunately, abuse and threats to women journalists in Pakistan have since then significantly grown (Avehart 2019; Free Press Unlimited and DRF 2018; Nusrat 2018), with long-lasting psychological and emotional impacts on women journalists that have impeded their productivity at work and silenced their freedom of expression with damaging effects on their personal life and career choices. As one of the first few studies on this issue in Pakistan, the findings of my research suggest that social media continue to be a volatile space for women journalists in Pakistan. It serves as a platform with unfiltered abuse, which has the full potential to deteriorate unless this issue becomes part of the mainstream discourse on feminist issues in media and contemporary scholarship in Pakistan.

Notes

1 www.ifj.org/media-centre/news/detail/category/press-releases/article/pakistan-and-syria-loom-large-in-violence-which-killed-118-journalists-and-media-staff-in-2014-says.html.
2 www.reuters.com/article/us-women-danger-factbox/factbox-the-worlds-most-dangerous-countries-for-women-idUSTRE75E32A20110615.
3 Globally, the feminist movement entered its fourth wave between 2012 and 2013. This wave sees women's empowerment through the use of internet tools. It focuses on issues such as rape culture, sexual harassment, body shaming, and online anti-feminism. The use of social media to highlight and address these concerns is a key component of this wave.

References

Ali, Tazeen S., Krantz, Gunilla, Gul, Raisa, Asad, Nargis, Johansson, Eva and Mogren, Ingrid. 2011. "Gender roles and their influence on life prospects for women in urban Karachi, Pakistan: A qualitative study." *Global Health Action*, 4(1), 7448.
Aslam, Rukhsana. 2015. "Pakistan: Media, politics and the threats to journalists in Pakistan". *Pacific Journalism Review: TeKoakoa*, 21(1), 177–194.

Averhart, Sandra. 2019. "Pakistan's women journalists face challenges in male-dominated field". *WUWF* (accessed 13 July 2019), www.wuwf.org/post/pakistans-women-journalists-face-challenges-male-dominated-field#stream/0.
Bruce, Toni, Hovden, Jorid and Markula, Pirkko. 2010. "Content analysis, liberal feminism, and the importance of mapping the media terrai n. Sportswomen at the Olympics." *Brill Sense*, 10 January 2010, 19–30.
Chemaly, Soraya. 2014. "There's no comparing male and women harassment online". *Time* (accessed 10 August 2019), https://time.com/3305466/male-women-harassment-online/.
Citron, Danielle K. 2009. "Law's expressive value in combating cyber gender harassment". *Michigan Law Review*, 108, 373.
Cudd, Ann. 2006. *Analysing Oppression*. New York: Oxford University Press.
Free Press Unlimited. 2018. "Haven from the trolls: A network for Pakistani women journalists" (accessed 26 September 2019), www.freepressunlimited.org/en/stories/safe-haven-from-the-trolls-a-network-for-pakistani-women-journalists.
Ghaffar, Omar. 2005. "Reporting under fire: Understanding psychopathology of war journalists". *Psychiatric Times*, 22(4), 31.
Herring, Susan C., Job-Sluder, Kirk, Scheckler, Rebecca and Barab, Sasha. 2002. "Searching for safety online: Managing 'trolling' in a feminist forum". *Information Society*, 18(5), 371–384.
Hess, Amanda. 2017. "Why women aren't welcome on the internet". *Pacific Standard* (accessed 19 August 2019), https://psmag.com/social-justice/women-arent-welcome-internet-72170.
Hocking, John E., Stacks, Don W. and McDermott, T. 2003. *Communication Research*. United States: Pearson.
IFJ. 2014. "Research study on media and gender in Asia-Pacific." *International Federation of Journalists* (accessed 26 September 2019), https://samsn.ifj.org/wp-content/uploads/2015/03/PAKISTAN.pdf.
Kian, Edward M. and Hardin, Marie. 2009. "Framing of sport coverage based on the sex of sports writers: Female journalists counter the traditional gendering of media coverage". *International Journal of Sport Communication*, 2(2), 185–204.
Khawaja, Asma S. 2017. "Women in security policy-making: A case study of Pakistan". *Strategic Studies*, 37(1).
Lindlof, Thomas R. and Shatzer, Milton J. 1998. "Media ethnography in virtual space: Strategies, limits, and possibilities". *Journal of Broadcasting and Electronic Media*, 42(2), 170–189.
MacKinnon, Catharine A. 1987. *Feminism Unmodified: Discourses on Life and Law*. Cambridge, MA: Harvard University Press.
Mahmood, Babak, Muhammad Sohail, Malik, Khalid, Salman and Babak, Iram. 2012. "Gender specific barriers to women entrepreneurs in Pakistan: A study in urban areas of Pakistan". *British Journal of Education, Society and Behavioural Science*, 2(4), 339–352.
McAdams, Katherine C. and Beasley, Maurine H. 1994. "Sexual harassment of Washington women journalists." *Newspaper Research Journal*, 15(1), 127–139.
Nusrat, Rabia. 2018. "The challenges of Pakistan's women journalists". *The Diplomat*, 13 July 2018.
Oberoi, Reshmi K. 2013. "UNESCO women journalists taking measures to protect women journalists from violence". *Huffington Post* (accessed 22 August 2019), www.huffpost.com/entry/unesco-womenjournalists_n_3991537?ir=Australia.
Okin, Susan M. 1979. *Women in Western Political Thought*. Princeton, NJ: Princeton University Press.
Perrin, Andrew. 2015. "Social Networking Usage: 2005–2015". *Pew Research Center*(accessed 19 August 2019), www.pewinternet.org/2015/10/08/2015/Social-Networking-Usage-2005-2015/.

Ricchiardi, Sherry. 2012. *Challenges for Independent News Media in Pakistan*. Washington, DC: Center for International Media Assistance.
Schultz, Vicki. 2003. "The sanitized workplace". *Yale Law Journal*, 112, 2061.
Shabir, Ghulam. 2012. "Pakhtunkhwa: A problems of women working journalists in Khyber case study in Peshawar City-Pakistan". *International Conference on Communication, Media, Technology and Design ICCMTD* 09, 11, 299–302.
Shaheed, Farida. 1986. "The cultural articulation of patriarchy: Legal systems, Islam, and women." *South Asia Bulletin*, 6 (1), 38–44.
Sommers, Christina H. 1994. *Who Stole Feminism? How Women Have Betrayed Women*. New York: Simon and Schuster.
Steiner, Linda. 2017. "Women war reporters' resistance and silence in the face of sexism and sexual violence". *Media and Jornalismo*, 17(30), 11–26.
Tuerkheimer, Deborah. 1997. "Street harassment as sexual subordination: The phenomenology of gender-specific harm." *Wisconsin Women's Law Journal*, 12(2), 167–206.
Yusuf, Huma, Dragomir, Marius, Thompson, Mark, Watts, Graham, Chan, Yuen-Ying and Nissen, Christian S. 2013. "*Mapping Digital Media: Pakistan*." Open Society Foundations. www.opensocietyfoundations.org/publications/mapping-digital-media-pakistan.

8

COUNTER-TERRORISM PERSPECTIVE AND THE PAKISTANI TV CHANNELS

A case study of Osama bin Laden's assassination

Amir Hamza Marwan

Headlines and related footage flashed on TV screen across the globe on 2 May 2011 struck viewers as a Hollywood thriller. Al-Qaeda's chief and the most wanted man on the face of the earth, Osama bin Laden, was shot dead by US Navy SEALS in a suspenseful operation, code-named Neptune Spear, on the outskirts of Abbottabad, a garrison town in the north of Pakistan.

Arguably, bin Laden's assassination was a massive blow to al-Qaeda as this secretive outfit lost its most branded public face. He was considered the alleged architect of the 9/11 terrorist attacks in the USA and 7/7 attacks in the UK. Two remarkable observations deserve special mention.

First, the curious fact that he was hunted down in Pakistan was indeed suggestive. Pakistan was a US ally in the War on Terror (WoT) unleashed post-9/11 and had suffered more causalities than any other country since 9/11 (The Express Tribune 2011; Raja 2013). Second, while the US administration, in league with the United Nations, NATO, the European Union (EU), and a cohort of governments, viewed bin Laden's killing as a success, and President Barrack Obama claimed that "justice has been done" (BBC 2011), things were radically different in the case of Pakistan.

Let us take, for instance, the official Pakistani reaction into account. At first, the then Prime Minister of Pakistan, Yousaf Raza Gillani, called bin Laden's assassination a "great achievement" (BBC 2011). Soon afterwards, possibly succumbing to public and military pressure, he began criticising Washington for the "unilateral" attack without taking Pakistan into its confidence (Syed 2011).

Elsewhere, the present author (Marwan 2016: 46) has established that Pakistan's political high-ups avoided an official public posture on bin Laden's assassination. Despite a planned official strategy to keep the citizens uninformed and confused, assuming that the dust would settle with the passage of time, it did not work. Arguably, the policy to shy away from manifestly allying with the USA on this matter was aimed at avoiding a possible violent reaction by al-Qaeda/the Taliban.

At the same time, Islamabad did not want to undermine the diplomatic rapport with Washington (Marwan 2016: 46–47) even if bin Laden's hiding place had damaged the bilateral relations to the point of embarrassment.

The Abbottabad Operation, vernacular *nom de plume* for Neptune Spear, also enlarged the cleavage between the civilian government, led at the time by the Pakistan People's Party (PPP), and Pakistan's all-powerful military establishment. The statements issued by the government high-ups were very confusing, evident from the contradictory positions stated by Prime Minister Gillani and President Asif Ali Zardari. For instance, the latter, in an op-ed published in the *Washington Post*, claimed that it was Pakistan's early intelligence assistance that identified a courier of al-Qaeda that ultimately resulted in the killing of bin Laden (Zardari 2011). Prime Minister Gillani, on the other hand, claimed that the "unilateral" US operation violated the sovereignty of Pakistan (The Express Tribune 2011). The statement issued by the then Federal Information Minister, Firdous Ashiq Awan, was an attempt to provide a cover for the operation by stating that the operation was conducted in line with the United Nations Security Council's (UNSC) resolution. The military establishment, on the other hand, came out into the open with the criticism of a "one-sided" US operation (Syed 2011).

Though the speculations about the contentious civil-military stance were unconvincingly rejected by government officials, including Prime Minister Gillani himself in his policy speech on the floor of the National Assembly, the tension was evident (translating into an article, penned by Mansoor Ijaz, in the *Financial Times*).

Mansoor Ijaz was a Pakistani businessman in the United States who had close links to the Obama administration. In his *Financial Times* essay, Ijaz claimed that the government was expecting a military coup in the wake of the Abbottabad Operation and they sent a "memo" to Admiral Mike Mullen, then Chairman of the Joint Chief of Staffs of the US, through him to seek help from the Obama administration (Ijaz 2011). It led to the "Memogate Scandal", and it further escalated tension between the civilian government and military heads. It even forced the Supreme Court of Pakistan to establish the "Memo Commission" to investigate the issue. The commission, in its report submitted to the Supreme Court of Pakistan, admitted that the memo was written. Hussain Haqqani, a Pakistani Ambassador in the US, was asked to resign from post and was called back home to face "treason" charges. He was indicted for treason, but the case later collapsed as Haqqani went back to the US (Gall 2014: 261).

Another proof of the civil-military row at the time was a statement Prime Minister Gillani delivered in his address to the National Assembly. The statement generated a lot of heat at the time. In his speech, he rhetorically asked: "I want to ask how Osama bin Laden lived here for the past six years? On what type of visa was he living here?" (Masood 2011). He implied that bin Laden was hiding in Pakistan with the connivance of secret agencies.

In light of the above, bin Laden's assassination and its coverage on Pakistani TV channels are singularly crucial as a case study in order to enrich an understanding of the Pak-US ties on the one hand, and civil-military relations in Pakistan, on the other, since all the stakeholders were deploying media outlets to communicate. It is still important to understand the issue, as bin Laden's presence in Abbottabad has haunted Pakistan for years, and the civil-military tension has turned to new dimensions.

Accordingly, the research questions answered in this study are the following:

1. Did TV channels cover bin Laden's assassination with a counter-terrorism perspective?
2. How did the coverage by news channels depict the positions held by the civilian government as well as the Pakistan military about bin Laden's assassination?

For the sake of empirical evidence, this chapter examines the coverage of bin Laden's assassination on three Pakistani TV channels: GEO News, Dunya News, and Pakistan Television Corporation (PTV). Justification for the selection of these TV channels is given below.

My thesis in this chapter is that the Pakistani media did not anchor its coverage of the Abbottabad Operation from a counter-terrorism perspective. On the contrary, the aim of the coverage of this episode was to rescue the Pakistan military from public criticism of its inability to defend against a border violation by the USA, a country viewed highly antagonistically in Pakistan.

The chapter is planned in the following manner: First, I will review the literature on the factors that shape media coverage. This brief review will help contextualise the thesis foregrounded in this study. I then lay out the scope and methodology of my research, followed by my detailed findings. Finally, before concluding, I briefly analyse the findings.

Literature review

Media outlets operating in different parts of the world (or even a country) usually report the same event in multiple ways. Several factors induce such diverse media coverage. For instance, "location" has the power to colour the "perspective and perception" of journalists (Singh 2002: 2). Likewise, "geography" is an important factor in shaping media coverage (Schaefer 2003). Pande (2010: 5), for instance, argues that "geographic proximity" has the power to influence the "nature" and strength of the coverage accorded to particular events. Another factor determining the direction of the reporting is the "nationality of victim" (Weimann and Winn cited in Schaefer 2003: 96). For instance, Schaefer (2003) claims, a local attack is usually covered with the perspective of rescue efforts, victims, investigation, and prosecution of the act and public reactions. But an attack on any foreign soil emphasises the causes of the attack, its political implications, the international context. Schaefer opines that the physical distances result in a "less material and more detached perspective" (Schaefer 2003: 96).

However, the above theoretical considerations should be viewed within the constraints imposed on the Pakistani media by way of violent threats to journalists' security, censorship, and self-censorship. Pakistan is considered one of the most dangerous zones for reporting in the world. The Committee to Protect Journalists (CPJ) reports that 61 journalists were killed in Pakistan between 1992 and 2019 (CPJ 2019). Journalists in Pakistan, understandably, fear retribution both by the establishment and militants, thus making it difficult for reporters to look independently into the issues, particularly when it comes to the Taliban militancy and WoT (IFJ 2014). Arguably, it is one of the most challenging tasks for journalists to keep both the Taliban and powerful establishment happy.[1] In such circumstances, little space is left for journalists to explore an issue in an investigative manner. It is one of the key reasons that most TV channels in Pakistan try to cover the events related to the WoT in an identical style by relying mostly on information sourced from the government and the establishment.

Azam (2008) has examined the relationship between radicalisation and the media. His research shows that 57% of the (Pakistani) journalists interviewed by him confessed that most media outlets were concealing the facts about radicalisation (Azam 2008: 11), while 69% think that radicalisation is antithetical to the freedom of expression (Azam 2008: 12). While radicalisation is one factor that restricts reporting, there is also an ideological factor: Pakistani journalists do not view the USA positively. At least 87% of journalists agree that the USA should not be allowed to intervene in Pakistan through its secret services; 85% hold the opinion that the Americans play a negative role in the region; and 84% say that Washington is unjustly interfering in Pakistan's politics. Only 23% somewhat favour US foreign policy (Pintak and Nazir 2013: 656–657).

In short, one may deduce that both "location" and "nationality of the victim" are instrumental in orientating the news coverage. Hence, an analysis of media coverage in the case of bin Laden's assassination requires that one takes into account Abbottabad's location as a garrison town. Likewise, threats to Pakistani journalists covering WoT-related stories must also be acknowledged. Similarly, the US image in the eyes of Pakistani media practitioners is a vital factor. Below, this research will examine the role these variables played in the Pakistani TV channels' coverage of bin Laden's killing in Pakistan. But before moving on to validate any claims, I will lay out the scope and method of my research.

Scope and methodology of research

This research looks at the coverage of three leading TV channels in Pakistan—GEO News, Dunya News, and Pakistan Television (PTV). The first two are privately owned commercial news channels, while PTV is state-owned. The selection of the different television channels in this research study is vital as it provides the opportunity to scan multiple responses to the coverage of bin Laden's assassination.

The channels examined for this research were selected owing to their broad outreach at the time of the present study (the situation has not changed since). Freedom Network Pakistan recently issued the data of the Top 10 News Channels in Pakistan. GEO News stood first with a 24.50% audience share, while PTV

News stood third with a 11.24% share, and Dunya News stood tenth with a 2.52% audience share (Freedom Network 2019). PTV, despite its reputation as a "mouthpiece" of the sitting government (Dawn 2014), has the second highest viewership in Pakistan (17%), second only to GEO News (28%) (Dawn 2017). The BBC also supports the view that it is the "most-watched television of Pakistan" and has the "largest newsgathering network" (BBC 2014). Likewise, Dunya News is one of the top ten channels in terms of ratings (Freedom Network 2019). The selection of PTV and two privately owned commercial channels also provides the opportunity to compare the media content in the state-owned channel and the so-called "independent" media.

To comprehensively examine various dimensions of the coverage accorded to the bin Laden episode, the content of these three TV channels has been studied for the ten consecutive days 2 May 2011 to 11 May 2011. The reason behind selecting consecutive days was to make sure all the data related to bin Laden's assassination and the possible variety of perspectives in the coverage were captured. As the author observed, the stories related to bin Laden decreased over time. Furthermore, the discussion also got limited to certain themes (Table 8.1).

In the case of every channel, two main news bulletins have been studied: the afternoon bulletin (3:00 pm) and evening bulletin (9:00 pm). The duration of both these bulletins was one hour. Every news story, in all these bulletins, containing the phrase "Osama bin Laden", was selected, studied, and coded.

Notably, 216 news stories aired on GEO News, 184 on Dunya News, and 63 on PTV News. There were a total of 463 bin Laden-related news stories aired on these channels.[2]

To analyse the above data, quantitative content analysis has been employed. This methodology was selected due to the nature of the research questions. In agreement with Riffe et al. (1998: 37), I argue that quantitative content analysis is the best methodology when an "explicit hypothesis and research questions" are examined.

According to Hansen et al. (1998: 95), "content analysis by definition is a quantitative method, and it stresses identifying and counting the occurrences of the specified characteristics or dimensions of the text and based on which one can say something about the messages, images, and representations of such texts and their wider social significance". Likewise, Berger (2000: 116) recommends the use of content analysis to better understand the comparative coverage since this method has the capacity to "quantify the silent and obvious features of a large number of texts".

TABLE 8.1 Decline in the strength of news coverage

TV channel	Number of stories aired during first three days	Number of stories aired during last three days
GEO News	95	47
Dunya News	74	46
PTV News (Script)	30	19

Source: Author

In line with the above methodology, for this research different specified themes were identified in the relevant news stories and later counted. The aim was to show the findings on the broader phenomenon—a counter-terrorism perspective.

Likewise, to code the different themes discussed in the introduction of news items, 102 distinct values were devised, which were later squeezed into 13 to understand the nature of the coverage better. Similarly, 167 different values (about the themes) were designed to code the additional themes discussed in the body of the news story (without the introduction), which were later collapsed into 14 to better understand the coverage.

Having described the scope of the research and research methodology, I will now proceed to demonstrate my research findings.

Findings

The findings of this research study are presented below in two sections. The first section looks at the coverage of themes in the introduction of the news items, while the next section deals with the first three additional themes discussed in the body of the story (i.e., excluding the introduction). In the subsequent analysis, centrality will be assigned to a counter-terrorism perspective in the coverage.

Themes discussed in the introduction of the news items

The themes thrashed out in the introduction of the news items will show the different aspects of the coverage highlighted by the three TV channels monitored for this study, i.e., GEO News, Dunya News, and PTV News. It will help pin down particular themes discussed in the opening of the news stories under investigation by these channels. Though all the themes related to the issue are important, the most critical point is to identify the themes when these were highlighted and/or marginalised.

This data will show us the importance given by the private TV channels as well as the official broadcaster (i.e., PTV) to different aspects of bin Laden's assassination. Keeping in view the importance of the lead (or introduction of the story) in the news items, it has been studied in isolation from the rest of the body of the story (which follows the lead). Table 8.2 summarises the results.

The above findings show that GEO News mostly focused on addressing the reaction of the Pakistani government/public/media/politicians to operation Neptune Spear. These reactions constitute 34% of its complete coverage of total themes. Details of the Abbottabad Operation constituted 33% of GEO's complete coverage. The channel also covered the global reaction to bin Laden's assassination (7% of the overall coverage). However, it didn't highlight in any considerable manner the failure of the armed/intelligence forces of Pakistan to trace/kill bin Laden (only 6%).

From the above data, it is evident that GEO News, in its coverage, focused more on the details about the Abbottabad Operation or the response of the Pakistani public/government to it, as together it totalled two-thirds (67%) of the

TABLE 8.2 Themes discussed in the introduction of the news item

	GEO News		Dunya News		PTV News		Total
Complete detail about the Abbottabad Operation.	71	33%	41	22%	7	11%	119
Pakistani govt/people/politicians/military/media response to the operation.	73	34%	75	41%	22	35%	170
US govt/people/officials' response to the operation/bin Laden's death.	9	4%	7	4%	4	6%	20
Security situation in different parts of Pakistan after the operation.	3	1%	9	5%	1	1.50%	13
Complete details about bin Laden's life.	7	3%	4	2%	2	3%	13
Reaction of world to bin Laden's death.	15	7%	4	2%	10	16%	29
Impact of bin Laden's death on the region.	0	0%	0	0%	0	0%	0
Bin Laden's death and the future of the War on Terror.	4	2%	8	4%	3	5%	15
Bin Laden's death and the future of al-Qaeda.	0	0%	4	2%	1	1.50%	5
Bin Laden's death and the failure of the Armed Forces of Pakistan.	14	6%	9	5%	7	11%	30
Bin Laden's death and the tense Pak-US relations.	13	6%	15	8%	4	6%	32
Impact of bin Laden's death on the coming US elections.	2	1%	0	0%	0	0%	2
Any other	5	2%	8	4%	2	3%	15
Total	216	100%	184	100%	63	100%	463

Source: Author

total coverage. It is also important to note that GEO News did not link bin Laden's killing to its impact on the region or the future of al-Qaeda after his departure from the scene. It indicates that the stories on GEO News avoided al-Qaeda from the analysis. For instance, the impact of bin Laden's death on the WoT's future made only 2% of the coverage. In other words, my findings support that the GEO News coverage of Abbottabad Operation did not take a counter-terrorism perspective.

Dunya News also followed the trend on GEO News and focused primarily on the reaction of the Pakistani government and public to the Abbottabad Operation—41% of the overall coverage—while details surrounding the operation constituted nearly 63%. The TV channel was also seemingly more interested in sharing the details about the Abbottabad Operation as it made more than one-fifth (22%) of its complete coverage. It also focused on the tense Pak-US relations after bin

Laden's assassination (8%). However, Dunya News, in general, avoided in introductions any reference to a failure of the armed/intelligence forces of Pakistan (only 5% of the coverage). Dunya News didn't cover the death of bin Laden in the context of the Af-Pak region, the WoT, or al-Qaeda's future. These topics comprised 0%, 4%, and 2% respectively of the complete coverage under study here.

Since Pakistan has been a critical country in the WoT context, one would have expected a debate expanding beyond official and public/audience comments. A narrow spectrum indicates that the so-called "independent" TV channels devoted their coverage to unproblematic and distracting questions. Round-the-clock coverage of what happened instead of exploring the whys, hows, and what next constitutes a safe bet in any country for the commercial channels.

The coverage on PTV News was hardly different from GEO News and Dunya News. The PTV coverage also emphasised the responses to the Abbottabad Operation by the Pakistani public and government (35% of the complete coverage). PTV also devoted some space to a global reaction (16%). Moreover, PTV flagged the operational details besides the failure of the armed/intelligence services (11% each). Like the private TV channels under study here, PTV News also shied away from linking the assassination of bin Laden to its impact on the region.

PTV was reluctant to discuss bin Laden's death in the context of either the "future of the War on Terror" or "future of al-Qaeda". Hence, in light of the above findings, the following conclusions can be derived:

1. The response of the Pakistani government/public/military made almost 37% of the entire coverage of the themes in the different news items on all three TV channels.
2. Details about the Abbottabad Operation constituted one-fourth (almost 26%) of the entire coverage across these three TV channels.
3. The discussion surrounding the failure of armed/intelligence forces of Pakistan to trace bin Laden made only 6%.
4. Highlighting the impact of bin Laden's death on the WoT, on the region, or on the future of al-Qaeda constituted 4% of the entire coverage on all the three channels.

Additional themes discussed in the body of the story

After studying the themes discussed in the introductions of the news items, it is now essential to look at the first three additional themes addressed in the body of the news stories (i.e., excluding introductions). Such findings will help us further determine the themes flagged in the coverage and vice versa (for details, see Table 8.3).

If we look at the coverage of GEO News, it transpires that the said TV channel mostly focused on the reaction of the Pakistani government/public/military even in the body of news items (24%), while details about the Abbottabad Operation

TABLE 8.3 First three additional themes discussed in the body of the story

	GEONews		Dunya TV		PTV News		Total
Complete details about the Abbottabad Operation.	94	14.50%	54	10%	14	7%	162
Complete details about bin Laden's life.	14	2%	9	1.50%	5	3%	28
Pakistani govt/people/politicians/military/media response to the operation/bin Laden's killing.	157	24%	119	21.50%	33	17%	309
Reaction of world leaders/public to bin Laden's death.	3	0.50%	6	1%	0	0%	9
American govt/people/military response to the operation/bin Laden's death.	40	6%	23	4%	4	2%	67
Bin Laden's death and the future of the War on Terror.	21	3%	16	3%	7	4%	44
Bin Laden's death and the future/response of al-Qaeda.	4	0.50%	4	1%	3	1.50%	11
Security situation in different parts of the country after the operation.	6	1%	11	2%	0	0%	17
Bin Laden's death and the failure of the security/intelligence agencies of Pakistan.	18	3%	19	3%	8	4%	45
Impact of bin Laden's death on the coming US elections.	2	0.30%	0	0%	0	0%	2
Bin Laden's death is important.	5	1%	5	1%	3	1.50%	13
Impact of Bin Laden's death on the tense Pak-US relations.	5	1%	4	1%	0	0%	9
Any other	5	1%	8	1%	2	1%	15%
No theme discussed	274	42%	274	50%	110	58%	658
Total	648	100%	552	100%	189	100%	1389

Source: Author

consumed 14.5% of the coverage. The other notable theme in this category was the reaction of the US government and the public (6% of the coverage). The themes consigned to marginality included the failure of the military and intelligence agencies in tracking bin Laden and the impact of bin Laden's assassination on the WoT's future (3% each).

The coverage of Dunya News was not much different from GEO News as they too devoted more coverage to the response of the Pakistani government/public/military (21.5% of the entire coverage). The details about the Abbottabad Operation were accorded considerable space (10%). Dunya News also allotted some air time to the American response (4% of the coverage). On the other hand, the least debated themes in the coverage included the failure of the Pakistani armed/intelligence forces to trace bin Laden, and the impact of bin Laden's death on both al-Qaeda and the WoT.

PTV News also followed similar trends. It highlighted the response of the Pakistani government/public/military to the so-called Abbottabad Operation more than any other theme (17%). The operational nitty-gritty of the Abbottabad Operation consumed 7% of the coverage, while the failure of the armed forces/intelligence agencies of Pakistan took up 4% of the news bulletins. It should be noted that the question of the WoT after the death of bin Laden made 4%, while the future of al-Qaeda constituted only 1.5% of the PTV coverage.

To sum up, the dominant themes discussed in the coverage of these TV channels are the following:

1. The reaction of the Pakistani government/public/military to the Abbottabad Operation: 22%.
2. Details about the Abbottabad Operation: 11%.
3. The WoT's future and al-Qaeda's response post-Abbottabad Operation: 4%.
4. Bin Laden's death and the failure of Pakistan Army/intelligence agencies: 3%.

After an exhaustive assessment of the findings, we will now move to the discussion and analysis.

Analysis and discussion

The above findings show that the three channels were identical in their coverage. A most notable aspect is their omission of any exploration of the failure of Pakistan's armed/intelligence forces. Likewise, while sounding patriotic, the three media outlets did not broach the topic of bin Laden's secretive stay on Pakistani soil.

Curiously, bin Laden was targeted in the garrison city of Abbottabad, and his villa was just a stone's throw away from the jealously guarded Kakool Military Academy (PMA). The PMA has significance similar to the Royal Military Academy Sandhurst in the UK or West Point in the US. Reportedly, bin Laden resided in the same compound for over six years and travelled to different parts of the country like Swat and Waziristan (Abbottabad Commission Report 2013). It confounds even common sense, let alone an informed analysis, that Pakistan's security and intelligence agencies didn't get wind of it all. Any independent or investigative reporting by the media outlets would have explored such apparent questions. Instead, the coverage was diversionary, mostly devoted to official and public reactions. While minute details about the operation were covered, vital questions of primary importance were ignored.

The prime explanation for such a skewed coverage seems to be that the TV channels self-censored their coverage to avoid the annoyance of the powerful military establishment. Independent reporting would also have invited backlash from al-Qaeda and its sympathisers. Given the situation in the country where bin Laden's loss was being mourned by Muslim radicals (evident from the funeral prayer offered in his absentia in Karachi, Peshawar, and many other cities), broaching a sensitive topic might have invited trouble.[3]

The job of the media is to make people and institutions accountable for their actions and explain the issue to their audiences in a critical manner. This is what was expected from them, but they stuck to the superficial lines attached to the story. However, fear was not the only filter blocking critical coverage. Widespread anti-Americanism, an ideological affinity with official narratives glorifying the Pakistan military, and sympathy for al-Qaeda/the Taliban among mainstream media practitioners (some of them openly associating with them), also explain the findings of this study.

Conclusion

This chapter examines the coverage given to the assassination of bin Laden in the news bulletins aired on GEO News, Dunya News, and PTV in the wake of the Abbotabad Operation. The findings establish that neither the public nor the privately owned TV channels in Pakistan highlighted the counter-terrorism perspective in their coverage, even when Pakistan is a frontline state in the ongoing War on Terror, besides being an official US ally.

Indeed, bin Laden's assassination could be emblematically called the most significant counter-terrorism action in the so-called War on Terror. Hence, one would have expected Pakistani news channels to ground their coverage of the episode in the counter-terrorism perspective by highlighting the impact of the Abbottabad Operation on the conduct of the War on Terror, the implications for the Afghanistan-Pakistan region, and the future of al-Qaeda itself.

However, the TV channels in Pakistan delineated the event for their viewers in patriotic tones by calling it an American attack on Pakistan's sovereignty and integrity. This "patriotism" played the role of an ideological pretext to avoid a debate on the part of the military. This state of affairs also shows the hegemony exercised by the powerful establishment over the media outlets, which helps men in uniform to control public opinion.

Notes

1 Since 9/11, the following prominent journalists have been assassinated: Musa Khan Kheil, Saleem Shahzad, Hayat Ullah Wazir, and Mukarram Khan Aatif. Among these, Saleem Shahzad and Hayat Ullah Wazir were killed while working on "sensitive" assignments related to the War on Terror (IFJ 2014; IMS 2009).
2 The following PTV bulletins could not be monitored: (1) 6 May, 9pm bulletin; (2) 7 May, 3pm bulletin.
3 In Peshawar, provincial capital of Khyber Pakhtunkhwa province, the funeral prayer was offered in the High Court premises.

References

Abbottabad Commission. 2013. *Abbottabad Commission Report*. Islamabad: Government of Pakistan (accessed 12 April 2019), www.aljazeera.com/news/asia/2013/07/20137813412615531.html.

Azam, M. 2008. "Radicalization and media: Who influences whom and how in Pakistan?". *Pak Institute for Peace studies*, 1(1), 1–20.

BBC. 2011. "Bin Laden's death: Political reaction in quotes" (accessed 21 August 2016), www.bbc.co.uk/news/world-us-canada-13256956.

BBC. 2014. "Leading Pakistani GEO TV channel is ordered off air". *BBC News* (accessed 6 October 2016), www.bbc.co.uk/news/world-asia-27733077.

Berger, A.A. 2000. *Media and Communication Research Methods: An Introduction to Qualitative and Quantitative Approaches*. 1 edn. London: Sage Publications.

CPJ. 2019. "61 Journalists Killed in Pakistan" (accessed 9 August 2019), https://cpj.org/data/killed/asia/pakistan/?status=Killed&motiveConfirmed%5B%5D=Confirmed&type%5B%5D=Journalist&cc_fips%5B%5D=PK&start_year=1992&end_year=2019&group_by=location.

Dawn. 2014. "Golden PTV", 30 November (accessed 6 October 2016), www.dawn.com/news/1147775.

Dawn. 2017. "TV viewership trends", 25 July (accessed 26 July 2017), http://aurora.dawn.com/news/1141935.

Freedom Network. 2019. "Media market: Money and control" (accessed9 August 2019), http://pakistan.mom-rsf.org/en/findings/market/.

Gall, C. 2014. *The Wrong Enemy: America in Afghanistan, 2001-2014*. 1 edn. New York: Houghton Mifflin Harcourt.

Hansen, A., Cottle, S., Negrine, R. and Newbold, C. 1998. *Mass Communication Research Methods*. 1 edn. Basingstoke: Palgrave Macmillan.

Ijaz, M. 2011. "Time to take on Pakistan's Jihadist Spies". *Financial Times, London*, 10 October (accessed6 October 2016), www.ft.com/cms/s/0/5ea9b804-f351-11e0-b11b-00144feab49a.html#axzz3h7GOdDo3.

IFJ. 2014. "Pakistan and Syria loom large in violence which killed 118 journalists and media staff in 2014, says IFJ" (accessed 17 May 2015), www.ifj.org/nc/news-single-view/backpid/1/article/pakistan-and-syria-loom-large-in-violence-which-killed-118-journalists-and-media-staff-in-2014-says/.

International Media Support. 2009. *Pakistan: Between Radicalisation and Democratisation in an Unfolding Conflict: Media in Pakistan* (accessed 12 April 2019), www.mediasupport.org/publication/pakistan-between-radicalisation-and-democratisation-in-an-unfolding-conflict/.

Marwan, A.H. 2016. "Pakistan's official stand on the killing of Osama bin Laden: A case study of the Daily Dawn". *PUTAJ Humanities and Social Sciences*, 23(1), 39–49.

Masood, S. 2011. "Pakistani Premier warns of plotting by military". *New York Times*, 22 December (accessed 21 September 2015), www.nytimes.com/2011/12/23/world/asia/pakistani-premier-yousaf-raza-gilani-lashes-out-at-his-military.html?_r=0.
Pande, K. 2010. *Domestic Conflict or Global Terror? Framing the Mumbai Terror Attacks in the U. S. Print Press*. MSc Dissertation, London School of Economics.
Pintak, L. and Nazir, S.J. 2013. "Pakistani journalism: At the crossroads of Muslim identity, national priorities and journalistic culture". *Media, Culture and Society*, 35 (5), 640–665.
Raja, M. 2013. "Pakistani victims: War on terror toll put at 49,000". *The Express Tribune*, 27 March (accessed 6 October 2016), http://tribune.com.pk/story/527016/pakistani-victims-war-on-terror-toll-put-at-49000/.
Riffe, D., Lacy, S. and Fico, F. 1998. *Analyzing Media Messages: Using Quantitative Content Analysis in Research*. 1 edn. London: Erlbaum.
Schaefer, M.T. 2003. 'Framing the US Embassy Bombings and September 11 Attacks in African and US Newspapers", in P. Norris, M. Kern and M. Just (eds) *Framing Terrorism: The News Media, The Government and the Public*. London: Routledge, 93–112.
Singh, R. 2002. "Covering September 11 and its Consequences: A Comparative Study of the Press in America, India and Pakistan". The Joan Shorenstein Center on the Press, Politics and Public Policy Working Paper Series, Fall 2001 (accessed 24 September 2019), http://shorensteincenter.org/wp-content/uploads/2012/03/2002_04_singh.pdf.
Syed, B.S. 2011. "Unauthorised raid must not serve as precedent, US told". *Dawn*, 4 May, 1.
The Express Tribune. 2011. "Abbottabad operation: US shouldn't have bypassed Pakistan, says PM". May 7 (accessed 9 August 2019), https://tribune.com.pk/story/163723/abbottabad-operation-us-shouldnt-have-bypassed-pakistan-says-pm/.
Zardari, A. A. 2011. "Pakistan did its part". *The Washington Post*, 2 May (accessed 6 October 2016), www.washingtonpost.com/opinions/pakistan-did-its part/2011/05/02/AFHxmybF_story.html.

9

THE JOURNEY OF PAKISTAN'S OSCAR SUCCESS

A Girl in the River: An insider's account

Haya Fatima Iqbal

This chapter spotlights the process behind the making of a documentary film, *A Girl in the River: The Price of Forgiveness*, that highlights the custom/crime of so-called "honour" killings in Pakistan. The film won an Academy Award in the Best Documentary Short category at the 88th Academy Awards in 2016 and an Emmy Award for Best Documentary at the 38th Annual News and Documentary Emmy Awards in 2017.

The purpose of this chapter is to navigate the Manichaean response it invoked at two levels: while the rest of the world generously appreciated the documentary, the reaction in Pakistan was mixed at best. While the then prime minister, Nawaz Sharif, and sections of media celebrated, the filmmaking team was vilified by several clerics, right-wing TV anchors, and social media users.

In many ways, the reception of the film was, arguably, reflective of Pakistani society, rife with complexities, complications, and enormous contradictions. It was not the first time that a film or a story drawing attention to a grave social problem in Pakistan was perceived as the continuation of the agenda of the West, or an attempt to showcase a "negative image of Pakistan". A case in point is the film *Saving Face*, directed by Sharmeen Obaid Chinoy, which highlighted the crime of acid attacks against women. Hateful reactions were not rare to find even when *Saving Face* won Pakistan its first-ever Oscar.

The vitriolic reaction of numerous Pakistanis towards women who dare speak the truth has a gender dimension as well. Any woman breaching the conservative code is a target. A strong manifestation of this venomous response is widespread suspicions, popularised by the mainstream media and amplified by social networking sites, towards Nobel laureate Malala Yousafzai, who is celebrated all over the world for her courage and activism. However, despite the global recognition she enjoys, many people across all socioeconomic classes in Pakistan are not just distrustful but utterly hateful towards the young woman.

This situation raises questions among people outside Pakistan and provokes considerable curiosity. Not merely to answer this "curiosity", the aim of this chapter is to discuss the role of Pakistani films to address a complicated question: should Pakistani documentaries depict Pakistan in a "positive" way (which in itself is a highly problematic characterisation) or should Pakistani filmmakers employ their art to help bring an improvement in the lives of marginalised citizens?

The rest of this chapter will be an attempt to answer this question by providing a personal account based on the observations and experiences of this author as the co-producer of *A Girl in the River: The Price of Forgiveness* (from now on we shall call the film *GITR*). Sharmeen Obaid Chinoy was the director of the documentary.

This chapter is organised in the following manner: it begins by contextualising honour killings in Pakistan; next, it documents the motives behind the making of the documentary; then it will narrate the aftermath of the Oscar award; and finally, it will offer the conclusion and suggestions.

Social contexts of honour killings in Pakistan

I begin by highlighting the gravity of the problem foregrounded in *GITR*. This exercise to flag the enormity and seriousness of honour killings in Pakistan will also help contextualise the debate and analysis in the subsequent sections. At the outset, let me also acknowledge that the question of honour killings is neither Pakistan-specific nor Muslim-centric. This cruel practice has defied temporal and spatial boundaries applied in human civilisation. In fact, across centuries and civilisations, the blood of innocent men and women has been shed for allegedly bringing disgrace upon their families. In ancient Rome, for instance, the law held men accountable if they failed to punish their women relatives for any perceived sexual misconduct. The Bible narrates the case of Phinehas who drives a spear through an Israeli man and his Midianite wife merely because Phinehas was outraged by their interracial marriage. Evidence of honour killings is also available in the case of China under the Qing dynasty, where men had the right to kill women relatives for any alleged breach of conventional morality (Pumbay 2016).

An honour killing is rooted in the patriarchal idea that men are the guardians of morality since women are incapable of rightly protecting their honour owing to an inferior intellect and poor capabilities. Consequently, men must bear this great responsibility. Indeed, several societies have fortunately moved on, thanks mainly to courageous struggles for gender equality. Subjecting women to physical violence in such communities, as a punishment for so-called moral/sexual transgressions, is a thing of the past. Nevertheless, a mindset imbued with male superiority, perpetuating the horrible practice of honour killing, dominates societal norms in various countries. Pakistan ranks rather high among such countries. According to the widely trusted Human Rights Commission of Pakistan (HRCP), an NGO that documents human rights abuses in the country, at least 16,498 men and women were killed in the name of honour between 2004 and 2017 alone. The majority of the victims were women (HRCP 2017).

Notably, weak legislation on honour killings has also played a pivotal role in the lack of deterrence for perpetrators. Before they changed the legislation on honour killings in Pakistan as a result of the international success achieved by *GITR* (more on the topic in a while), the existing law provided a convenient escape route for the perpetrators of honour killing to go scot-free. Lawyer Asad Jamal explains:

> In 1989, the Shariat Appellate Bench of the Supreme Court declared the then existing punishments on offences relating to the human body un-Islamic and made eight specific directions in the way the criminal law must be changed to make it Islamic.
>
> As a consequence, the option of compounding (compromise as a result of payment of diyat—blood money—for the offence of killing or arsh, etc. in the case of bodily hurt) and waiver (pardon accepted for the offence of killing or bodily hurt) were introduced in the Pakistan Penal Code (PPC). Since these options were left entirely—even though in cases of qisas only—to the discretion of the legal heirs of the victims, it has had a serious adverse impact on the whole of the criminal justice system.
>
> This has been called the "privatisation of justice", which has impacted even where the court has the discretion to impose secular punishment prescribed in the statute as taazir. It isn't that compromise between parties was not allowed for certain offences before 1989. But with the Islamic sanction assigned to it, each instance of every offence against human body—including killing, and the so-called "honour" crimes—is now considered to be de facto pardonable or compoundable.
>
> *(Jamal 2016)*

Over 90% of cases of honour killings registered in the Punjab, the country's largest province, ended in some compromise—with the perpetrators let off the hook.

Arguably, this is the "spill-over effect" of *qisas*,[1] *diyat*,[2] and *arsh*[3] laws. Hamstrung by such legalities, the trial courts do not use discretion to award punishment in honour killings (Jamal 2016). Pakistani law follows the principle of *Fasaad fil Arz*,[4] which allows an offender to be punished with a sentence of up to 14 years' imprisonment even if the victim's party pardons the perpetrator under the *qisas* and *diyat*. Additionally, *taazir*[5] may be inflicted by the imposition of fines, imprisonment, death, compensation, warning, or reprimand, etc.

While the existing law on honour killing was a considerably severe impediment in the way of penalising perpetrators of honour killing, the purpose of the film was not to amend the law. The sole purpose was to film a documentary on the burning question of honour killings in Pakistan. The team (henceforth Production Team[6]) behind *GITR* arduously scanned and analysed the data. We concluded that a stimulating documentary film on an important issue was necessary also because the question of honour killings is often ignored on the pretext that "it only happens in the villages" or "oh! It's a tribal thing!". Within this context, the next section will focus on the real-time process of making *GITR*. Additionally, the next section will also, by default, demonstrate the importance of engaging cinematic work in an age of social media and commercial television whereby ephemerality and superficiality discourage serious exploration of critical social issues.

Making the documentary

The coverage of honour killings in the mainstream Pakistani media is usually fleeting, with seldom any follow-up stories. Footage, in the case of news channels, or a pictorial display, in the case of the press, finds some space only if a particular case is either particularly outrageous or bears a nuisance value.

Here are two examples. The media covered the case of Ambreen Riasat (more below). She was killed and set ablaze in a van, in Abbottabad district. Likewise, media devoted considerable coverage when Farzana Parveen was stoned to death by her family members right outside the Lahore High Court.

At times, news stories about honour killings in the countryside do not make any headlines also because the details are not always accurate. Since many media outlets depend on ill-trained stringers in rural areas instead of professional reporters because of economic reasons, the victims often remain nameless and faceless individuals.

However, the Production Team also decided to make this film because all the members found telling stories revolving around human rights violations as something close to their hearts. It was an issue the Production Team had not covered before, even if promoting the women question had been a cause célèbre for every team member. The Production Team has worked together on numerous documentary films that are socially engaging, aimed at building a more just society.

Being the focal person to investigate the incidents of honour killings for this film, I travelled across the country to meet families affected by the crime and gain first-hand knowledge of their side of the stories. Understandably, in every case I explored, the most significant barrier remained that there was no way to plausibly document the accounts of the women (and men) killed in the name of honour. The actual victims had no voice. The Production Team realised that a compelling film requires a convincing case study. But how could I locate such a case? This far into the process, the families I had met would either speak fondly about the dead or would defend their brutal act of committing the murder to save their "honour".

Abruptly, on a sweltering hot summer day in June 2014, my director Sharmeen Obaid Chinoy stumbled upon the story of an honour killing survivor, Saba Maqsood. Saba, then a 19-year-old from Gujranwala district in north-east Pakistan, eloped to marry the love of her life, 21-year-old Qaiser Ali. The same day the couple registered their marriage in court. After a lapse of a few months, Saba's parents visited her at her in-laws' home and convinced her to return to her father's house. Saba, as usually is the case, was promised that her parents would wed her off to her husband in an "honourable" manner if she came along.

Saba made the common mistake in such cases of trusting her parents and returned to her parental home. The feisty and otherwise street-smart Saba got the shock of her life when she realised that the vehicle she was traveling in with her parents and other relatives was moving in an unknown direction. When she asked where they were taking her, she was told that someone in the family had an errand to run in the area their motorcar was heading. When the group drove to a sparsely populated area by the stream running alongside Hafizabad Road in the middle of the night, they dragged Saba out of the vehicle. She was slapped several times by her father, Maqsood Ahmed, and uncle, Ashfaq Ali, before her father shot her in the face. In the heat of the moment, he thought Saba had passed away. He proceeded to dump what he believed to be her dead body into a gunny bag and threw it in the river. The family left in the vehicle, thinking they had "gotten rid of" Saba.

As luck would have it, the bullet had grazed Saba's cheek. She was bleeding profusely and had initially fainted. But the cold river water helped her regain consciousness quickly. She managed to wriggle out of the river and walked a long distance in the direction of a well-lit gas station where she was finally rescued.

Somehow, this extraordinary story of a woman's survival in the face of gruesome violence didn't make it big on national TV news. I immediately made calls to the police and found out which hospital Saba had been admitted to. The Production Team flew to meet Saba in Hafizabad right away.

I met Saba for the first time on 12 June 2014—almost a week after the violent attack—but her spirits were high. She expressed her wish that people should know her story. It was hard to ignore her courage and confidence, even when she was 19. She explicitly said that she wanted justice for herself and wanted to see everyone involved in the murder attempt behind bars.

With Saba's consent, our camera began following her. I remember filming Saba when she went into a safe house to hide from her father right after she was released from the hospital. After a few weeks at the safe house, she moved back to her in-laws' place.

By that time, we knew that HBO had approved the documentary and we were aware that the documentary would be aired to an international audience, primarily viewers in the USA.

Matters took a complicated turn once Saba moved with her husband to his parents' house. For me, it was not difficult to notice that Saba would avoid talking during the interviews. Perhaps she was traumatised. Our presence probably reminded her of her close call with death each time we met.

Saba's neighbours wouldn't heckle as we filmed, but they would religiously congregate atop their rooftops to stare at the shooting process taking place in the small courtyard. Saba's mother-in-law, Bibi Rehmatay, once told me that their curious neighbours asked a lot of uneasy questions once the film crew left every night. The characters in our documentary were visibly upset. A spark of gossip, they feared, might become a devouring flame. They did not want a repeat scandal.

Curiously, getting access to Saba's parents—Maqsooda and Maqsood—and their home was unexpectedly smooth. As the primary person responsible for reaching out to them, I treated them with respect and empathy, and in return, Saba's parents readily spoke on camera. From the first day of filming until the last leg of the shoot, Saba's father was very respectful and hospitable. He would frankly talk to the Production Team and seemed to believe that he had done the right thing by trying to kill his daughter. The performance of the Hafizabad police throughout the case was stellar. Filming with them was an unexpectedly positive experience.

Throughout the months I spent producing the film, I distinctly felt the existence of a class barrier while interacting with our documentary characters. There are so many documentary shoots where the filmmakers become insiders almost immediately. However, in this case, it took a considerable time for our characters to open up to the Production Team. We had their consent from day one, but a bond based on trust grew only with the passage of substantial time. Perhaps the shock that Saba and her in-laws had experienced was far too immense for us even remotely to imagine, or maybe we asked them too many questions rooted in a very urban sensibility that brought them discomfort.

We quizzed them about court proceedings. There were questions about the forgiveness procedure. We asked them why the family was deciding not to pursue the case. We enquired about the motives behind pressurising Saba to pardon her father. We even asked Saba if she had forgiven her father.

We had to navigate a delicate space: ensuring the family's comfort while managing to film the quickly changing landscape inside Saba's home was a learning experience that is going to stay with me forever.

A couple of months into filming, there was one off-camera conversation between me and Saba's brother-in-law, Shafaqat, that personally turned things around for me. In a candid discussion I asked him to explain why he and his family were asking Saba to forgive her father when he was already imprisoned for his crime and posed no threat to them anymore. Additionally, they also had access to a brilliant lawyer willing to fight Saba's case on a pro bono basis. Shafaqat's response reshaped my concept of forgiveness and compromise.

According to Shafaqat, even though Saba's father was in prison and they had legal help available to them, they still preferred to forgive the man because their *biradari* (community) expected them to do so. The community's say mattered to them the most because Saba's in-laws belonged to the lowest rung of the ladder in terms of financial and social capital. They depended on the community at every critical step of their lives—whether dealing with paperwork when buying, selling, or renting a property, or getting documents attested, or dealing with the courts and the police if they were caught in a legal matter. They were unlettered and navigating complex bureaucratic procedures could be a dangerously confusing business. Since no institution or representative of the state was there to hold their hand and facilitate them, they would seek their community's help. The community served as the sole source of guidance. Also, the *biradari* was always there for them. It would not demand money in exchange for support; however, the *biradari* expected obedience, submission, and compliance from the members in return.

When Saba left her parents' home to marry Qaiser in court, the community was furious because she had breached its unspoken rules and mores. The community pressure was the primary motivation for Saba's father to kill his daughter. When Saba survived the attack, Saba and her in-laws initially decided to take the father to court. But this did not sit well with the community elders either. It implied that Saba's in-laws did not regard the *biradari* highly. In other words, we should not drag a matter considered the jurisdiction of *biradari* to the courts. The community immediately began convincing Shafaqat to quit pursuing the courts and resolve the issue under the sight of the community elders.

The community elders urged that publicising a family matter would bring further shame to both parties. Second, they claimed that even if Saba's father received a prison sentence from the court, he might begrudgingly try to harm Saba after his release on the completion of his prison term. The community patriarchs wanted to ensure Saba's safety in the future, they reminded Shafaqat. After all, the state would not offer protection to Saba forever. Shafaqat explained to me that forgiving Saba's father was not one of the options they had, but the only option they had.

For the above reasons, Shafaqat and his family pushed Saba to "forgive" her father. In all of this, the perpetrators were men, the community members who pushed Saba's father to kill his daughter were men, the people who then pushed Shafaqat to stay away from the courts were men, and the people who persuaded Saba to forgive her father were also men. The men first violated a woman's right to live. Afterwards, the community's men took all the vital decisions that mattered.

The conversation with Shafaqat changed my perspective altogether. It taught me how Pakistanis with little influence in society must very carefully scrutinise the possible consequences of every step they take, lest it renders them even more vulnerable.

The more I interviewed them, the more I realised that it should not be anyone's prerogative to judge people for their actions. I was able to listen to both parties of the case with more care and open-mindedness. While knowing right from wrong is essential for a documentary filmmaker, it is equally crucial to examine what drove someone to carry out a wrong act and why someone else chose to refrain from it.

This sort of thought process also directly influenced the interview design I crafted for Saba's father just before the filming was about to end. I interviewed him when he was set free from prison. He spilled his heart out about how the community respected him for his actions and how he still felt comfortable with his actions.

The shooting of the film consumed a full ten months, whereas the editing and post-production required another six months. The film was ready by October 2015. It was immediately shortlisted for the Academy Award in October 2015. Nothing noteworthy happened during that period. However, when the film got nominated into the list of top 5 films in January 2016, the then Prime Minister Nawaz Sharif congratulated the filmmakers. Prime Minister House's reaction to the film and its nomination was not only very positive, but it was also uncharacteristically swift. The impression was that the prime minister wasn't shying away from the fact that the issue of honour killing existed in the country. Most politicians in Pakistan would have avoided such a bold gesture.

The film was not a favourite to win in the Oscar predictions. The two front-runners were *Body Team 12*, a film on the Ebola crisis in Liberia; and *Claude Lanzmann: Spectres of the Shoah*, a documentary about a filmmaker who made an epic film on the Holocaust. *GITR* was occasionally covered under the "films that could surprise you" headline.

The Production Team was not entertaining any hopes for a win either. What, however, ensued in the country right before the Oscars ceremony was that the Punjab Assembly introduced the women protection bill. The bill discussed punishment for perpetrators of domestic violence, among other issues. Unsurprisingly, the proposed bill polarised the country. The political parties were also divided along ideological lines. The firebrand clerics were vociferously flaying the proposed bill. A day before the Oscars, in an interview regarding the bill, Mufti Naeem (who is one of the leading Muslim scholars in Pakistan) went off track in his conversation and called Sharmeen Obaid Chinoy a *faahisha* (Daily Motion 2016), a highly derogatory word in Urdu literally meaning "vulgar woman" but is also an implicit reference to a prostitute. The filmmaker had absolutely nothing to do with the proposed bill. It was a jab at the women who dare raise their voice for women's rights in the country (Nasir 2016).

On the day of the Oscars, to our surprise, our film won. The initial reaction on the Pakistani news channels was celebratory. But then as we sat through the ceremony, I received a text message carrying a very shocking update from Pakistan. Mumtaz Qadri, a police officer who assassinated the Punjab Governor, Salman Taseer, on blasphemy charges, had been hanged. Despite sitting thousands of miles away from my home country, it felt as if suddenly the climate in Pakistan had changed. Qadri's execution suddenly grabbed media attention. Pakistan's second Oscar victory was not accorded the media limelight, unlike Pakistan's first Oscar win. When I look back, I feel that after Qadri's hanging the overall public sentiment believed that the state was anti-Islam; the support from the Prime Minister for the film as well as Qadri's execution was interpreted as gestures aimed at pleasing "the West".

The aftermath of the win

The first expression of high-profile praise came when Prime Minister Nawaz Sharif issued a congratulatory statement. "Women like Ms. Sharmeen Obaid-Chinoy are not only a pride for the Pakistani nation but are also a significant source of contribution toward the march of civilization in the world," Mr. Sharif observed in his statement (Zahra-Malik 2016).

Likewise, an upbeat global media lauded the unique moment in Pakistan's film history. There was an appreciation for the short but upfront speech Obaid-Chinoy delivered at the Oscars ceremony. In her acceptance speech, she proudly declared, "This is what happens when determined women get together". In her article for *The Cut*, Hilary Weaver commented:

> The ceremony might have gone on forever, but this speech was not one to fast-forward. As a woman of color, Obaid-Chinoy's words might have carried extra weight this year, as she brings visibility to the stories that often go

untold, about people rarely seen onscreen. The filmmaker added that the Pakistani prime minister said he would change the law on honor killing after watching the film. "That is the power of film," she said.

(Weaver 2016)

Others praised the filmmaker for shining a spotlight on the issue of honour killings in Pakistan once again—something that activists in the past had also been doing—but now that the promise of a change in the law on honour killings was attached to the film, the stakes were even higher. "Obaid-Chinoy's film and its Oscar win have brought the issue of honour crimes back into the public consciousness", read an article in *The Guardian* (Hasan 2016). A news story in the *National Post* observed: "Qaiser and Obaid-Chinoy's vision has offered a rare platform for women in similar situations, and have acted as a catalyst to create governmental change" (Ahsan 2016).

The media in Pakistan were equally thrilled initially and lavishly celebrated another Oscar for Obaid-Chinoy. The country's leading English-language broadsheet with a liberal ideological bent, the daily *Dawn,* considered the Oscar win important enough to comment editorially:

> For Pakistan, it was a moment to be proud of, and for Sharmeen Obaid Chinoy herself, it was nothing less than a triumph: on Sunday night, after a glittering Los Angeles ceremony, she once again brought home the coveted Oscar. Both the subject of the documentary and its director deserve to be commended. Ms Chinoy has indeed established herself amongst the ranks of those Pakistani filmmakers, from Mushtaq Gazdar to Samar Minallah and Sabiha Sumar to name just a few, who have used their camera to highlight issues that society tends to paper over, and in some cases, even justify.
>
> *(Dawn 2016a).*

However, the *Dawn*-style celebrations proved short-lived. Within two days of the win, social media exploded with messages of hate and condemnation both for the film and the filmmaker. #WeDisownSharmeen became a significant trend on Twitter in Pakistan. Journalist Sanam Maher described what was being posted under this trend:

> Two memes featuring Obaid-Chinoy were widely circulated by her critics. One features a woman filming another woman performing oral sex on a man. "Still better than Sharmeen Obaid-Chinoy," reads the text of the meme. In the second, the creators use Chinoy's photograph and refers to Indian adult entertainment star Sunny Leone. "Sunny Leone is better than this Pakistani Oscar auntie," the text in Urdu says. "Sunny f★★★s you for sure, but at least she doesn't say her country is bad." The memes are often tweeted with a link to a video—a supercut of many of Chinoy's documentaries—that lays out Chinoy's "propaganda." "Sharmeen is the CIA's pet b★★★h," wrote one Twitter user in response to the video. "She keeps disgracing Pakistan".
>
> *(Maher 2016)*

Ironically, the "concerned" citizens of Pakistan worried about Pakistan's image tarnished by the documentary film did not realise that their online posts marked by naked misogyny were endorsing by default the message the Production Team had flashed on the screen.

The virtual vitriol soon found allies in the mainstream media. In his TV talk show *Harf-e-Raaz* on NEO TV, Orya Maqbool Jan (OMJ), a popular ultra-conservative TV talk show panellist and former bureaucrat, claimed that Obaid-Chinoy was neither his idol nor for anyone else in Pakistan. According to OMJ, she was artificially iconised by the West to penetrate Pakistani society. He observes: "The fundamental problem is that the entire issue of honour killings has been overblown by this film. Is this the only problem left to be highlighted in Pakistan? And is honour killing only a problem in Pakistan?" (NEO TV 2016).

There were supportive voices too in the Pakistani media countering the criticism spearheaded by the likes of OMJ. Kamal Siddiqi, for instance, editor-in-chief at the daily *Express Tribune* (an English-language subsidiary of the *International Herald Tribune*) commented:

> What is worrisome is that these are not the views of the uneducated and the under-privileged. These comments come from our educated middle class. Pakistanis who cry themselves hoarse over other issues like what is happening in Gaza, drone attacks or the country's VIP culture. They have been strangely silent over both Pakistan's second Nobel laureate, and our two-time Oscar winner. The charge-sheet against both Malala and Sharmeen is long, while facts do not come in the way. In any other country, Sharmeen's return would have been met with a public welcome. Instead, we were all silent.
>
> *(Siddiqi 2016)*

Likewise, Ali Afzal Sahi, in *The News* observed:

> Instead of bombarding the documentary with an onslaught of negative criticism, one should realise that the real message underlying the movie is an outright condemnation of those atrocities by Pakistanis themselves. Simply put, the opposition that is being leveled against those who struggle to reveal the bare realities should be rerouted to the real perpetrators of the heinous crimes. If we still feel that movies such as these are damaging the reputation of the nation, what should perhaps be done is to weed out these evils from society.
>
> *(Sahi 2016)*

Commenting in *The Nation* on rampant patriarchy in strong words, columnist Kunwar Khuldune Shahid suggested:

> Unlike a "true Pakistani woman" Sharmeen did not hush up the violence against "men's possessions", because she didn't know how to exist like one. Her fight is to help as many Pakistani women as possible experience what it is

like to be an individual whose choices don't impact families, clans, communities, nations, or anyone but her own self. It is this long-held fear of Pakistan's most privileged demographic, of seeing their own human properties being freed into individuals, which pushes them to disown liberated women.

(Shahid 2016)

What is evident from the above quotations is the familiar fact that the English-language press supported *GITR* with a niche and minuscule audience. The vernacular press and news channels commanding mass audience were in general hostile.

As is the case with Pakistan's news cycle, conversations about the film, and the prospects of changing the law, tapered off as soon as the Panama Leaks, exposing corruption by bigwigs, happened. The ruling Sharif family was implicated in the scam. All the media's attention was now devoted to the Prime Minister as well as the first family and their alleged corruption.

The Panama Leaks elbowed out the (mis)coverage of *GITR*. The mainstream media also changed the debate on amending the legislation on honour killings. By May 2016, a leading source from Pakistan's civil society mentioned that the civil society advocates of amended legislation on honour killings had wilfully taken a backseat because the Sharif government, post-Panama Leaks, wouldn't be able to rally support for the amendment.

Amidst all of it, more news of honour killings made it to the national media. Each new case was more gruesome than the other. In Karachi's Orangi area, on 28 April 2016, 16-year-old Sumaira was murdered by her brother after he found her talking to a man. He used a kitchen knife to stab his sister inside their home. He then dragged her out on the street where she continued to bleed and writhe in pain on the steps as neighbours gathered (Dawn 2016b).

Sixteen-year-old Ambreen Riasat (mentioned above) was set on fire as punishment for helping her friend escape the village to marry of her free will in Abbottabad district on 5 May 2016. They brought her to an abandoned house where she was drugged, killed, and placed in the backseat of a parked van. The van was then doused with petrol and set on fire. A 15-member *jirga* [7] decided her fate (Javed 2016).

The most high-profile case of honour killing was the murder of famous social media celebrity and model Qandeel Baloch on 15 July 2016. She was strangled to death at the age of 26 by her brother, in her own home in Multan district of the Punjab province (Gabol and Subhani 2016). Her brother was not happy with the snaps and videos that Qandeel Baloch used to post on social media platforms (Gabol and Subhani 2016). Her case made global headlines and became the topic of a popular biographical screenplay *Baghi* aired on entertainment channel Urdu 1 in 2017.

Another case was reported from Jhelum district in July 2016: a 28-year-old British-Pakistani woman, Samia Shahid, trapped into visiting Pakistan by her family, was killed by her British-Pakistani father in connivance with her ex-husband. She was strangled to death because she had brought "dishonour" to the family by divorcing her first husband and marrying a man she loved (Mortimer

2016). Again, the case provided fare for spicy headlines to the newsrooms in the "infidel West".

Meanwhile, with the increased reporting of honour killing cases in the mainstream media, the pressure to do something about the honour killing law regained intensity. The Anti-Honour Killing Law was finally passed in October 2016. One may view the amendment as a watered-down version of the intended amendment to satisfy the right-wing political parties. The amended law does not make honour crimes non-compoundable, which implies that heirs can still grant amnesty to the perpetrator, even where crimes are committed in the name of honour.

The new law provides for mandatory life imprisonment; however, the mandatory life imprisonment is applicable if, despite the heir's compromise, the court decides to use its discretion to punish the offender. Previously, the minimum punishment for honour killings in such cases was ten years. One may point out other lacunae in the amended law, yet a laudable development is the fact that offenses committed in the name of honour are included now in the definition of *Fasad-fil-arz* (Omar 2016).

Meanwhile, after the release of the documentary, Saba's father and an uncle started threatening her again. The police arrested the two again. The threats were made despite the promise at the time of amnesty that there would be no further attack on Saba.

Saba and her husband have now sought asylum outside Pakistan, where they live with their two children (a boy and a girl). Her father and uncle were released from prison because Saba and her husband decided not to press charges against them. While the Panama Leaks led to the ouster of Prime Minister Nawaz Sharif in the summer of 2018, the law against honour killings has stayed.

The above sequence of events answers the question posed in the introduction by establishing that it is not artistic expressions like *GITR* that tarnish the global image of a country in the global south; on the contrary, one may argue rhetorically, brutal practices make juicy headlines internationally. However, the most important lesson to learn is that inhuman practices are self-destructive. Socially engaged cinematic endeavours such as our documentary are crucial also because they may help usher in a positive change.

However, there are several other dilemmas and questions one needs to explore and answer in the context of such countries as Pakistan. Below I will frame a few questions for future debates in the light of my own experience.

First, let me state the obvious: documentary filmmakers are necessarily storytellers who use the canvas of reality to convey a message. We use our cameras to take viewers into worlds they have never seen before so that their perspectives on life expand. Often we are unable to imagine how far a film will go when we start shooting it. The Production Team never thought that the film would gain global recognition by winning the Academy Award. Nobody ever imagined either the media limelight Saba would receive when we launched the project. Likewise, it was neither intended nor conceived by the Production Team that the documentary would put Saba in harm's way. Going into the film's production, no one knew that Saba would end up forgiving her father instead of continuing her fight for justice.

Her uncle happened to watch the trailer of the documentary, and interestingly he knew all along that we were filming Saba's story. Infuriated by the trailer, he went to Saba's home to attack her again. Because of the threats, Saba and her husband went into hiding. The Production Team facilitated the couple throughout this ordeal.

Such a situation poses several important questions: if a filmmaker's job is to tell stories, how far ahead should they think about an unfavourable situation arising in their characters' lives before deciding to make a film? How intricately does a filmmaker have to plan a character's exit strategy in case things go wrong? What if the filmmaker tries to protect their characters but fails to do so? Who is responsible for any harm that happens to one's documentary characters—the filmmaker, or the state institutions accountable for protecting citizens in the first place? If a film's success leads to a change in legislation, but the film's characters must go into hiding to ensure safety for a certain period, what is the filmmaker supposed to make of their activism? Can thoughts about a film's consequences result in filmmakers avoiding making films on critical subjects? Where do filmmakers have to draw the line between caution and duty?

Similarly, films that challenge the status quo can potentially end up in increased risks for their filmmakers as well. For instance, in a country like Pakistan, if a filmmaker (especially in the case of a woman) plans to make a film about a social problem, the person is immediately labelled as a Western agent working to fulfil the somewhat enigmatic "Western agenda". Online hate speech is becoming more visible all over the world, but in Pakistan, trolling of women assumes an unprecedented intensity. The examples of hateful content against the director of our documentary shared earlier in this chapter, offer a prime example of the situation.

Concluding remarks

The above account has not been written to discourage filmmakers from taking up uneasy, contested, or controversial themes in their film projects. My statement above is not a commentary on the effectiveness or infectivity of activism stemming from the film genre either. In a country like Pakistan, where burning issues remain off-limits in the public sphere and mainstream media, documentary filmmakers are in a unique position to flag them up. Documentary filmmakers should not shut themselves down for fear of vilification/trolling. A metropolitan perspective may provide clues to the work we do as filmmakers: as stated above, our purpose as filmmakers is to tell stories through the medium of films that build empathy and understanding for people, places, and practices across borders. The goal of our work should not necessarily be to please our viewers. Instead, our work should provide viewers with a deeper understanding of the topics we spotlight. If we can achieve this goal at the expense of some cognitive dissonance on the part of our viewers, we should strive for it.

Our stories aim to tell the truth, and the truth can be bitter at times. In a country where the freedom to express ourselves is shrinking because of restrictive laws and heightened surveillance, it would be very damaging for the social fabric of

Pakistan if its filmmakers and journalists bowed down to pressures and started practicing self-censorship. It would not be an exaggeration to say that making hard-hitting documentary films as a woman is an even more complicated undertaking in Pakistan. Male Pakistani documentary filmmakers have also produced brilliant cinematic social commentaries on topics deemed subversive by the ideological establishment, for the country's global image. But mainstream media, as well as social media platforms, have not hounded them.

Notes

1 *Qisas*: It follows the principle of an eye for an eye. This is where the perpetrator of the crime is punished with the same injury that he caused to the victim. If the criminal killed the victim, then he is killed. If he cut off or injured a limb of the victim, then his own limb will be cut off or injured if it is possible without killing the criminal.
2 *Diyat*: In Islamic law, it is the compensation that is payable to the heir of the victim by the offender.
3 *Arsh*: It is compensation for offences relating to various kinds of hurt. It is a compensation for organs and parts of the body. It is to be assessed at a certain percentage of the value of *diyat*. It is to be paid in a lump sum or in instalments. In case of default, the convict is liable to simple imprisonment.
4 *Fasaad-fil-Arz*: To commit mischief or corruption in the land.
5 *Taazir*: It comprises such punishments that are not covered by *Hadd* or where the conditions necessary for enforcement of *Hadd* are not fulfilled. In such cases, the judge is authorised to fix the term, nature, and extent of the sentence awarded to the culprit.
6 Our Production Team comprised 1. Sharmeen Obaid Chinoy who is the director of the film, and it was her vision for the content of the film that guided us throughout the making of the film. 2. Asad Faruqi who is the Director of Photography. He was responsible for shooting the film and taking decisions related to the visual look and feel of the film. 3. Nadir Siddiqui is the Sound Engineer. All decisions and ideas related to how on-field sound should be recorded were his. 4. Haya Fatima Iqbal, this author, is the Co Producer. I was solely responsible for conducting all on-ground research prior to the production of the film, gaining access to all characters of this film, and conducting on-camera interviews with all characters of the documentary.
7 *Jirga*: A tribal council that makes decisions on social issues and crimes in the community.

References

Ahsan, S. 2016. "Pakistani-Canadian Sharmeen Obaid-Chinoy wins her second Oscar commends the power of film". *National Post* (accessed 8 August 2017), http://nationalpost.com/entertainment/movies/pakistani-canadian-sharmeen-obaid-chinoy-wins-her-second-oscar-commends-the-power-of-film.
Daily Motion. 2016. Mufti Naeem calls Shareem Obaid-Chinoy a "Fahisha Aurat" added by Jadu TV (accessed 8 August 2017), www.dailymotion.com/video/x3uiwql.
Dawn. 2016a. "Editorial 'Another Oscar'". 1 March 2016 (accessed 8 August 2017), www.dawn.com/news/1242791.
Dawn. 2016b. "Karachi police arrest man for gruesome 'honour killing' of sister." 28 April 2016 (accessed 8 August 2017), www.dawn.com/news/1255016.
Gabol, I. and Subhani, T. 2016. "Qandeel Baloch murdered by brother in Multan: police". *Dawn*, 26 July 2016 (accessed 8 August 2017), www.dawn.com/news/1271213.

Hasan, Y. 2016. "*A Girl in the River*'s Oscar win gives Pakistan chance to end honour killings". *Guardian*, (accessed 8 August 2017), www.theguardian.com/global-development/2016/mar/04/a-girl-in-the-river-oscar-win-pakistan-end-honour-killings.

HRCP. 2017. "Media monitoring of human rights violations and concerns in Pakistan". *Human Rights Commission of Pakistan* (HRCP) (accessed 31 July 2017), http://hrcpmonitor.org/.

Jamal, A. 2016. "The dishonour of compromise." *News International* (accessed 31 July 2017) www.thenews.com.pk/print/101537-The-dishonour-of-compromise.

Javed, R. 2016. "16-year-old girl set on fire as 'punishment' by Abbottabad jirga". *Dawn*, 5 May 2016 (accessed 8 August 2017), www.dawn.com/news/1256448.

Maher, S. 2016. "Oscar-nominated documentary about 'honor killings' exposes filmmaker to witch hunt". *New York Times* (accessed 8 August 2017) http://nytlive.nytimes.com/womenintheworld/2016/02/24/oscar-nominated-film-about-honor-killings-exposes-filmmaker-to-witch-hunt/?mcubz=1.

Mortimer, C. 2016. "SamiaShahid: British woman who died in alleged honour killing texted friend about fears she would not return alive". *Independent* (accessed 8 August 2017), www.independent.co.uk/news/world/asia/samia-shahid-honour-killing-pakistan-violence-against-women-murder-crime-a7232271.html.

Nasir, A. 2016. "Prime-time shame". *Dawn*, 27 February 2016 (accessed 8 August 2017), www.dawn.com/news/1242172.

NEO TV. 2016. "Harf E Raaz With Orya Maqbool". *NEO TV Network* (accessed September 2019), www.youtube.com/watch?v=t9SCrhijJYw.

Omar, R. 2016. "A compromised law". *News on Sunday*, 16 October 2016 (accessed 31 July 2016), http://tns.thenews.com.pk/compromised-law-2/#.WXlguyN96AM.

Pumbay, M. 2016. "Honour Killings in Afghanistan and Pakistan". *Diplomat*, 30 December 2016 (accessed 31 July 2017), http://thediplomat.com/2016/12/honor-killings-in-afghanistan-and-pakistan/.

Sahi, A. 2016. "Our distorted sense of 'honour'". *The News*, 8 March 2016 (accessed 8 August 2017), www.thenews.com.pk/print/103621-Our-distorted-sense-of-honour.

Shahid, K. 2016. "Owning Qadri, disowning Sharmeen" *The Nation*, 3 March 2016 (accessed 8 August 2017), http://nation.com.pk/columns/03-Mar-2016/owning-qadri-disowning-sharmeen.

Siddiqi, K. 2016. "Welcome back, Sharmeen". *Express Tribune*, 6 March 2016 (accessed 8 August 2017), https://tribune.com.pk/story/1060486/welcome-back-sharmeen/.

Weaver, H. 2016. "The Oscars needed Sharmeen Obaid-Chinoy's speech." *The Cut*, 29 February 2016 (accessed 8 July 2017), www.thecut.com/2016/02/oscars-needed-sharmeen-obaid-chinoys-speech.html>.

Zahra-Malik, M. 2016. "Pakistan praises Oscar for film denouncing 'honor killings'". *Reuters*, 29 February 2016 (accessed 8 July 2017), www.reuters.com/article/us-awards-oscars-pakistan/pakistan-praises-oscar-for-film-denouncing-honor-killings-idUSKCN0W21CF.

10

WHAT FREEDOM?

Reflections of a working journalist

Farah Zia

It was a lazy Sunday afternoon on 15 April 2018. The weekly edition, both print and online, of *TNS* (*The News on Sunday*) that I used to edit at the time was already out. *TNS*, a part of Jang Group, the largest media house in the country, is a weekend magazine that comes out every Sunday with the English daily *The News*.

I was casually looking at my cell phone every now and then to gauge how our content was doing on social media, fixing small errors here and there, when I got a WhatsApp message from an unrecognised number. It asked me to remove all articles about the Pashtun Tahaffuz Movement (PTM) from the online edition and all e-papers. We had published three articles on the PTM in *TNS* that week, all carefully assigned or picked for their journalistic relevance (PTM was the name of a newly emerged movement, led and followed by young Pashtuns, for the constitutional rights of the Pashtuns especially in the tribal regions). One article in the main section addressed how the political parties in Khyber Pakhtunkhwa province were realigning their politics for the upcoming general election in the wake of PTM's growing popularity, while the other two in another section were about the genesis of the movement itself.

Even though I knew the message was from someone in management, I tried talking with a senior management person. I asked him about the logic of having the articles removed when they had already been printed and warned him of the embarrassment we would face on social media. The reply from him was short and clear: it was a matter of survival for the group, which was fighting a constant battle with the country's security establishment. We had no option but to pull the articles.

Soon, as expected, social media started to heat up. The writers began tweeting about their forcibly removed articles. It was ridiculous because only three weeks before we had published a long profile interview of the PTM's main leader, Manzoor Pashteen, and no one from management was talking about removing it. That interview was and still is part of the magazine's online archive.

The person in management I spoke to had said the social media reaction would convince all and sundry about the constraints faced by the group. Looking back, I think it was the best way the state could tell media people everywhere that the PTM was the absolute red line they dare not cross. Electronic media were already doing the necessary by ignoring the PTM's sit-ins and public meetings. Henceforth, we were careful not to commission another piece on the PTM. If the name appeared at all, we on the desk replaced it with "a civil rights movement". Some may be tempted to call it an exercise in "self-censorship" but, a year down the line, I still think about it in terms of blatant censorship. Most newspapers got overt or covert hints, and soon the name PTM disappeared from the mainstream media discourse.

This was, of course, not the first instance of censorship for us at *TNS*—we who were believed to be exceptionally lucky insofar as media curbs go in this country. With the year 2019 drawing to a close, a time which is arguably the worst for freedom of expression in this country, when the powers that be have muzzled the media houses through financial and existential threats in a way that they are forced to change their content and silence independent voices (Hashim 2019), it may be instructive to trace the history of media freedom through a personal journey of roughly 27 years.

My journey began in the so-called decade of democracy, i.e., the 1990s—the interregnum between the draconian military regime of General Zia-ul-Haq and the enlightened moderation of another military ruler General Pervez Musharraf. It continued through the post-9/11 world that affected Pakistan as much as Pakistan affected it, to the current times.

It started—in 1992 to be precise—when journalism meant only print because the state dominated all forms of broadcast. In the 2000s, I carefully watched the opening of the airwaves to private players and how it affected the media landscape, followed by the onslaught of digital and social media in the same period, which became a lot more influential after 2010; I persisted with print in the company of all other forms of media.

As an observer and consumer of all forms of media, in this chapter I will also trace the trajectory of print media, which I have remained associated with throughout, and look at the possibilities of its relevance or otherwise and the reasons too.

I begin by narrating a personal and collective journey of journalism in the 1990s and connect it briefly with the history that preceded it. In the next section, a sketch of the structure of what journalism—both English and Urdu—looked like is drawn, along with the political developments in the so-called decade of democracy. The section after that recounts the Kargil War, followed by the next military rule; the structure of media changed with the opening of private television and radio channels while the most significant political development of the time was the events of 9/11, which changed the world. Next, the post-9/11 world with terrorism and its retaliation all relayed on television is recounted. I briefly talk about gender in journalism and the final section crystallises the debate on freedom of expression through personal experiences as editor of a news magazine, and ties it with the future of print media.

Censorship—A personal and collective history

Of course, we the journalists understood freedom of expression as an essential democratic value, and as the fourth pillar of the state, we considered ourselves part of the struggle for democracy. In a country that had already seen three martial laws before the 1990s, it was both an exciting and frustrating time to be a journalist: to partake in the joys of a relatively free press, political activity, and elections, and the sorrows of the so-called media freedoms being exploited against elected governments by non-democratic forces who felt no qualms in sending them packing. The stories of corruption, fed to journalists by the same unelected forces, were used in courts against the elected governments, keeping the whole idea of procedural democracy fragile and vulnerable. (The brief-case carrying investigative journalists became shining stars in those years and then faded. The briefcase was a symbol of the corruption story handed over to them often by some bureaucrat, while they were supposed to sit on the desk and turn it into a news item.)

Memory is fickle, no doubt, but the 1990s was a decade when journalists' trade unionism was more a matter of nostalgia than anything else. There was a confused conflation between trade unionism and press club politics, and a young journalist saw the press club election gradually gain ascendancy and successfully push back all trade union activity by the end of the decade. In Lahore, for instance, the press club was relocated to a purpose-built fancy building that still did not attract senior and serious-minded journalists, least of all women.

The few times I went to the club, I found some permanent male faces playing board games, leaving the impression that women weren't welcome in this space. By the beginning of the 2000s, the press club's was the only election that was talked about. Soon, press club politics in Lahore, and elsewhere too, was all about a housing society and residential plots for journalists. The ascendency of press clubs signifies in the Pakistani context a corresponding decline of trade unionism in the media sector.

As a working journalist, my generation was never a part of the political struggle and unionisation efforts that our senior colleagues had waged for their freedoms since Partition in 1947. What was worse was that this generation only had a vague sense of its own history. We did know all along that Gen. Zia's military courts actually flogged at least three journalists and imprisoned many; that a certain Dastoori (Constitutional) group had broken the unity of the Pakistan Federal Union of Journalists (PFUJ), an umbrella organisation for local unions; and that some publications often left the space blank in protest against censorship.

Zamir Niazi had done ground-breaking work in writing a history of journalism aptly titled *The Press in Chains* (1986) and was a part of the collective consciousness of every journalist entering the profession. It documents a history of repression, glorious struggle, courage, and also collusion in journalism, and has led to many more works in its wake. In fact, from the start, there were attempts to promote "a unitary outlook, prioritising one language (Urdu), one religion (Islam) and a one size fits all cultural identity" thus "creating brittle conformity and discouraging the projection of a nuanced and realistic picture of the country" (Cheema 2019).

As senior journalist and human rights activist I. A. Rehman (2017), in an interview for this study, acknowledged, more in the context of recent media curbs, that "all these [restrictions] are leading to a conformist society whereas society develops and evolves with difference of opinion, debate, controversy, and discourse". Little wonder that freedom of the press has remained an unpalatable idea to the state all along. Ayub Khan's stringent laws were followed with martial law regulations under Yahya Khan, the military dictator who came after Ayub, and even the elected government of Zulfikar Ali Bhutto went after journalists with a vengeance (Niazi 1986: 79–131). The Zia dictatorship that ousted Z. A. Bhutto's popularly elected government proved an unmitigated disaster for media freedoms.

Back to the 1990s

So, what was the 1990s, the era of print journalism in Pakistan, like?

On the surface, it seemed as if Gen. Zia had broken the spirit of individuals and institutions in the media alike. As for me, I was young, straight out of university and full of idealism. Even though the institutions had weakened considerably in the face of the might of the state, the journalists' trade unions stood divided and ineffectual, and many journalists and intellectuals were in forced exile, there still were some towering figures around us. Some of the best editors were kept away from newspapers but, thankfully, their voice was available through their columns. In my personal interviews with senior journalists like Zafar Iqbal Mirza, Tahir Mirza, and Nisar Osmani in 1992–93, everyone lamented the professional editor being replaced by the proprietor. Journalists trained in a variety of disciplines joined the profession which worked on the principle of "on the job training", through what we colloquially know as *Ustadi Shagirdi*. Unfortunately, there weren't many *asaataza* (teachers) left to learn from.

With all this happening, journalistic ethics took a plunge as well. For every journalist still ready to join the profession and work for a better, plural, democratic Pakistan, there was an owner/editor who was more than ready to employ him/her on an ad hoc and contractual basis.

I had opted to work for an English-language paper, *The Frontier Post*, because that was where, for me, salvation lay. In a largely illiterate populace, Urdu-language papers were the first priority for the majority of literate people; it would not be incorrect to say they were in the line of fire because of their mass readership. The pre-censorship (later changed to Press Advice) practices of earlier decades, as well as the continuing self-censorship, took their toll on the standard of Urdu-language journalism. This, along with the burden of tradition from colonial times ensured that the Urdu-language press remained beholden to the nationalistic and religious ideals propagated by the post-1947 security state shaped in Pakistan. The English-language press, on the other hand, was ideologically secular and progressive, more professional, ready to take on issues like human rights, women, minorities, and discriminatory laws that were largely ignored by the Urdu press. It was easier to uphold standards in the English language precisely because there was less censorship, and also because it catered to a different market, or class if you like. In fact, market was a consideration for both the Urdu and English press, both of which remained urban-centric.

But the relative freedom, ideology, and professionalism of the English-language press were enough grounds for fresh graduates like me who saw a career away from civil service or teaching. We also sought consolation in the fact that our work was more effective since it reached the international audience and policymakers alike.

The early 1990s was a time when newspaper offices regularly subscribed to Indian newspapers and magazines, and the middle classes had access to Indian channels, including news channels through the newly introduced dish antennas. But 24/7 live television was not yet there. I still remember the demolition of Babri Mosque on 6 December 1992, which became known to most people in Pakistan through the next day's newspapers. Babri Mosque was one of the largest mosques in Ayodhya in Uttar Pradesh state, said to have been built on the orders of Mughal Emperor Babar. Some oral accounts stated that the mosque was built on the site of an old temple of Rama. The Ayodhya Dispute, as it came to be known, has been going on between Hindus and Muslims for two centuries.

It was on 7 December that many in Pakistan retaliated to the demolition in ways that were depressing, to say the least. We who were desk-bound went onto the rooftop of *The Frontier Post Lahore*'s office on the Queens Road (a progressive and liberal English daily from Peshawar that had opened an office in Lahore that I had joined) and saw thick black smoke emitting from at least four, five places, not too far from where we were. Meanwhile, news trickled in from reporters and photographers that most Hindu temples in the city had been set on fire by angry mobs. Even as a young journalist, I could feel the sadness in the air that day. Memory is fickle, so I can't remember if Jain Mandir in Lahore's old Anarkali was burnt the same day or later. Lahore, a cosmopolitan city before the Partition of 1947, had a considerable population of Hindus and Sikhs (more than 35%) and boasted many Sikh gurdwaras and Hindu temples, some of which stayed functional while others were put to other uses.

I distinctly recall meeting Shafqat Tanveer Mirza, another senior journalist, a little later who expressed deep sorrow over the destruction, particularly of Jain Mandir: "They [the mob] don't know who the Jains are [referring to them as a sensitive community]; they destroyed even *their* worship place" is I think what he said with a clear sense of loss.

Another incident from 1993 that stayed with me for a long time was when a woman journalist (I am concealing her identity) who wrote an op-ed column for our paper managed to get an interview with the then interior minister Chaudhry Shujaat Hussain, a politician belonging to the conservative Pakistan Muslim League. A remarkable interview, it was carried on the front page as anchor with the journalist/columnist's byline. A male journalist, who wrote leaders and was a stop-gap editor of the magazine that I worked for, came upstairs to our office, not too happy to see the interview with a woman's byline, and told us that everybody knew *how she got the interview*. As a young journalist who felt strongly about and wanted to report or comment on politics, this was the single most discouraging remark. For a long time, I used to think that even if we the women made it to the top in reporting on politics, *this* is how we will be seen by *everybody* beginning with our own colleagues.

Outside, in the political arena, a game of musical chairs was played in the so-called two-party system, none of which was allowed to complete its tenure in office. This is what 1990s politics looked like. Those were weak coalition governments, powerless to start with, and prone to conspiracies wrapped in legally sanctioned "votes of no confidence" from their opponents. Each dissolution of parliament in the 1990s was challenged in courts of law and a lot of time was spent on reporting the hearings and judgements. Realpolitik, however, was the order of the day, even in the courts. Print journalism will have to partly share the blame for reinforcing the image of the political class as wholly corrupt; while the political class must share the other half of the blame—for doing nothing to contradict this image.

When I started out, the English language press had its own "no-go" areas. There were references to budgetary allocation for the military, but like parliament, you could not debate it in the press. The Zia dictatorship coincided with the big powers waging a proxy war in Afghanistan, and Pakistan's role, especially those of its intelligence agencies, was outside the media's purview. The intelligence agencies, clearly involved in politics, were instrumental in forming a political alliance (Islami Jamhoori Ittihad) to counter Benazir Bhutto's and her Pakistan People's Party's (PPP) popularity and potential success in election. But no one dared to tread in that territory.

The freedom of the press was in danger also because of many structural constraints. As always, the newspapers depended for their economic viability on government advertisements, and these formed a significant chunk of their advertisement share. They were also dependent on the government for their newsprint quota (Pakistan imports most if not all of its newsprint). Thus, there weren't many investigative stories in the dailies, while some monthly periodicals and magazines—*Herald* and *Newsline* immediately come to mind—did delve into that territory. Investigation was not attempted into the affairs of the corporate sector, the other source of advertisements for the newspapers. This, coupled with a diluted institution of the editor, was responsible for an environment that made journalists, for want of a better word, lazy. In 1998, when the Jang papers ran some stories about a financial scandal that involved the Ittefaq group of companies owned by the Sharifs—a business family that was brought into politics by Gen. Zia and whose public face was represented by none other than Mian Nawaz Sharif, by then the twice-elected prime minister of the country—all hell broke loose (Menon 2000). Their offices were raided by the Federal Investigation Agency (FIA), they were issued tax notices, the staffers were harassed, and newsprint was withheld. I vividly remember how both *Jang* and *The News* were forced to reduce the number of pages and took out skeleton papers; this included our magazine *TNS* as well. Our workload considerably reduced, we got a lot of time in the office to discuss politics, though deep down we were distressed at the state of affairs. The editor-in-chief was asked by the government of the day to get rid of many of his staffers, which to his credit he did not, although some staff members were advised to stop writing for some time.

These incidents only showed how fragile and vulnerable the hard-won freedoms were. The Jang Group was able to withstand the pressure, but many smaller publications were closed down along the way. Among the many high-handed actions of the Nawaz government was the ignominious arrest of Najam Sethi, editor of the English-language weekly *The Friday Times*.

Kargil War, Musharraf, 9/11, and the aftermath

The Kargil War in 1999, which followed closely (it began in April) the Lahore Declaration in February the same year, after Indian prime minister Atal Bihari Vajpayee's maiden and euphoric visit to Pakistan on a peace bus, exposed the wide civil-military gap—and that the decision-making regarding relations with India rested with the military. In the case of Kargil, the military kept the civilian government completely in the dark (Zehra 2018) until the operation was in full swing. But when the tensions became too high and endangered the mainland with a full-blown war between the clichéd "nuclear powers", Prime Minister Nawaz Sharif was forced to go to the United States to seek mediation and normalcy. It wasn't just the civilian government; the Pakistani media were equally oblivious to what was happening in Kargil and could not report from the field as the Indian media could. One isn't sure if Pakistani journalists weren't allowed access to the Northern Areas or they did not even try. In the absence of actual information, even some senior journalists were peddling the state narrative (Abbas 1999)—that it was Kashmiri mujahideen who had taken hold of Indian posts and Pakistani forces had nothing to do with it. Because many in Pakistan had access to Indian news channels, the security establishment found it hard to propagate their one-sided narrative. Soon, the role of the Northern Light Infantry, a regiment of the Pakistan army, became known; even the state acknowledged its martyrs whose valour is now part of our textbooks.

Following the events of Kargil, the military coup of 12 October 2009 that ousted Nawaz Sharif as prime minister and installed Gen. Musharraf as the head of the country, was a foregone outcome. Like always, the Supreme Court validated martial law, but this time gave Gen. Musharraf three years to hold the election. Some publications like *TNS* where I worked refused to address him as "chief executive" and "president" on their pages and instead kept using the title "General" Pervez Musharraf for a long time. It was an act of discreet resistance on the part of English-language journalism which did not have any real bearing on the country's politics.

The Kargil War taught one key lesson to the military government in Pakistan: it needed to create more space for electronic media to have bigger propaganda tools at its hand. The state broadcasters had little or no credibility. Musharraf's liberalising of the broadcast industry and issuing licences to private channels is generally assumed to be a progressive act, meant to free the media of all curbs. There is no shortage of naive analyses trying to prove that (Amir 2013). Note that India had started the process of liberalising the media almost a decade back, in 1992, and by 1997 its television viewership had phenomenally increased. The Kargil War was televised in India in every manner possible. This comment by Maroof Raza, strategic affairs expert for the leading Indian English-language TV channel *Times Now*, is telling: "Kargil was a watershed mark in the militarisation of the Indian mind" (Bose 2011). Here in Pakistan, we thought that the militarisation of the Indian mind happened with the live-televised 2008 Mumbai attacks; it happened long before that—during the Kargil War.

By July 2001, the media were held responsible for the failure of the much-publicised Agra summit, a two-day summit that aimed to resolve all outstanding issues between India and Pakistan, including the reduction of nuclear arsenals and the Kashmir issue. The media were found guilty for having hyped up expectations about the results of the meeting between Musharraf and Vajpayee.

To come back to the opening up of the airwaves, Musharraf had set up an electronic media regulator, the Pakistan Electronic Media Regulatory Authority (PEMRA), which was not really accepted by the private media. The private media were more in favour of self-regulation and thought of it as a tool in the hands of government to control the media, also because PEMRA excluded the state broadcasters from its purview. Another development was that PEMRA had originally prohibited cross-media ownership, but the Musharraf regime was soon pressurised by the bigger media groups into changing the laws and allowing it. This fact alone changed the entire media landscape and its ethos. In a matter of a decade, the privately owned commercially driven TV channels multiplied from three to a hundred and then even more between 2005 and 2015. According to a recent study by Reporters Without Borders (2019), "Most of the ownership of top 40—by audience share—news television channels, radio stations, newspapers and websites in Pakistan are concentrated in only a few hands, aided by lax legal restrictions on cross-media ownership. This environment, increasingly, restricts sources of information available to the public thereby limiting news-and-opinion diversity and pluralism in country's media landscape". When it comes to news media, both ownership and audience share are even more concentrated: "Top 4 television channels, radio stations, newspapers and news websites, in each category have over 50% of country's entire audience share" (Reporters Without Borders 2019).

In the 2000s, everyone had switched to television it seemed, and you could not enter a drawing room or office without hearing people talk about a recent talk show. The erstwhile moderator of the state-run PTV had become the "anchor" of these political talk shows, whose job it was to keep the viewers glued to his or her channel. These anchors went beyond information and analysis and tried to create high drama to improve the marketing potential of their programmes.

The newsrooms in the print media were a part of this discussion as well. Some saw television as the medium of the future and were keen to join at the first opportunity; others like us considered television as too lowbrow. Because of the nature of the medium, television offered women this rare opportunity to become anchors. I too was lured into joining it, but this is a pressure that I have resisted so far.

Terrorism and television side by side—Media in the 2000s

However, in the post-9/11 world, impacted by the Afghan and Iraq wars, it was terrorism that was the real elephant in the room. Pakistan's tribal belt or FATA region,[1] bordering Afghanistan, was considered a hub of collusion of militants belonging to al-Qaeda and the Taliban. Thus, in response to US President Bush's famous statement that there was no neutrality in the war on terrorism and "you are either with us or against us", Musharraf had no option but to be on the side of the US.

The war in Afghanistan had its fallout within Pakistan, with sporadic incidents of terrorism taking place. The government, making use of the carrot and stick policy, was busy making peace deals with militant Taliban commanders in FATA. Meanwhile, the writ of the government was challenged in the settled area of Swat and other places. The watershed moment was when the Lal Masjid students in the capital Islamabad held a Chinese health centre's staff hostage, and there was pressure on the government from the Chinese government, as well as the citizens voiced through media, to take action. The year was 2007. The developments were reported live till the complex, believed to be heavily armed, was besieged and captured, with lots of deaths whose figures remain contested (Hussain 2017). Thereafter, the country came under unending terrorist attacks, with the security and intelligence forces' headquarters in big cities, and shrines, marketplaces, and media houses in the tribal belt as targets (after 2010, even universities and schools have not been spared).

A rapidly expanding electronic media that thrived on sensationalism and spectacle could not have asked for anything better. Ill-equipped in every sense of the word, it started live coverage of these suicide blasts, sending their all-too-vulnerable reporters and photographers to these sites and later hospitals in their DSNG (Digital Satellite News Gathering) or OB (Outside Broadcasting) vans. The planners of these terrorist attacks could not have asked for anything better either. It became a sort of cycle, where such attacks would happen with regularity in the afternoon/evening so that they got live coverage till late night. Some sane voices from within the electronic media got together to develop a code of ethics on how to report terrorist incidents—the guidelines included refusing live coverage. By and large, terrorism and television stood side by side for many years.

The Musharraf government became known for its liberal leanings, pro-women legislation (even he couldn't touch the controversial blasphemy laws made stringent during the Zia dictatorship), putting in place a local bodies system (as all military dictators had done in the past but with more fanfare this time), and creating a political party—Pakistan Muslim League-Quaid-e-Azam (PML-Q)—to give his rule a civilian face. And yet it was a politically dead era because the leaders of two major political parties—Pakistan People's Party (PPP) and Pakistan Muslim League Nawaz (PML-N)—were in exile. To their credit, they had both signed a Charter of Democracy, a document for civilian supremacy in the country, in London in May 2006 which was duly reported and well received back home.

Another important event of 2006 was the publication of satirical cartoons of Prophet Mohammad (pbuh) in a Danish newspaper, condemned most strongly by Pakistan and Turkey among other countries of the Muslim world. The protests in Lahore on 14 February, followed by the worst rioting and burning of state and private property, were entirely unexpected. This was a diverse mob; some of them were motivated by Barelvi thought (but whose show of strength in this manner was unanticipated), but most of them seemed the regular, mostly unemployed, youth who saw an occasion to vent their frustration. This protest was reported in the media no doubt, but its details remained unexplained and unanalysed.

August the same year saw the brutal killing of Nawab Akbar Bugti, a tribal leader from Balochistan who had always sided with the state of Pakistan but finally stood against it, and settled in protest in the mountains of Dera Bugti. Balochistan was in the grip of insurgency in Musharraf's time and the security forces were dealing harshly with the insurgents. Many of them went missing, some recovered in the form of dead bodies. The media were under severe curbs to report what was actually happening on the ground. Private television did not really care about Balochistan. But some of the channels did try going to Quetta on Bugti's first anniversary when there was a shutdown call in the province. Munizae Jahangir, a television anchor from Lahore who was brave enough to go to Quetta that day, narrated sometime later that someone on the Quetta streets looked at her holding a microphone and said: "*Aap logon ne apna banda hi maar diya* [You killed your own man]". He was referring not just to Bugti's earlier association with the state but also the Baloch alienation from the rest of Pakistan, especially Punjab. In other parts of the country, it was kind of accepted that media in Balochistan was under threat from both militants and the military, the same narrative that was conveniently held for the tribal areas where the military was by then engaged in military operations that became more potent with passing years and displaced huge swathes of the population.

It was the 2007 Lawyers' Movement for the restoration of the chief justice of the Supreme Court (CJP) that brought together the political opponents and civil society in their collective anger against the Musharraf regime. Because it picked it as a major issue, the media's—or television's—role is said to be that of a catalyst for this movement, which shook the foundations of the Musharraf regime. It took some time before he actually quit, first as army chief, and then for the president of the CJP to be restored to his office, but the power of the media was firmly established. It was this power that the media (from the 1990s to the 2000s the terms "press" and "journalism" were replaced with "media") exercised with a vengeance—in becoming part of the political turmoil, and sometimes creating it, instead of maintaining its neutrality.

There also was violence committed on sectarian grounds and even though Punjab was a hub where such incidents against Ahmadis were common, terrorist attacks against Hazara Shias in Balochistan and Ismailis in Karachi were continuously reported. In Punjab again, Christians were at the receiving end of complaints leading to mob violence, incidents that had surged after the controversial blasphemy laws were put in place. As an English-language paper, *TNS* tried to make these issues a priority but they had to be covered very sensitively. We didn't want to give the extremist elements negative publicity, so even the photographs of people like Mumtaz Qadri were used with discretion. One incident that happened in May 2015 at Safoora Goth in Karachi comes to mind where eight gunmen shot and killed all 46 Ismaili Muslims. Soon after, there was a suggestion to do a special report on the role of various Ismaili Muslims in the country, in their individual and institutional capacity. But the suggestion was rejected because we did not want to assign them a "special" "minority" status when they are equal citizens under the Constitution.

Gender and journalism

I have often been asked questions about the challenges for women journalists—and later women editors—which are perfectly legitimate considering the male dominance in most fields in Pakistan. I can only speak from personal experience. When I joined the profession in 1992, there were structural barriers almost cast in stone. Women were discouraged from joining as reporters and even in the newsrooms, largely because these sections maintained late hours. Women were considered more suitable for magazines or for specialised beats. In the power hierarchy, reporting figured on top followed by deskwork, putting women at a natural disadvantage. By the time I joined, women journalists had already established themselves as the finest editors of monthly magazines of high standard. When I, too, was consigned to the magazine section of the paper, luckily there were positive role models to look up to. Around that time, women became editors of newspapers too, and the Jang Group took the lead in doing this.

In later years, as I grew comfortable in the magazine section of *The News*, also because it happened to be the best weekly, I always thought how unnecessary those barriers were, how easy it was to close the edition much earlier than it usually is (as is done in the West), and how useful it was to employ women in every section of the newspaper. Almost three decades later, print journalism continues to be the male-dominated dinosaur, extremely slow in bringing gender diversity into its reporting and newsrooms. Electronic media, I am told, is not too dissimilar, especially when it comes to having more women in its influential sections.

However, once at work, I honestly felt gender had ceased to exist, at least in certain respects. I may have been structurally pigeonholed into working for a particular section, but I was looking at issues with a journalist's mind—from a gender-neutral perspective, you could say. However, as editor, I was always conscious of women representation in our newsroom, in the stories we published and wrote, in the comments we got from women experts, and in presenting the women's side of the picture that went beyond mere tokenism.

My experience has been peculiarly rewarding for me to conclude that it is one of the best professions for women. It may sound patronising or not so true to those women who work in the field or, say, in Urdu-language media, but within the office environment in the papers that I worked for, I felt there was less harassment. Of course, there is still a lot of ground to be covered. The media need to realise that they can't preach to the world about gender balance without setting their own house in order first.

More on censorship—The future of print in the times of other mediums

It was January 2007 when I took charge as editor of *TNS*. My first thought was I had some really big shoes to fill. But those were heady days (I wonder what days are not if you happen to live in Pakistan) and there was no time to think. The magazine was set up and led in 1994 by Beena Sarwar, a very strong woman editor, so I did not need to fret about that. I also looked up to Razia Bhatti, that shining star of journalism and the editor of the *Herald* and *Newsline*, as an inspiration. Besides, it was an English-language weekly (newspaper magazines were considered soft journalism), so censorship was not at the top of my mind either; high professional standards were.

I was more worried about the structural problems: the arrival and mushrooming of private television had diluted the talent base; many of the print journalists had found lucrative jobs in television channels, largely because of cross-media ownership; there weren't as many universities churning out trained personnel to feed media this size. Standards were becoming lax; no organisation was bothered about investing in training, least of all in print, or specialisation. The struggle began, in minds and on pages, to keep the progressive and pro-people outlook of the magazine; challenge the state narrative for the cause of democracy; speak for the marginalised; and bring *TNS* to the helm of the national debate. The real fight was against our laziness. The red lines were drawn in the minds, but we kept trying to push the boundaries.

There were political red lines that stood out sharply. Balochistan remained uncovered, and so did FATA; this is where post 9/11, all military operations took place to expel the "terrorists". We assigned articles to reporters in Karachi on the Muttahida Qaumi Movement (MQM), an ethnic outfit infamous for employing thug violence against political opponents, but all we got was excuses in return. We published an interview of MQM founder Altaf Hussain after editing out the self-promotional parts, but were asked by the management to publish another instalment of the interview, including everything we had edited out; otherwise, the management feared or was told, the Jang publications would not be distributed in Karachi.

The military operations in Swat and FATA were not covered by the media or us because there was only the ISPR version to rely on. When Hamid Mir, an anchorperson at *TNS*'s electronic cousin GEO, was attacked in 2014, GEO blamed the military. Consequently, the establishment became a permanent enemy of the Jang Group. The struggle for survival began in earnest, taking away our remaining freedoms one after the other. In January 2015, an article on the then army chief Raheel Sharif was pulled out of *TNS* while it was being printed. In 2018, a story on the forced closure of Radio *Mashaal* was filed by a reporter in the Peshawar bureau who requested it to be run without his byline. In 2018 again, a young intern who did a detailed piece in *TNS* on the crackdown on the NGOs and INGOs for our magazine was hounded by intelligence officials. No analyst or reporter was ready to write a profile of Maulana Masood Azhar after the "Pulwama attack" in February 2019 that brought India and Pakistan to the verge of war. The suicide bombing targeting the Indian military in the Pulwama district of Indian-held Kashmir was claimed by Jaish-e-Muhammad, an outfit led by Azhar.

Other than politics, the advertisers, especially in the real estate sector, were our major worry. And of course, we could not print nudes or semi-nude pictures with art reviews, even for a painter like Jamil Naqsh.

The sad part is that, especially since 2013–14, there wasn't any unity seen among the media houses; they would rather collude with the state against other media groups for their survival. The good part is that despite this cannibalistic tendency, the fight for the freedom of expression is still being waged—from electronic to print to digital to blogs to social media. The retaliation from the state has followed in the same order.

Laws and regulations were made stricter, but even those laws were not used when the five bloggers from the Punjab and capital territory were forcibly disappeared in January 2017. For once, there was extreme fear even on social media. However, the outrage was such that the bloggers were all returned. They were not just badly tortured; social media had been used to spread blasphemy allegations against them, forcing them all to leave the country as soon as they were released. The ill-conceived cybercrime law did not help matters. And now, under the new government headed by former cricket star Imran Khan and constituted in 2018, there is talk of one common regulator for all kinds of media.

It is against this backdrop that we must discuss the relevance or fate of different media, including print. In the same interview for this research, I. A. Rehman asked an important question: when we talk of curtailment of freedom of expression, we talk of content, but what happens to people? "Generation after generation of journalists is suffocated because they want to say something but cannot, because of the restrictions. The society turns against them; half the readers don't understand what they are trying to say and the other half complains they don't say things openly" (Rehman 2017). This way, he says, their talent is wasted and the overall standard of journalism declines.

Rehman, who has remained associated with print media, acknowledges that print, despite its drawbacks, has had a longer time to mature in this country, whereas electronic media is "still in its adolescence if not infancy". He dwells on the "linguistic relationship that is established between the reader and the words, phrases and concepts used in the print media". Electronic media, he says, are quick and easy to understand, give instant coverage, but have no deliberation or analysis. Electronic media are understood as a medium of the masses and therefore, Rehman says "there are more efforts to infiltrate it".

At this point in time, all the different media coexist and apparently feed on each other, and it is difficult to predict if one or all will survive. It definitely has changed the face of journalism. Technology has made many things easier, not least for the subeditor. But, one is tempted to add, it is making journalists lazier; whatever little spot reporting is done or views from the field are available are excessively celebrated on social media. For journalists working in the mainstream media, the problems are systemic. In the absence of or weakened trade unions, even their fat salaries do not provide the security they need. They seek it in technology, on social media where they are able to curate "their brands" (Zia 2018).

It is essential to understand that whether it is print, electronic, digital, or social media, its values will remain the same: "Whatever media survives in the end, it should be free," says I. A. Rehman. Today, he laments, there is no thinkable space left. That should be a real cause for worry, because no one wants to live in a conformist society.

Note

1 FATA denotes Federally Administered Tribal Areas. The FATA districts were merged into Khyber Pukhtunkhwa province in 2018.

References

Abbas, Z. 1999. "When Pakistan and India went to war". *Herald*, 7 February 2017 (accessed 30 August 2019), https://herald.dawn.com/news/1153481.

Amir, A. 2013. "Musharraf and the media". *The News*, 6 December 2013 (accessed 5 September 2019), www.thenews.com.pk/print/88367-musharraf-and-the-media.

Bose, D. 2011. "Journalism caught in narrow nationalism: The India-Pakistan media war". University of Oxford: Reuters Institute Fellowship Paper (accessed 2 September, 2019), https://reutersinstitute.politics.ox.ac.uk/sites/default/files/2017-10/Journalism_Caught_in_Narrow_Nationalism_The_India-Pakistan_Media_War.pdf.

Cheema, N. 2019. "Why Pakistan's official narrative is not serving it well". *Herald*, April 2019 (accessed 15 August 2019), https://herald.dawn.com/news/1398851.

Hashim, A. 2019. "Silenced: Pakistan's journalists decry new era of censorship". *Al Jazeera* (accessed 10 August, 2019), www.aljazeera.com/indepth/features/pakistan-journalists-decry-era-censorship-190813064754381.html.

Hussain, Z. 2017. "The legacy of Lal Masjid". *Dawn*, 9 July 2017 (accessed 10 September 2019), www.dawn.com/news/1344098.

Menon, K. 2000. "Pakistan: The press for change". Committee to Protect Journalists (accessed 5 September 2019), https://cpj.org/reports/2000/02/pakistan07feb00br.php.

Niazi, Z. 1986. *The Press in Chains*. Karachi: Royal Book Company.

Rehman, I. A. 2017. "Stringent measures for a dangerous lot". *Dawn*, 30 December 2017 (accessed 1 September 2019), dawn.com/news/1379761.

Reporters Without Borders. 2019. Media ownership monitor (accessed 6 September 2019), http://pakistan.mom-rsf.org/en/findings/concentration/.

Zehra, N. 2018. *From Kargil to the Coup: Events that Shook Pakistan*. Lahore: Sang-e-Meel.

Zia, F. 2018. "A developing story". *The News on Sunday*, 24 June 2018 (accessed 21 September 2019), http://tns.thenews.com.pk/developing-story/.

11

COVERING THE PERIPHERY

Balochistan as a blind spot in the mainstream newspapers of Pakistan

Adnan Aamir

"We are still demonising communities yet no activism on the part of citizens is there. Balochistan represents one such population which is not being covered properly because it does not guarantee good ratings to the media" (Mansoor 2014). These words by I. A. Rehman, former Secretary General at the Human Rights Commission of Pakistan (HRCP), summarise the concerns of media scholars, journalists, and intellectuals who feel Balochistan, the largest province of Pakistan geographically, is being widely ignored by the mainstream Pakistani media.

This chapter, in investigating the coverage of the province, further explores the widely accepted but rarely researched phenomenon of insufficient, shallow, and sometimes biased coverage of Balochistan province in the mainstream media outlets with a Pakistan-wide outreach. However, this study restricts itself to the coverage of Balochistan in two mainstream Pakistani newspapers. Specifically, it analyses the coverage of two incidents—a terrorist attack killing members of a minority community and a financial scandal in Balochistan—before and after these incidents.

This chapter has a two-fold aim. First, the media landscape of Balochistan is mapped. Second, based on two case studies, this chapter argues that Balochistan is covered by the mainstream media only when it offers tabloidised fare for what can be called "disaster journalism" (defined below). Instances of such topics include terrorist attacks or sensationalised corruption scams.

To provide a holistic picture and delineate Balochistan's marginality, this chapter will begin by exploring the nature and issues related to media outlets in Balochistan province itself within the context of history, growth of the media, and political dynamics in the province. Additionally, the status of different forms of media, including TV, newspaper, radio, and the internet, are examined, along with the media linkages to the government and civil society, and training of journalists.

The final section investigates coverage of the province in *Dawn* and *Daily Express*, newspapers published in the federal capital of Islamabad, with the assumption that Balochistan is insufficiently covered, without socio-cultural and historical contexts of the area, by the mainstream press both in the English and Urdu languages.

Balochistan as periphery

Balochistan, located in south-west Pakistan and sharing borders with Iran and Afghanistan, is the largest province of Pakistan in terms of area, with six administrative divisions and 33 administrative districts (Government 2018). Paradoxically, despite being the largest province of Pakistan area-wise, Balochistan is the smallest province in terms of population. According to the census of 2017, the population of Balochistan was 12.34 million (Statistics 2017). Balochistan is also an ethnically diverse province where 65% of the population consists of Baloch, 25% are Pashtun, while the remaining 10% includes such diverse ethnic groups as Hazaras, Punjabis, Urdu-speaking, and Seraikis (Statistics 2008).

The economy of Balochistan is dependent upon agriculture, natural resources, and government jobs. There are hardly any large manufacturing units and private-sector organisations which may provide mass employment (Government 2018). Balochistan is considered to be the least developed province of Pakistan. This under-development can be traced back to British rule. Arguably, under the British Raj, Balochistan was deliberately kept underdeveloped (Baloch 2014). However, Balochistan's lack of political representation and exploitation on a nationalist basis, post-1947, has only prolonged Balochistan's economic misery.

Different economic indicators can further gauge the economic underdevelopment of Balochistan. On the Multidimensional Poverty Index (MPI), Balochistan is at the top in Pakistan: 71.2% of the population lives below the poverty line (Pakistan 2016). According to the Planning Commission (2011), the maternal mortality rate in Balochistan is 785 out of 100,000 mothers giving birth, while the same rate is 272 for the national average of Pakistan. Likewise, according to the Pakistan Bureau of Statistics (2016) the adult literacy rate in Balochistan is 38%, which is the lowest in a country where the national average is 57%. The unemployment rate of Balochistan is just 3.92% according to the labour force survey of Pakistan. However, research conducted in Balochistan shows that up to 1,500 jobs are available to almost 30,000 job seekers in Balochistan on an annual basis (Aamir 2016b).

Balochistan's economic underdevelopment has been aggravated by concomitant political turmoil ever since Pakistan's independence in 1947. The starting point of the insurgencies was the accession of Balochistan to Pakistan in March 1948 (Ahmer 2016). Currently, Balochistan is going through the fifth round of an armed separatist insurgency. This phase started in 2005 and has been in progress ever since. Earlier, four insurgencies took place in Balochistan in 1948, 1958–59, 1962–69, and 1973–77.

Balochistan has 65 members of its assembly, while 20 members represent the province in the National Assembly and 23 members in the Senate of Pakistan.

Politicians in Balochistan routinely complain about Balochistan's inadequate share in the federal structure of Pakistan. For instance, since the creation of Pakistan, only two Baloch have held the office of prime minister for short stints. Mir Zafarullah Khan Jamali served as prime minister from 2002 to 2004, while Mir Hazar Khan Khosa served as caretaker prime minister in 2013 for only three months (AFP 2013). Currently, there are only two Baloch in the 48-member federal cabinet of Pakistan (Assembly 2019).

Historically, an ideologically diverse set of political parties have ruled the province of Balochistan. In general, the political parties can be divided into two main categories: (1) federalist parties that work as the provincial chapter of Pakistan-wide parties; (2) nationalist parties who base their politics on the rights of ethnic groups in Balochistan. Since the creation of Balochistan as an administrative province in 1970, nationalists have been at the helm for merely six years (Aamir 2017b).

Balochistan's political marginality is mirrored in its media sphere too. Chronologically, the history of the mass media in the province can be traced back to1888 when Albert Press, a printing press, was established by Dadabhai Golwala, a Parsi businessman based in Quetta, the provincial capital. Albert Press is considered the founding stone of all media organisations in Balochistan. In the same year, the monthly *Balochistan Advertiser* was launched, which was the first newspaper in Balochistan. This newspaper, as the name suggests, only carried advertisements and classified ads (Tahir 2006).

After the Partition of India in 1947, the weekly *Zamana* (*Period*), launched by Barkat Ali Azad in 1948, was a pioneering media venture in the province. By the 1960s, *Zamana* moved on to a daily broadsheet (Khan 2010). The driving force behind *Zamana*'s progress was Syed Fasih Iqbal, the co-editor. In 1955, he bought its ownership rights, and *Zamana* reigned supreme as Balochistan media's flagship publication until the early 1970s. *Zamana*'s period was not yet over, yet its monopoly was subverted. The challenge arrived from other competitors.

From 1972 onwards, national newspapers began publishing their editions from Balochistan (Tahir 2006). For instance, in 1972, Karachi-based daily *Jang* (*War*) as well as the daily *Mashriq* (*East*), also a Karachi-based chain paper, launched their Urdu-language editions from Quetta. To this day, *Jang* and *Mashriq* remain the leading Urdu-language newspapers published from Balochistan.

The 1970s are important for another reason, as the decade marked the start of English-language publications. The initiative, yet again, was taken by *Zamana* proprietor, Syed Fasih Iqbal. In 1976, the *Zamana* group of newspapers launched the *Balochistan Times* as the first English-language daily newspaper from Balochistan. In 1991, Siddique Baloch founded the *Balochistan Express,* yet another English-language daily newspaper from Balochistan (Tahir 2006). Siddique Baloch (1940–2018) was a veteran journalist whose journalistic career spanned over five decades. Prior to launching the *Balochistan Express* he worked as a staff reporter of *Dawn* for 20 years. He is considered the father of English journalism in Balochistan (Ghori 2018).

It will not be a huge digression to briefly acknowledge here Syed Fasih Iqbal's contributions to Balochistan's media. Considered as the founder of the modern press in Balochistan, he not only founded the important newspapers mentioned above, he is also credited with introducing commercial logic to the press. Before Iqbal, the concept of revenue generation through commercial advertisements was rather alien to the press in the province. During his illustrious career, he was elected as the president of the All Pakistan Newspapers Society (APNS) as well as the Council of Pakistan Newspapers Editors (CPNE). The former is a newspaper-owners' guild, while the latter, as the name suggests, is a platform for editors. He was also elected as the president of the South Asia Editors Forum (SAEF), a body of editors of press organisations across South Asia (Notezai 2014).

Currently, among the widely read newspapers, one may include the daily *Jang*, the daily *Express*, the daily *Mashriq*, and the daily *Intehkhab* (Relations 2014).

Beyond the press, state-owned electronic media also arrived Balochistan early on. With the launching of Radio Pakistan in 1956 in Quetta, radio transmissions began in Urdu and regional languages of Balochistan, including Brahvi, Balochi, and Pashtu. Radio Pakistan still commands a sizeable audience in the province, despite a declining trend in the rest of Pakistan. Television, unlike radio, began to infiltrate Balochistan airwaves with a delay compared to the rest of Pakistan. A Pakistan Television Corporation (PTV) station was first established in Quetta in 1975.

However, with the decline of state monopoly over the airwaves from 2002 onwards, several privately owned radio and television networks began broadcasting in the province. Presently, out of the seven privately owned FM radio networks, five are commercial, while two are non- profit (PEMRA 2019). Likewise, 19 news channels are operating in Balochistan (Relations 2014). Almost all national news channels have a bureau office in Quetta, while no such bureaux are maintained in the rest of the province.

In addition to the print and electronic media, social media are also penetrating Balochistan and the internet has spurred on a few e-zines. *Baloch Hal* was the first such online initiative in Balochistan. Launched on 10 November 2009, *Baloch Hal* was edited by Malik Siraj. It soon established itself as a source of candid reporting at a time when insurgency in Balochistan was worrying the authorities. Consequently, it was officially blocked inside Pakistan on 1 November 2010. *Baloch Hal* primarily had two goals: to play the role of an agitator on behalf of the Baloch nationalist cause and to train a new generation of young journalists and writers. Many Baloch journalists whose initial writings were published in *Baloch Hal* eventually ended up writing for the national and international media. *Baloch Hal* was officially closed on 10 February 2015, when it was no longer economically affordable (Akbar 2017).

Meanwhile, a few online newspapers have sprouted up in the blogosphere. These are all not-for-profit ventures. Notable among these online ventures are the *Balochistan Point, Balochistan Voices, Balochistan Times,* and Urdu-language *Haal Hawal*. There are several news websites too, but operated anonymously, such platforms lack credibility, quality, and authenticity.

Online journalism also offers new opportunities to young journalists who start with a blog or online platform and keep writing persistently. In some cases, editors from national and international publications reach out to talented writers and invite them to report for them (Akbar 2017). However, online journalism in Balochistan does not have any sustainable revenue model, which makes it difficult for online media platforms to survive in the long run.

Media, government control, and media training

It can be claimed that the provincial government is effectively running, in terms of political economy, the media industry in Balochistan. The survival of print media in the province solely depends upon the advertisements provided by the provincial government, which allocates a large sum of money for government ads to be distributed among the print media, based on their recorded circulation. From July 2017 to June 2018, the Balochistan government spent Rs 548 million ($3.41 million) on advertisements (Finance Department 2018).

Hundreds of newspapers and magazines have been registered with the Directorate General of Public Relations (DGPR), the provincial authority to coordinate with the press. The overwhelming majority of these publications are what in vernacular journalistic lingo one calls "dummy publications". A dummy publication has no real circulation. A few dozen copies of the dummy publication are published and submitted to the DGPR for record-keeping. Such dummy publications are not available to the public in the newspaper market. According to the DGPR data analysed for this study, there are 163 dailies in Balochistan, 107 monthlies, 18 fortnightly publications, and 52 weeklies.

How many of these publications registered with the DGPR are apocryphal dummy' publications? Hard to guess. But the majority of these publications lack any considerable audience, if at all. A high proportion of dummy publications corresponds to a high level of corruption since these dummy publications also claim huge circulations and claim a considerable share in the government-sponsored ad spend.

Moreover, the DGPR issues accreditation cards to journalists, which is official recognition for journalists in the province. The DGPR has issued accreditation cards to 380 journalists, and most of them are family members of publishers and not working journalists. Many working journalists who are active in the field are deprived of accreditation cards (Unnamed 2016). Many national newspapers based out of Balochistan, such as *Jang* and *Express,* receive large sums of money as advertisements from the Balochistan government, but they don't give proper coverage to the province in their national editions (Shah 2017).

Press clubs are centres of journalistic activities in any town where journalists not only socialise, but they also provide a known venue as a source of news and publicity for the public, organisations, and the government. Press clubs provide operating space for the journalists who either don't have offices or work on a freelance basis. The presence of a press club, thus, is also a barometer of the level of journalistic activity in that area. There are 27 registered press clubs in Balochistan

(Ahmad 2015). The oldest and most developed one is the Quetta Press Club, established in 1959 (Tahir 2006). Since 1989, elections are regularly held for office bearers every two years.

Journalist unions based in the provincial capital Quetta are strong and have the power to exert influence on the government. There are more than 1,000 journalists in Balochistan, and 200 of them are based in the provincial capital of Quetta. However, Quetta Press Club only has a membership of 130 journalists, and 400 journalists from the province are members of Pakistan Federal Union of Journalists, PFUJ (IFJ 2015).

In Balochistan, journalists fall into two categories: those who are working in Quetta and those in the interior areas of the province. Most of the journalists working in Quetta are provided with salaries and other facilities, whereas their employing organisations almost never pay journalists in the interior. Some of these are involved in business, while others are government employees. In several cases, the journalists who have other jobs are also involved in blackmailing and corruption (Zulfiqar 2016).

In Balochistan, journalism is taught at three universities: the University of Balochistan, Sardar Bahadur Khan Women's University (SBKWU), and Balochistan University of Information Technology, Engineering, and Management Sciences (BUITEMS). The University of Balochistan (UoB) was the first university to start teaching Mass Communication in the late 1980s. Most journalists in Balochistan have graduated from UoB. While SBKWU's Mass Communication Department is still in its infancy, BUITEMS' Department of Mass Communication was established in 2010, and over 150 students have enrolled there (Zakir 2016).

The dynamics of media are complex in Balochistan. Ongoing insurgency, the strong tribal system, and the prevailing social fabric have made it very difficult for journalists to operate beyond certain boundaries. Journalism has thus been limited to event reporting, reporting only the official viewpoint using press releases and conducting harmless interviews. Therefore, media outlets are unable to play the role of idiomatic fourth pillar or the apocryphal watchdog. Within the context of the above mapping of the media sphere in Balochistan, the next section focuses on the coverage of Balochistan in the two mainstream newspapers of Pakistan.

Coverage of Balochistan in the mainstream media

There is a perception that Balochistan does not get adequate coverage in Pakistan's mainstream media. Meanwhile, ever since 2005, Balochistan has been undergoing a low-intensity insurgency, and the matter has become globalised to some extent. Still, the province and the vital problems facing the Baloch people, as well as other ethnic groups in the province, do not get media attention that can be described as either fair or sufficient.

The lack of news coverage in the case of Balochistan can be traced back to the British Raj when the colonial rulers discouraged the development of news media in the province. In their view, a free press would have undermined their interests in countering the USSR (Shah 2017). This trend has, unfortunately, persisted post-1947. In fact, Balochistan's exclusion in the mainstream media has become a huge political question for the Baloch people.

Balochistan's political leadership, particularly with a nationalistic bent, has complained on a fairly regular basis about the inadequate coverage of the province in the mainstream media. For instance, Sardar Akhtar Mengal, who heads the Balochistan National Party (BNP) and has served as Balochistan's Chief Minister (1997–98), has been flagging Balochistan's exclusion in the mainstream media. He said that media in Pakistan is doing the same with Balochistan, which the federal government always does, which is to ignore Balochistan (Aamir 2017a). Likewise, BNP stalwarts have protested the media blackout of Balochistan on several occasions. In December 2014, television cable service providers shut down all news channels in Balochistan for two weeks after the BNP announced a boycott of news channels (Anon 2014).

Even some of the prominent Pakistani columnists have endorsed the criticism mounted by Akhtar Mengal Abbas Nasir, former editor of *Dawn*, who argues that Balochistan is not getting its due attention in the mainstream media of Pakistan. He wrote that what the Baloch see as a burning issue, i.e., disappearances, has more or less been "disappeared" from the media thanks to the cloak of invisibility (Nasir 2016).

The debate that Balochistan is not getting adequate coverage has, in turn, triggered the debate about the reasons behind this shallow and insufficient coverage of Balochistan. I. A. Rehman claims that Balochistan is not being covered in the media because it does not guarantee good media ratings (Mansoor 2014). In other words, Balochistan is not an attractive market either for advertisers or media bosses.

TV ratings have become a decisive factor in media coverage in the case of commercially driven news channels (Aamir 2015a). There are more than 4,000 rating meters in Pakistan, and only 20 of them have been installed in Balochistan, most of these in Quetta. This means only less than 1% of TV rating meters are installed across Balochistan (Shah 2017).

Interestingly, in 2016 a delegation of newspapers and media owners visited Balochistan to investigate the problems facing the journalist fraternity in Quetta. Mujeeb-ur-Rehman Shami, the then CPNE chairperson, correctly observed that the miniscule coverage devoted to Balochistan province in the mainstream media was due to so-called "national security" concerns. He also attributed the lack of Balochistan's coverage to the fact that the province is not an attractive media market for commercially driven media outlets (Zulfiqar 2016).

Insurgency is yet another explanation for restricted coverage of Balochistan. As mentioned earlier, Balochistan is witnessing a low-intensity insurgency, and an overall tense environment is stifling for media practitioners. Media operations in a conflict-ridden region are always problematic. For instance, any news report covering a security-related event is viewed with scepticism by the security establishment. Consequently, the news channels or newspapers discourage such reporting (Aamir 2015b). In certain other cases, a media outlet may invite the wrath of the militant groups unhappy over the coverage of their activities. Like journalists in any other conflict-hit region, the reporters in Balochistan usually find themselves between the security establishment's hammer and the militant's anvil.

Quantitatively, the situation of insecurity among journalists results in reduced coverage of the province. That 38 journalists have been killed in Balochistan from 2007 to 2019 speaks volumes about the security situation. Understandably, journalists practice fairly intensive self-censorship (IFJ 2015). In fact, since 2015, the journalist community has observed 28 August as the day of Martyred Journalists to honour the journalists who lost their lives in the line of duty in the province of Balochistan. This commemoration was a response to the target-killings of Irshaad Mastoi, a noted journalist, gunned down along with two of his colleagues, Abdul Rasool Khajjak and Muhammad Younas, in his office on 28 August 2014 (Aamir 2015a).

To recapitulate, a mapping of media in Balochistan establishes the following key features. First, this province is not a lucrative media market. Second, the media in Balochistan is operative in a situation of conflict. Third, a lack of professionalism and media corruption has also hindered the growth of media in Balochistan. Finally, and most importantly, Balochistan's under-development implies that the province is not an attractive market for commercially driven mainstream media outlets based in such metropolitan centres as Lahore and Karachi. Hence, Balochistan's marginality. In the following, this exclusion will be established through two case studies. I will begin with a brief sketch of my research methodology.

Research methodology

This study examines the coverage of two events in Balochistan which received considerable attention in the mainstream media. First, a suicide attack on the Hazara community in January 2013. Ethnically Hazaras people migrated to Quetta (and surrounding areas) in the nineteenth century from Afghanistan. By faith, Hazaras are Shia Muslims. The other event, in May 2016, was the recovery of Rs 630 million (US$3.92 million) from the residence of Mushtaq Raisani, a top bureaucrat, in a raid by the anti-corruption agency NAB. This research has monitored the coverage of these two events four days prior to as well as four days after these incidents in two dailies. The broadsheets examined are the Urdu-language *Express* and the English-language *Dawn*, which were established in 1998 and 1941, respectively. *Dawn* is published from 3 cities, whereas the *Express* is published from 12 cities. These two newspapers were chosen because they are among the most read newspapers in Pakistan in Urdu and English. For the purpose of this research, their editions from the federal capital Islamabad were scanned for data gathering because the regional editions from provincial capitals mostly carry regional news of those cities. Any news about Balochistan on the front page, national page, back page, and the editorial page of these newspapers was counted.

Both these events, I argue, constitute ready topics for "disaster journalism". Coined by Sulehria (2018: 87), the term "disaster journalism" is "a variant of what Canadian author Naomi Klein describes as 'disaster capitalism' under the 'Shock

Doctrine'" (Klein 2007). By "disaster journalism", Sulehria implies tabloidised media content "that is cheap to produce and predictable in the sense that it is likely to draw a regular audience and generate advertisers' interest through a certain amount of shock. Sex, violence, and spectacle constitute concrete personifications of tabloidised television" (Sulehria (2018: 87).

Tragedy in Balochistan makes headlines

On 10 January 2013, 81 people were killed in two bomb explosions at a market in Alamdar Road in Quetta. The majority of the victims belonged to the Hazara community who practice Shia Islam. Members of the Hazara community immediately staged a sit-in and refused to bury the dead until their demands were met (Shahid 2013). The symbolically powerful and unique but tragic protest began to attract attention beyond the province, and it created a political crisis for the provincial government. It led to the imposition of the so-called Governor's Rule, whereby the provincial cabinet of Balochistan was dissolved, and a federally appointed governor replaced the chief minister as the chief executive of the province.

This attack was reported in the press on 11 January, one day after the bomb explosion. For the purpose of this research, I documented the news coverage from 7 January to 13 January 2013. For the sake of brevity, I present my findings in Table 11.1, which shows the number of news items related to Balochistan published by the newspapers on the given dates.

The findings show that during the four days preceding the explosions on Alamdar Road, Balochistan was covered just once by the *Express* while it ran 25 news stories and op-eds in the four days in the wake of the tragic attack on Hazaras. Similarly, *Dawn* covered 12 stories and op-eds related to Balochistan in the four preceding days, while 24 stories appeared on the next four days.

The data indicates that both these newspapers considerably, in fact, dramatically for any Baloch observers, increased coverage of Balochistan after the terrorist attack. Incidentally, the number of news stories covered by both newspapers remained almost the same: 25 for *Dawn* and 24 for the *Express*. The assumption that Balochistan only gets the attention of the mainstream media when an extraordinary incident of terrorism happens holds true.

TABLE 11.1 Number of stories published about Balochistan before and after Hazaras bomb explosion

Newspaper	7 Jan	8 Jan	9 Jan	10 Jan	11 Jan	12 Jan	13 Jan	14 Jan	15 Jan
Dawn	1	3	5	3	5	7	4	3	5
Express	0	0	0	1	1	3	5	6	10

Source: Author

A financial scam in Balochistan makes headlines

On 6 May 2016, the National Accountability Bureau (NAB), a team of the federal accountability watchdog in Pakistan, raided the residence of Mushtaq Raisani, Secretary Finance of Balochistan. The NAB squad recovered a whopping sum worth Rs 630 million in cash. The currency notes were hidden in various nooks and corners of his palatial residence. Mushtaq Raisani was arrested and the Advisor to the Chief Minister of Balochistan on Finance, Khalid Langove, resigned. He was later also arrested. This was the biggest anti-corruption raid in the history of the country (Aamir 2016a).

This incident was sensationally reported in the press on 7 May. For the purpose of this study, the coverage of Balochistan was scanned from 3 May to 11 May in the two dailies selected as case studies. Table 11.2 shows the number of news items related to Balochistan covered by the newspapers under study.

Table 11.2 shows that in the four days preceding the day of the incident, Balochistan was covered just twice by the *Express* and included eight news stories in the four days after the news of the scandal was broken. Similarly, *Dawn* covered Balochistan 9 times in the four preceding days, while 14 stories were featured in the following four days after the incident. Overall, both newspapers considerably increased coverage of Balochistan after the scam, although the number of stories covered by *Dawn* was higher before and after the incident as compared to the *Express*. The total number of stories covered by both newspapers were 23 for *Dawn* and 10 for the *Express*. Obviously, the Urdu-language newspaper paid less attention to the province than the English-language newspaper.

Further analysis of the data shows that over the nine-day period of data analysis, both newspapers combined published an average of seven news stories per day during the attack on Hazaras and four news stories per day during the Finance Department scandal. This indicates that Balochistan doesn't get much coverage in the mainstream Urdu and English newspapers. Likewise, the data also shows that both newspapers covered more stories related to Balochistan during the attack on Hazaras as compared to the financial scam. This strongly indicates that Balochistan gets more coverage when there are terrorism-related incidents as compared to other stories. Moreover, the attack on Hazaras dominated both newspapers during the period of analysis. Overall, 51% of the news stories in *Dawn* and 83% of the news stories published in the *Express* related to

TABLE 11.2 Press coverage of Balochistan before and after the financial scandal

Newspaper	3 May	4 May	5 May	6 May	7 May	8 May	9 May	10 May	11 May
Dawn	4	2	0	3	3	3	1	4	3
Express	0	1	0	1	1	2	1	2	2

Source: Author

Balochistan were about the attack on Hazaras. However, in the case of the financial scandal, the coverage of the scandal made up 25% of news published in *Dawn* and 55% of news published in the *Express* related to Balochistan.

The research also indicates that *Dawn* gave relatively balanced coverage to Balochistan during these incidents, whereas the *Express* overwhelmingly focused on these two issues during the period of analysis, excluding other stories related to the province. Similarly, the data indicates that the other news stories related to the target killings of the Hazara community were the second major focus of the newspapers. These target killings made up 15% of the coverage of *Dawn* and 10% of the coverage of the *Express* during the period in question. Corruption in Balochistan was the third major issue covered in both newspapers, which made up 10% of the total Balochistan-related coverage in both newspapers.

Conclusion

Based on the results of this study, it can be concluded that the coverage of Balochistan in the national media increases for a short period of time when a major incident of national importance takes place in the province. The Urdu press routinely gives almost negligible coverage to Balochistan, and coverage increases in the case of any terrorist attack or a government scandal. Also, the English press, particularly *Dawn*, routinely gives reasonable coverage to Balochistan, which increases when an extraordinary incident takes place.

The study also indicates that terrorism in Balochistan is the main subject which gets coverage on a regular basis. When a major incident happens, the coverage gets out of proportion for a few days, and other news items get buried. Likewise, the coverage of the English press is relatively better in terms of covering Balochistan on a routine basis. Content analysis also reveals that the coverage of Urdu newspapers is more sensational and melodramatic as compared to the English press. Content analysis of individual news stories published in both Urdu and English newspapers shows that most of the news stories only cover the information which has been released in the form of a press release or already reported by the TV news channels. We can say that most of the coverage is based on official versions of the incidents, avoiding the critical analysis of these news events within the context of history, law and order, administration, and socio-cultural issues.

There is hardly ever a detailed news story on the event with new information not known to the audience. Overall, the news coverage of Balochistan in the national press is insufficient, shallow, and scanty, without any socio-cultural and historical contexts of the province and its population. The province gets space in the national press only when something negative happens, such as the terrorist attack or an extraordinary scandal in the area.

Interestingly, online journalism has become more challenging for news editors of the mainstream media in covering Balochistan. Ignoring certain important stories, which are already reported online, can be embarrassing for news editors as people can easily find out which stories are not covered by them. It seems, however, the national media are more concerned about their ratings and economic benefits than objectivity and fairness in covering news stories.

References

Aamir, Adnan. 2015a. "28th August declared as Day of Martyred Journalists" (accessed 25 July 2019), http://thebalochistanpoint.com/28th-august-declared-as-day-of-martyred-journalists/.

Aamir, Adnan. 2015b. "Why does the national media ignore Balochistan?" (accessed 25 July 2019), http://nation.com.pk/blogs/29-May-2015/why-does-the-national-media-ignore-balochistan.

Aamir, Adnan. 2016a. "Anti-corruption drive: Secretary Finance arrested and advisor resigned" (accessed25 July 2019), http://balochistanvoices.com/2016/05/anti-corruption-drive-secretary-finance-arrested-and-advisor-resigned/.

Aamir, Adnan. 2016b. "Balochistan: Gainlessly employed". *Newsline*, October 2016.

Aamir, Adnan. 2017a. "Baloch people not taken on board on CPEC: Akhtar Mengal" (accessed 25 July 2019), http://balochistanvoices.com/2017/03/baloch-people-not-taken-board-cpec-akhtar-mengal/.

Aamir, Adnan. 2017b. "The deprivation card". *Newsline*, February 2017.

AFP. 2013. "Justice (r) Mir Hazar Khan Khoso, named interim PM of Pakistan" (accessed 25 July 2019), https://tribune.com.pk/story/525608/justice-r-mir-hazar-khan-khoso-named-interim-pm-of-pakistan/.

Ahmad, Gulmina B. 2015. *The Press Clubs of Pakistan*, Islamabad: Individualland.

Ahmer, M. 2016. "Politics: Why is the current Baloch Nationalist Movement different from the rest". *Dawn*, 6 November 2016.

Akbar, Malik S. 2017. Founder and Editor-in-Chief, The Baloch Hal [Interview] (25 July 2017).

Anon. 2014. "Protest by BNP and BSO: News channels shut down in all Balochistan" (accessed 4 August 2019), http://thebalochistanpoint.com/protest-by-bnp-and-bso-news-channels-shut-down-in-all-balochistan/.

Assembly, National. 2019. "National Assembly of Pakistan" (accessed 25 July 2019), http://na.gov.pk/en/index.php.

Baloch, Siddique. 2014. *Balochistan: It's Politics and Economics*. Quetta: Gosha e Adab.

Finance Department, Government of Balochistan. 2018. *Annual Budget Statement—Volume-1*. Quetta: Finance Department, Government of Balochistan.

Ghori, H.K. 2018. "Journalist Siddique Baloch passes away" (accessed 25 July 2019), www.dawn.com/news/1387826.

Government, Balochistan. 2017–18. *Budget White Paper*. Quetta: Government of Balochistan.

IFJ. 2015. *The Freedom Frontier—Press Freedom in South Asia 2014–15*. https://www.ifj.org/fileadmin/images/Asia_Pacific/Asia_Pacific_documents/IFJ_South_Asia_2014-15_Web_low_res.pdf.

Khan, Aurangzaib. 2010. *Media in Balochistan: Blighted but a Brave New World Beckons*. Islamabad: Intermedia.

Mansoor, Hassan. 2014. "Media ignoring the Balochistan issue due to ratings" (accessed 25 July 2019), www.dawn.com/news/1085134.

Nasir, Abbas. 2016. "Case of the missing news" (accessed 25 July 2019), www.dawn.com/news/128164.

Notezai, Akbar. 2014. "Rest in Peace—Syed Fasih Iqbal" (accessed 25 July 2019), https://akbarnotezai.wordpress.com/2014/06/13/rest-in-peace-syed-fasih-iqbal-sahab/.

Pakistan Bureau of Statistics. 2016. *Pakistan Social and Living Standards Measurement Survey (2014–15)*. Islamabad: Government of Pakistan Statistics Division (accessed 27 April 2020), www.pbs.gov.pk/sites/default/files//pslm/publications/PSLM_2014-15_National-Provincial-District_report.pdf.

Pakistan, Planning Commission. 2016. *Report on Multidimensional Poverty in Pakistan*. UNDP, OPHI.

PEMRA. 2019. "PEMRA" (accessed 25 July 2019), www.pemra.gov.pk/.

Planning Commission. 2011. *National Nutrition Survey 2011*. Islamabad: Planning and Development Division, Government of Pakistan (accessed 27 April 2020), https://pndajk.gov.pk/uploadfiles/downloads/NNS%20Survey.pdf.

Relations, Directorate General of Public. 2014. *Media Directory*. Quetta: Directorate General of Public Relations, Government of Balochistan.

Shahid, Saleem. 2013. "At least 93 lives lost in Quetta explosions" (accessed 25 July 2019), www.dawn.com/news/777830.

Shah, Syed A. 2017. Bureau Chief, Dawn News Quetta [Interview] (25 July 2017).

Statistics, Pakistan Bureau. 2008. *Pakistan Statistical Year Book*.

Statistics, Pakistan Bureau. 2017. "Province-wise Provisional Results of Census—2017" (accessed 25 July 2019), www.pbs.gov.pk/sites/default/files/PAKISTAN%20TEHSIL%20WISE%20FOR%20WEB%20CENSUS_2017.pdf.

Tahir, Seemi N. 2006. *Balochistan me Ablaaghe Ama—Aghaz o Irteqa*. National Language Authority.

Unnamed. 2016. Senior Official of DGPR Balochistan [Interview] (14 December 2016).

Zakir, Sumaira. 2016. Chairperson, Mass Communications Department, BUITEMS Quetta [Interview] (12 November 2016).

Zulfiqar, Shahzada. 2016. Former President, Quetta Press Club [Interview] (22 December 2016).

12

INTERVIEWS WITH I. A. REHMAN, MEHDI HASAN, AND ERIC RAHIM

Freedom of expression and sham democracy

Qaisar Abbas and Farooq Sulehria[1]

We can describe the state of the fourth estate in Pakistan in different ways. Here are three statements about the mass media in Pakistan:

- The mass media are some of the few institutions in Pakistan that have grown at a tremendous pace.
- Overall, the Pakistani news media are moderately free.
- Pakistan is one of the most dangerous countries in the world for journalists and media personnel.

Although they seem to be contradictory, these statements are unbelievably accurate. The mass media have grown in unimaginable proportions in Pakistan. However, "moderately free" only means that the media work under better conditions as compared to the worst kind of monarchies and dictatorships in the world. The last statement also seems to be true as according to the 2016 Journalists Without Borders Report, journalists and media workers routinely become the target of intimidation and violence by state agencies and non-state terrorist groups in Pakistan.

To further explore several burning issues related to the freedom of expression and censorship, we interviewed three extraordinary intellectuals and journalists in Pakistan. These include a well-respected journalist; a reporter who became an academic scholar; and an activist and reporter who left the country to become a professor in England.

I. A. Rehman is known for his well-researched and scholarly analyses. During his distinguished journalistic career, he always strived for social justice, democratic values, and human rights while maintaining impartiality at the same time. He served as editor-in-chief of the *Pakistan Times* from 1989–1990. Since 1990 he has been serving as a director of the Human Rights

Commission of Pakistan. Before this, he worked as managing editor of the Urdu daily *Azad* and executive director of the weekly magazine *Viewpoint*. In addition to numerous articles and papers, Rehman has to his credit three books. He won the Nuremberg International Award for Peace and Human Rights in 2003, and the Magsaysay Award for Peace and International Understanding in 2004.

Dr Mehdi Hasan is a leading scholar, political commentator, and media expert who started his career as the News Bureau Chief for the Pakistan Press International (PPI). With a PhD and Master's degrees in Mass Communication from the University of the Punjab, Lahore, he retired as Dean, School of Media and Mass Communication at the Beacon House National University, Lahore. He also worked as Professor of Mass Communication at the University of the Punjab. He was a Fulbright Scholar at the University of Colorado, Boulder, in the US and also taught as Visiting Faculty for Kinnaird College, Administrative Staff College, Civil Services Academy of Pakistan, and the National Institute of Public Administration (NIPA).

Dr Eric Rahim became a target of state repression in the early days of independence and was jailed for 11 months. He joined *Dawn*, Karachi, in 1949 as a sub-editor, and remained there until 1953 when he became the Karachi correspondent of the *Pakistan Times*. In 1958, around the time when Ayub Khan imposed martial law, he moved to England and received a PhD in economics at University College London. He was appointed a lecturer in economics at the University of Strathclyde, Glasgow, Scotland, in 1963. In the late 1980s and early 1990s he was, for several years, a member of a team in Bangkok producing the United Nations annual economic and social survey. During the same period, he was adviser to the Development Studies Institute at the University of Sindh, Jamshoro, and coordinated links between the economics department of Strathclyde University and the University of Peshawar and Government College University, Lahore. He is currently honorary economics lecturer at Strathclyde University. He is convener of the Scottish charity Solas Educational Trust which financially supports community-based schools in the district of Chitral, Pakistan. He lives in Glasgow, Scotland, and has recently completed his book *A Promethean Vision—Formation of Marx's Worldview*.

These interviews offer significant perspectives on the freedom of expression, training, and education of journalists, social responsibilities of media personnel, and the state and non-state patterns of censorships. Their views also explore distinctions and similarities of censorship in private, public, digital, electronic, print, Urdu, English, and the news and entertainment media contents. While we asked the same questions to these scholars, their responses are reproduced here without any changes.

How do you define freedom of expression within the cultural, political, and historical contexts of Pakistan?

I. A. REHMAN: I define freedom of expression as given in Article 19 of the International Covenant on Civil and Political Rights. But I am prepared to be pragmatic in Pakistan and refrain from criticising Islam, the Holy Prophet, Jinnah (up to a point), until society develops to a stage that free debate on all matters and personalities is possible.

MEHDI HASAN: Every nation defines freedom of expression within the context of its history and cultural traditions. In Pakistan, unfortunately, freedom of expression is defined by the establishment that elaborates this constitutional right to protect its interests. All administrations in Pakistan, military or civil, have justified censorship on the pretext of national security, religious sanctity, and good relations with other countries. They were only interested in strengthening their power and control.

ERIC RAHIM: The definition of "freedom of expression" is the same in the context of Pakistan as in any other settings. It is the right (human right) to hold an opinion and express it without fear of state retaliation, threat, etc., and social sanctions. There are well-recognised limits to this freedom which relate to slander, obscenity, incitement, and people's private lives. I suppose the context refers to social acceptability and sanctions. What is socially acceptable as free speech and expression will be different in Pakistan from some other countries such as the UK. What may be considered as, say, obscene in one may be acceptable in the other.

As they say, media are supposed to be socially responsible. Who defines these tenets of social responsibility? Media, society, or state?

REHMAN: In a rational society, the state and the social elite arrive at a consensus on social responsibility, and the media follows these guidelines.

HASAN: Journalists' code of ethics becomes their declaration of social responsibility. These codes are generally evolved out of the well-established conventions, traditions, and practices in their profession. It is wrong to think that codes precede or create conventions. Moreover, codes have a moral sanction behind them, not legal. In a democratic society, the area of moral codes should continue to expand, and the range of legal codes should steadily shrink. The Pakistan Federal Union of Journalists (PFUJ) formulated a code of conduct to guard themselves against the misuse of their power. But this code has lost much of its validity now. What is needed now is not a set of "don'ts" but something more positive to enable journalists to discharge their social responsibilities.

RAHIM: What is "socially responsible" is defined, in the first instance, by society (general, public opinion), by the state, and also by the media. The criteria considered in each case may be different. And therefore there may be conflicting definitions.

Do you think media contents of entertainment programmes have rarely been a target of state censorship as compared to the news and current affairs? Do you believe it's just a myth or reality? Why?

REHMAN: In the case of Pakistan, weak governments have been and are afraid of open debate, and hence censorship of news and current affairs programmes is stricter than in the case of entertainment programmes. In the latter programmes, too, the state is allergic to criticism of its policies but mostly it follows the conservative clerics' obsession with fighting vulgarity and obscenity. The situation is changing, though. Music items and women's roles in plays that were once taboo are now allowed.

HASAN: Somehow, our governments, civil or military both, have been obsessed with their domestic and external image. News has always been a tool for them to improve their public image to project positive publicity and curb negative information as they define them. This is the reason why news and current affairs programmes have been the target of censorship in Pakistan more than entertainment programmes.

RAHIM: Don't know.

Journalists and writers have been the target of state censorship and suppression in Pakistan in the name of national security, law and order, religion, or good relations with other countries. Is there a borderline that journalists should not cross when it comes to these justifications and who should draw this line?

REHMAN: I believe journalists should draw the line under the Johannesburg Principles. But governments in Pakistan interpret Article 19 of the Constitution much too broadly and target media persons whimsically.

HASAN: There are several ethical standards that journalists have to follow. The most important include excluding confidential information from stories; ensuring objectivity and maintaining balance; becoming sensitive to issues of genuine national security and potential loss of human life; the accuracy of news; privacy of citizens, especially vulnerable members of society; and not demanding total immunity from criminal and civil liability for journalists. These and other principles should be the borderline for journalists.

RAHIM: The "borderline" in each case is decided by the government and then made into law. Journalists cross the borderline at their peril. (The "borderline" may, of course, have no genuine reasons relating to national security.)

When media were mostly owned or regulated by the autocratic regimes in Pakistan, journalists were working under unwritten rules and draconian laws. Now, when electronic media are privatised and journalists have the freedom to criticise everyone (except the army and religion), why do they still complain of restrictions and dangers involved in reporting?

REHMAN: The army and the judiciary are protected under the Constitution. Media are afraid of non-state actors (jihadis). Now laws are not used to silence journalists; they are either co-opted, or they are frightened into silence, or they "disappear".

HASAN: Privatisation of media means nothing when the establishment is coming up with innovative ways of curbing information using economic, political, and legal pressures. Imposing the recent limits by PEMRA on media content and introducing the so-called Cyber Crime Act to control digital information are only some examples.

RAHIM: "Restrictions" and "dangers" may come from various sources. The media owners for their reasons may be aligned with one centre of power or the other (the army or the central government, etc.), there may be threats, implicit or explicit, expectations of media owners regarding benefits from one source or the other. And so on. In general, there is always a line that the media people, owners and journalists, know that they should not cross because there are legal and illegal sanctions that the authority can apply.

In this age of digital media, information has become a global phenomenon where states appear to lose their control of information dissemination. Do you think the recently enacted Cyber Crime Act is an attempt to regain information control through restricting digital media and their contents in the name of terrorism and security?

REHMAN: Yes. The Cyber Crime Act has been designed to control/censor the digital media in the name of security. The sweeping powers given to officials are likely to be abused. Worse, it will lead to self-censorship, discourage people from expressing their views, and eventually from having any opinions.

HASAN: The Cyber Act has been widely criticised by human rights organisations and journalists internally and globally. With its vague definitions of cyber-crimes and unlimited powers given to the administration, the act has become another method of limiting the freedom of speech.

RAHIM: This is a universal problem. All governments are trying to get some control over the flow of information on digital media. In America and Europe, these efforts to access data are justified on the grounds of terrorist threats.

Several media associations and human rights organisations say Pakistan is one of the most dangerous nations for journalists and media workers. In your view, when most media outlets are not state-owned, why is it a dangerous world for reporters and media workers?

REHMAN: The fact that most media outlets are privately owned makes them more vulnerable to indirect control by a state apparatus that is obsessed with security. Besides, media are under attack from non-state actors. In and around conflict areas (KP, FATA, Balochistan) media persons are caught in a crossfire between security forces and militants; each side wants its version of events published/broadcast. Noncompliance could mean death.

HASAN: I think the non-state extremist groups and political violence have become more dangerous for journalists today than the traditional methods used by the establishment. Journalists now are a target of double jeopardy: state and non-state violence and pressures.

RAHIM: My answer here is on the lines of the answer to the question above.

Every profession needs sound training and education for its workers. Do you think media professionals, including journalists, managers, producers, technical staff, and other workers, get quality education and training before they start working in the trenches? What kind of training do media professionals need to ensure the quality of news and entertainment programmes?

REHMAN: This is an old complaint. Those entering media now have far better training possibilities than their predecessors. Many universities and arts institutions offer courses in news and entertainment areas. Some of the young graduates have made their mark as documentary filmmakers. Now the problem is the lack of a culture of open discourse and development of work ethics and aesthetics by media houses.

HASAN: The importance of social sciences is directly related to and has a bearing on democratic dispensation. In a country like Pakistan, where democratic culture has remained fragile, the teaching of social sciences and research in various fields connected with social science needs serious consideration.

I can say, based on my teaching experience, most journalism and broadcasting courses are theory oriented, and there are insufficient facilities for practical work and training. I remember when a sponsorship opportunity came up to establish a photography lab in my department at a university, the administration was not sure we should have it and asked us to provide strong justifications to have it in the department. There is a need to connect communication courses to applied training and provide future journalists a real experience in the field.

Basic courses like Media History, International Relations, Public Relations, Pakistan Studies, Comparative Economics and Politics, and Theory of Mass Communication are the norm at a typical Pakistani university. Students should be well versed in these fields, but our communication curricula should also be receptive to the changing world of communication technologies, global communication, and cyber journalism.

After the introduction of the internet and satellite technologies, our communication world has drastically changed, but our education has not adjusted to these developments. Every media organisation has an online edition now. We should offer courses on web-based and digital media journalism for businesses, government departments, and non-profit groups.

An option of Urdu and English journalism has been available since 1969 at our universities, but most students prefer to opt for the Urdu medium, with the exception of Kinnaird College in Lahore, which offers only English journalism courses. Similarly, only a few doctoral theses are in English. To compete with the current global trends, our students should be trained in culturally based English and Urdu journalism.

RAHIM: Don't know.

As an intellectual, writer, and journalist, were there occasions when you were asked to censor your piece or change your position on specific issues? Also, can you tell us some examples, situations, and cases when you applied self-censorship?

REHMAN: No editor has asked me to delete anything from my writing. But self-censorship cannot be avoided. It is not possible for me to write what I think of mullahs and generals. I avoid appearing on TV because they have problems. Once I was invited to speak about the fall of Dhaka on TV and what I said was completely deleted.

HASAN: It happens all the time in newspapers and electronic media. Media organisations have their routines to write under defined guidelines determined by financial and political boundaries. Extremist groups, politicians, and state agencies are also busy in muting media voices through various mechanisms.

RAHIM: I worked as a journalist in Pakistan in the 1950s. There was self-censorship exercised with respect to the armed forces and the Kashmir issue. On the latter, you toed the government line.

Your editor allows you to write on a given topic, but under an invisible pressure, you are asked later to change your position. What are these mysterious pressures that media organisations have to deal with daily? Can you give specific and concrete examples?

REHMAN: This has not happened to me. But I know that editors have withheld columns written by their well-known contributors.

HASAN: Take the recent example of the *Dawn* reporter whose name was included on the exit list so he cannot leave the country, for reporting a meeting of army officials and government representatives. Under the military pressure, the government is further investigating who leaked the news, and the federal Minister for Broadcasting had to resign because he could not stop publication of the story. In this case, the military is exposing itself to unnecessary criticism in an attempt to show its power to political leaders. In most cases, however, the mysterious hand is successful in curtailing or preventing publication of "undesirable" information.

RAHIM: In my limited experience, this did not happen. Maybe if I had written something critical of the army, it would have been suppressed. You knew what was acceptable.

If you are Minister of Information and Broadcasting in Pakistan, what kind of policy changes would you suggest in the areas of freedom of information, working conditions of media professionals, wages of journalists, code of ethics, and security of media workers?

REHMAN: The Minister for Information in Pakistan will not be a free agent for a long, long time. Laws are in place to protect freedom of information, wages, and working conditions. These need to be enforced. The only issue is right to information. The government is delaying adoption of a bill because it is too good to win the establishment's approval.

HASAN: The seventeenth- and eighteenth-century thoughts in most of Western Europe and America turned to the public rights to receive information as the basis for governance. Thus, people needed access to the maximum flow of information and opinion to make decisions. The freedom of speech and press was considered indispensable to the life of a public capable of self-governance. Freedom is essential to the individual's development, and it is a natural right to which every person has a claim in exploiting his or her talents. Every national communication strategy should be based on these principles.

RAHIM: To answer this question, I would need a good deal of information—which I do not have.

Television now symbolises the media in Pakistan. Since liberalisation of the airwaves post-1999, a change has occurred in terms of free expression on screen. In the case of PTV, there was a strict censorship regime. Now we have manipulation by the establishment and fear of attrition in the case of non-state actors. From the viewpoint of media audiences, don't you think manipulation is more dangerous than censorship?

REHMAN: Censorship is of two kinds. Total censorship means complete suppression of news while partial censorship means offering a doctored version of the truth. It is as bad as manipulation. The most unacceptable form of manipulation, which is far worse than censorship, is the dissemination of falsehood/disinformation.

HASAN: Direct censorship or manipulation, both forms of muting mass media messages, have devastating effects on the free flow of communication and people's right to know in a democratic society.

RAHIM: I would say "manipulation" and censorship are equally bad.

The so-called Taliban, militant groups, and sectarian outfits have emerged as dominant players in Pakistani polity. How has the rise of militant confessional outfits impacted free expression? What other violent groups have posed a threat to free speech?

REHMAN: As said earlier, militant groups threaten media persons in two ways. They threaten reprisal if they are exposed and they want their version of events to be published/broadcast.

HASAN: We have seen political workers threatening media organisations and attacking journalists demanding favourable coverage. Extremist groups have made the free flow of information, especially in the tribal belt, virtually impossible. These dangerous trends are, to some extent, already limiting media contents.

RAHIM: I am sure they have impacted. They have their spokesmen in the media. I know of no other violent group threatening free expression.

When profit becomes the primary motive for media, can the idea of free expression be served in any real sense? In other words, can we delink the debate on free media and media's political economy?

REHMAN: We cannot. Business controls the media, but companies are afraid of the establishment too. The more moneyed an owner is, the more vulnerable he becomes.

HASAN: Media in the modern age have become business- and profit-based enterprises. Media business, however, is not similar to selling goods and services.

Media tend to feed the human mind, and that's how communication is different than retailing business or banking. It works for the public good. Free flow of information and providing an independent platform for public debate should be the primary goal of media organisations.

RAHIM: Media are generally controlled/owned by business corporations who wish to make a profit and influence opinion and government policy in favour of business or particular sectors of it. The greater the diversity in the ownership of media and the greater the competition, the greater the scope for free expression.

Can we claim the English-language high-brow press enjoys more freedom and is less manipulated compared to the popular media (news channels, vernacular press)? If yes, why?

REHMAN: Yes. The government allows the English-language media some concession for two reasons. 1. These media have a relatively smaller audience than the vernacular media, and hence they pose little threat of fostering mass opposition. 2. These media can be offered to the diplomats and the world abroad as evidence that the media are free. Still, even English-language media are punished (by withholding ads), if it is truthful about Balochistan, for instance.

HASAN: It's true that the English press has a special status in Pakistan based on the fact that English is the language of bureaucrats. It has enjoyed more prestige and credibility as compared to the Urdu press. The English press is still an important symbol of superiority for the elite through which they draw a line between the ruler and the ruled. This cultural difference has helped sustain the English-language press. By the same token, the English press becomes an important tool of publicity for the elite, and whenever it tries to become the voice of the people, the establishment never hesitates to curb it effectively. When Faiz was the editor of PPL, he was arrested in 1951. PPL was finally dissolved when Martial Law was imposed in 1958. These are just a few examples.

RAHIM: My impression is that the claim would be wrong. I suppose governments would try to manipulate those sections that are more popular, have wider reach, and are more "manipulable".

Note

1 The editors would like to thank the three scholars for their interviews included in this chapter. These email interviews were conducted on the following dates: Eric Rahim, 3 March 2017; I. A. Rehman, 10 October 2016; and Mehdi Hasan, 1 November 2016.

INDEX

Abbas, Q. 8, 24
Ahmed, U. 109
Alavi, H. 2–3, 24
Al-Qaida 76, 135–136, 141–145
Althusser, L. 47–48
Aurat March 112–113

Bugti, A. A. 172

Carey, J. 26, 28–30
Chinoy, S. O. 148
Chomsky, N. 96
CPJ 5, 13, 138
Cyber Crime Act 11, 18, 194
Cyber Crime Law 123

Daman, U. 44
Dutt, B. 88–90, 92

Faiz, F. A. 43–44
feminism: liberal 61–63, 117–121, Muslim Pakistani 63; neoliberal 62–63
Freedman, D. 4

Gazdar, M. 41, 156
Gitlin, T. 85
Gramsci, A. 47

Hall, S. 96
Hamelink, C. J. 83
Hasan, M. 190, 24
HRCP 149, 177

IFJ 120–121
Islamification 45–47
Islamisation 22, 39–41, 45, 53–54, 67
Islamism 63
Islamophobia 61–63, 65–68
ISPR 13–14, 41, 47, 52, 174

Jalib, H. 44
jihadification 22, 39–40, 42–45, 47, 52–54

Kargil War 11, 45–47, 89, 164, 169–170
Kashmir 50–53, 56, 57, 58

Lal Masjid 106–107, 171

Mai, M. 22, 61–72, 74–79
Maududi, A. 101
Memogate 136
Mir, H. 14, 89, 174
Mirza, S. T. 167
Mirza, T. 166
Mirza, Z. I. 166
model: disposal and replacement 4–5; political parallelism 4–7
Mushtaq, F. 102

Naqsh, J. 175
Niazi, Z. 7, 165

Osmani, N. 166
overdeveloped state 2

Pashteen, M. 163
PEMRA 11–13, 170, 180, 194
PFUJ 165, 182, 192
PTM 13, 163–164

Qadri, M. 155

RAWA 71

Siddiqa, A. 12, 42
Sulehria, F. 3, 25, 88, 184–185
Suleman, S. 9, 25

Thanawi, A. A. 101–103

War on Terror 28–29, 32, 34–36, 105, 108, 135, 142, 145–146, 171

Yesil, B. 4
Yusufzai, M. 22, 32–33, 61, 63–64, 69–72, 74–80, 120, 148, 157

Zaidi, A. 3

For Product Safety Concerns and Information please contact our EU
representative GPSR@taylorandfrancis.com
Taylor & Francis Verlag GmbH, Kaufingerstraße 24, 80331 München, Germany